MANHOOD

For my father
For the memory of my mother, Rachel Shapiro
For my brother
For the memory of my uncle, Seymour Shapiro
For Morag Hann, who encouraged me
*   every step of the way*

CONTENTS

PREFACE

This is a book for men and women, but it is about men. The discussions of moral maturity and heroism apply to women as well as to men, but this point is not emphasized because I feel it is vital for my argument to keep male attention focused on male tasks. My intention is not to slight women but to respect their capacity to understand the differentness of the male effort to achieve manhood as well as its similarity to the female effort to achieve adulthood. There is no precise equivalent for the term manhood in the history of women.

When I tell stories about clients in this book, I have followed the now standard practices to preserve confidentiality and the protection of privacy. That is, the stories are true, but the characters are composite figures. No single client referred to is an actual person. The names, professions, and other identifying marks of persons have been altered. The effect I aim at in these stories and character sketches is the truth of fiction, not the truth of journalism.

Some of the ideas expressed here were developed during the preparation of special programs for men at the Volunteer Counseling Service of Rockland County. I am grateful to Gail Golden, Marjorie Lipson, and especially to Phyllis Frank for helping to keep me honest. Any book is partially an argument with one's friends, and I hope my friends will forgive me for making some of our private arguments public. Any book is also an argument with one's editors. For editorial assistance—

and argument—I thank Harriet Blacker, Faith Sale, and Sara Blackburn.

The women's movement helped me to become a feminist, and that helped me to find myself needing to go beyond that borrowed position to a renewed sense of manhood. There is an ancient gnostic story that keeps me conscious of the arrogance and narcissism of the Judaic-Christian-Islamic paternalist tradition. It is said that God the Father was a jealous God, saying there is no one but him because he was ignorant of his mother.

INTRODUCTION

Hiking on Mount Rainier with another couple, our best friends, my wife and I suggested that we explore the valley left by the retreating Nisqually glacier. The landscape was lunar: pumice stone, ash, gray on gray, nothing living. We ignored the warnings, the sounds of crashing in the distance, and kept clambering over the slippery rocks of the moraine in the bottom of the U-shaped valley, following the Nisqually River back to its source in the glacier.

About half a mile from the muddy brown face of the glacier, we knew we were in trouble. The rocks sliding and crashing down into the valley were not stones, but boulders, some as big as cars. It seemed just as dangerous to go back as forward, so we pushed on. Then my wife fell and twisted her ankle badly, crying out with fear and pain.

In that moment, I felt a hairline crack in my heart. I felt an impulse of rage toward her. I wanted to run and leave her there, but I went to her and helped her up, thinking that Dan and I could carry her out. That would be faster than the slow pace of her limp, which would make us even more vulnerable to rock slides. We could make a sling, I thought quickly.

I looked around for my friends. They were gone. My fury at their betrayal of our friendship veiled the little fracture in my own solidarity with my wife.

What kind of friends flee from your side when you are

most in danger? We hobbled out of that valley of death learning later that several people had died in rock slides that day. The friendship did not survive the unraveling of loyalty in the face of danger.

Mistrust ruled that day in 1964 on that mountain. I did not trust the signs of danger I sensed. I could not trust my best friend to stand by me in my need. I could not trust my own heart to stay whole. It felt like the beginning of a new ice age.

The experience confirmed the message of the important fiction of the 1960s, of Updike's *Rabbit, Run,* Bellow's *Herzog,* Lessing's *The Golden Notebook*: men were divided in their hearts, untrustworthy, ambivalent about making commitments.

Men are falling off the mountain. The mountain is not just Rainier, or Mount Saint Helens. We are all walking on the mountain now, making marriage vows that are empty words, giving signs of friendship that are empty gestures. When words split from feelings and deeds, the cords of trust that bind us together in a living community fray and break. When the bonds of trust break, the mountain that thunders is Sinai.

When men are divided in their hearts—from their wives and from their friends—they can make only a divided world. It is now urgent that we men read the signs of danger correctly. Those distant warnings of unraveling families, of the contamination of the food chain, of environmentally caused cancer, of growing depersonalization in social life, of military solutions to social problems, of immense credibility gaps in government—all point to a crisis of mistrust that may be lethal, not only to the soul of men but to the values that have up to now sustained this nation as a people.

Men are always in short supply. By men, I mean good men, tempered to hold steady in times of stress and danger. Such men keep trust alive for the whole community. Men who can solder word, feeling, and deed together can help us to repair our broken bonds of trust.

It is so easy to violate trust now. The trustees of labor unions "invest" the pension funds entrusted to them in the coffers of organized crime, replacing them with counterfeit documents. Why not double your money? White-collar crime is a parasite on social trust. But counterfeit dollars are valuable only because of social trust in the real currency. Con men only parody social trust. The question is, do we have confidence men instead of confidence *in* men? Both politics and business slide so easily into the gray zone between truth and lies.

Some presidents have made it a matter of policy to say what is not the case and then later to assert the contrary, hoping no one will remember the contradiction. But duplicity masked by a smile remains duplicity.

Who can forget the images of the evacuation of Saigon, U.S. friends and allies clinging to the struts of helicopters until their hands were viciously pried loose? But we could see before then that something was awry with men. All those lies about Vietnam. And Cuba. And Chile. All the violence. The secrecy. All the signs that men with cracked hearts were inflicting their agony, shame, and violence on others. Truth has suffered. Trust has suffered. Faith in manhood has suffered. The ground splits under our feet.

It is a long way back up that mountain. It is difficult to create trust, easy to damage it, hard to repair it. That is the work I will ask men to do, beginning with our fathers, our brothers, our mates. For that is the work of men and the meaning of manhood. What each man does in his inner world, with his own speech, his own heart, his own hands, on his own mountain, will be reflected in the kind of family, community, and political life we have. We have been running away, and now is the time to stop running.

This book means to chart a way back to strengthening trust, first by examining the personal crisis we face as individuals and then by exploring the means to resolve it. It begins by repairing our relationships with those who are closest to us.

"Never say 'I am only a boy!' . . .
Don't be afraid . . .
For I am with you . . ."

Then Yahweh stretched out his hand
and touched my mouth. And Yahweh said to me:
"There! I have put my words in your mouth . . ."

Jeremiah, I.
John Bright translation

1

FROM NARCISSISM TO HEROISM

When Narcissus reached
His sixteenth year he seemed to be a boy
As much as man; both boys and girls looked to him
To make love, and yet . . .
Proud Narcissus had little feeling . . .
His love was cursed. Only the glancing mirror
Of reflections filled his eyes, a body
That had no being of its own . . .

OVID, *The Metamorphoses,*
Horace Gregory translation

Manhood is a term of honor that has fallen into dishonor. Men desperately need clarification about who they are trying to be after they stop playing basketball and before they have their first coronary. Men who feel politically powerless have become embroiled in political struggles at home—over laundry, over who drives the car, over sex. We have lost a personal language at the same time that we have lost political self-confidence. We have taken flight from love, protectiveness, and mutual involvement, showing neither strength nor need, which women and men require to trust one another.

In a climate of widespread mistrust of our political "fathers," revulsion against militarism, and legitimate feminist critique of male chauvinism, men need to recognize that there is an honorable tradition of manhood and heroism. To discover that tradition means to embark on a process of rediscovering trust and repairing old wounds that have been sustained and nourished by years of silence and mistrust.

This book proposes that male self-mistrust is caused by narcissism and reinforced by male silence, emotional inhibition, and puerile attitudes and behavior. The division inside men, in the male psyche, has the drastic social consequence of weakening trust in all other relationships—father and son, brother and brother, husband and wife, lover and lover, citizen and citizen. The weakening of the bonds of trust in these relationships causes still further decay in male self-trust. We have only to regard our social world to see a mirror image of this growing mistrust, a tragic reflection of the inner world of men. When trust diminishes, the power of death to deprive life of meaning grows.

Overcoming self-mistrust means facing one's own violence, silence, and dishonesty. Suffering one's own pain is the metamorphosis that turns childish males into men. And the task of men is to repair trust—in themselves, their families, and in their social world. Either we govern our own violence or violence will govern us. If men can learn to suffer their own pain, fear, and violence, instead of withdrawing into fantasy or inflicting their violence on others, they can overcome shame and guilt. Then they will be free to learn the power of living speech, of dialogue. They will be able to grow in self-respect and respect for others. To respect others includes respecting their pain and according them status and deference. We attain moral heroism when we are able to devote acute attention to the reality of other human beings who suffer like ourselves and to engage in the effort to sacrifice our impulse to distance ourselves from those who are most vulnerable to suffering. The measure of manhood is creation of trust, repair of trust.

Vast numbers of us are silent, enraged, insecure, and consumed by self, qualities that have come to be considered together as elements of a narcissistic character. Narcissism begins as a defense against childhood feelings of dependency, and eventually it becomes a grandiose illusion of independence, of self-sufficiency, of being above needing others, who are perceived as inferior. Other people are not fully real to narcissistic men, who blindly aspire to realize only their own egocentric fantasies. As narcissistic men approach mid-life, they become increasingly isolated and depressed because their reality has failed to match the dream, and they are ashamed of the human damage they have caused. Such men can repair their lives by the hard task of acknowledging their narcissism and then setting out to revise their values and reset their goals. In doing so, they may encounter for the first time the real pleasures that begin with genuinely responding to others, with taking responsibility, with wanting to make sacrifices, with giving up the old urgency of "I want."

Manhood begins with the repudiation of narcissism, cynicism, and immaturity. We attain heroism not when we display ourselves or become famous, but when we make a commitment to live our own values here, now, in the flesh of a single person and when we accept responsibility for our own tasks and for the people who love and depend on us. The values of heroism include a fully developed concern to protect others from violence, the will to suffer and sacrifice for others, and a passion for the sacred quality of human life.

If we are to recover the pride men once took in their manhood, we must rediscover some traditional values: respect for our forefathers, brotherhood, commitment to marital love, responsibility, sacrifice. And if it is to flourish and survive, our respect for these values cannot be based, as it was so often in the past, on submissive conformity to their false authoritarian forms but on realizing the fullness of their meaning for our personal moral development and for our democratic community life.

If men are ashamed of their fathers, they will be ashamed of themselves, because every man is partially identified with his father. When men are ashamed of themselves, they emphasize their differences from others, alienating themselves from their own feelings and from people. When men overcome this kind of shame, they learn to love, which means they learn to minimize the distance between their fathers, brothers, and mates, and themselves. Men who achieve moral heroism strive to minimize the differences that divide them from those people who seem *most* different. What we need most, I propose, is to overcome our tendency to withdraw into silence and fantasy, because noninvolvement makes us ashamed and guilty and costs us self-respect.

It is difficult to write about manhood. If I had to be heroic myself in order to write about heroism, I could not write this book. I, too, am searching for the truth of manhood, a truth I have failed many times to understand or to live.

My purpose is to illuminate the reality of a man's life as best I can. I am very much like most men in my struggle to overcome immaturity, and I understand others mainly through my own suffering of myself. I have learned by experience, as a psychotherapist and as a man, that personality is mainly a defensive mask that divides us from knowledge of ourselves and contact with others. We are all more alike than we are different.

To write about manhood is to write of despair and hope. The *scale* of the problem of male self-doubt puts tremendous pressure on language, for if one is denied the self-indulgence of being grandiose about manhood, then there ensues a powerful tendency to be negative. I have found that the only words to use are hard words, earned words most closely related to actual experience. We men must face our own destiny, must make a better world in the midst of violence and loss, without the illusions that sustained men in the past, by renewing the meaning of manhood.

The philosopher Alasdair MacIntyre has described our current condition as a vacuum of hope, marked by a loss of faith in our own social institutions and in the language that is the voice of those institutions:

> The founders of atheist humanism hoped for and predicted secularization not merely in the sense of abandonment of religious belief and practice, but in the sense of a transformation of human goals and hopes from other worldly to this worldly. The present was to be judged and transcended, not by looking to the justice of heaven but by looking to that of the future. The hope of glory was to be . . . replaced by the hope of Utopia.
>
> But we have neither glory nor Utopia to hope for. The hope that a secular Utopian tradition, whether liberal or Marxist, sought to provide was never realized. The routines of working class life, the competitive ladders of the middle class, absorb us into immediacy. We are dominated by a present to which the idea of a radically different future is alien. What conventional politics promises is always a brighter version of what we have now. This is why political talk about ends and aims is always doomed to become rhetoric. In this situation the substance of religious belief is no longer with us, but in our ordinary secular vocabulary we have no language to express common needs, hopes, and fears that go beyond the immediacies of technique and social structure.
>
> What we do have is a religious language, which survives even though we do not know what to say in it.[1]

Only one thing has changed since MacIntyre wrote these words more than twenty years ago, and that is the hope that computers and the language of IBM could somehow replace the hope of heaven, utopia, and the need for personal communication. But "personal computers" are impersonal. Insofar as it is an object of hope, the computer is only a new tower of Babel. It evolved as a tool of male violence, intended to secure the military control of information, and it now has the status of an idol. But antitechnological fantasy, the fantasy of pastoral escape to the simple, is not a real option for men in the face of the technical world, as so many naively believed in the 1960s. It only perpetuates our distance from the world around us and divorces us from it even further.

We have lost faith in the future, in ourselves, in our fellows. We need to resist the deadening quality of both routine work and total all-out competitiveness. We need to resist the seductiveness of regressing to juvenile "lifestyles." We need to speak to each other.

We live in a time when the presence of the human voice threatens to vanish from the earth. When men fall silent, violence grows upon the earth. And because part of the narcissism of men is preferring silent monologue to speaking as a vulnerable person, a man, to other men, we men need to renew our common language.

The absence of a common language for men is powerfully dramatized by John M. Del Vecchio in his novel about the war in Vietnam, *The 13th Valley*. In this book, the divisions in our culture can be heard as differences in language. The men, the "boonierats," can comprehend each other only under the stress of combat. Their group life is meaningless without violence, and even then, the threat of division is there. The lower ranks do not understand the orders of the officers; the blacks cannot be understood by the whites; the Hispanics cannot be understood by the whites. The boonierats are so estranged from what they call "the world" that they have no hope of being understood by their families, by their wives, or by the antiwar public.[2] The novel conveys in striking metaphor that being a man means being isolated.

Michael Herr, in his Vietnam book, *Dispatches,* also focuses
on language, on the horrible gaps in communication between
isolated, terrified men, gaps filled by drugs and by "mad
minutes" of panicked gunfire. One soldier cannot understand
why his girlfriend stopped writing to him after he sent her
the gift of an ear cut off the head of a Vietnamese soldier.[3]
This bizarre episode presents a telling portrait of male behavior in our time. How many contemporary men, pressed
by loved ones to listen to them, to speak to them, present
them instead with the "ear" of someone else—a video re-
corder, perhaps, or a TV or video game? In 1952, the story
goes, General MacArthur's aides were afraid to interrupt him
with news of the disastrous invasion of South Korea during
the ritual of his watching an after-dinner movie.

Speaking, revealing myself, must be the first sacrifice I make
as I set out toward being a man today. The Latin root of
"sacrifice" means "to make holy." Sacrifice generally signifies
the destruction of a victim or an offering made to maintain
or restore the proper relationship of a person or a group to
the sacred powers that are felt to organize the cosmos. Speaking is required of all men today, as a beginning, because we
must repair the trust that has been damaged by our own
private withdrawal into irony and fantasy. The truth about
men is a truth about violence. And silence, the silence of men,
is the core of the problem of our violence, of our narcissism.

Before there was speech in the world, there was magic, and
where there is no speech, there is magic still. Before we could
speak of our fears to one another and protect each other, there
were amulets, incantations, magic spells to kill enemies. The
belief in the magical power of wishes persists, as does the
belief in the omnipotence of the silent will. It is impossible
to exaggerate the importance of speech, and it is very difficult
to fully realize how little personal speech we men actually
experience in our lives, either as speakers or listeners. It is a

truth that begins with the poverty of our abilities to truly speak, to truly be present.

Men are continually being asked for their presence. Sometimes they are too busy to be present with mates or children. But when they are at home, they imagine that they are present, only to find to their chagrin that they are not really there, according to their mates. This absence is denied vigorously. A man will protest that he can hear every word his wife is saying to him, even if he is reading the newspaper, watching the ballgame, changing the spark plugs, or looking at *Penthouse* magazine in the bathroom and masturbating. He confuses "I am here," meaning that he is physically nearby, with being present, just as he confuses "I can hear" with being engaged and responsive.

"Presence" is a term of mystery if it has not been experienced. As a psychotherapist, I may say to a bewildered new client that the goal of psychotherapy is to enable him to be in the room, here with me, fully present—just two of us. The client usually does not realize just how difficult that is. He may still be raging at the sheriff who just gave him a speeding ticket, counting his money, speaking to an invisible judgmental parent hovering over my shoulder, or straining to get on with his day and call his investment broker. The parts of him that are not there do not know they are not there, because they are otherwise engaged. It is no accident that common speech describes the emotionally disturbed person as someone who is "not all there."

It is somewhat easier for people to grasp that they are not fully attentive than it is for them to comprehend that there is a state of being *all there*. Being *all there* is what I mean by presence. It is not the same as social poise, which is a mask of presence, not the real thing.

"Presence" is a word with theological overtones, one of those terms that must be reinvested with substance if we men

are to renew our common language. Jehovah is the God who
is present with his people. Jesus promises not only the presence
of God on earth as a person but a personal revelation of his
presence that enriches that person's own capacity for presence.

Presence has to do with the appearance, or the revelation,
of love, attention, and protection. It means reduced fear, reduced "absence of mind," reduced fragmentation of the person. It cannot be assumed that when a body fills space a
person is present, because anxiety or rage may dim that presence to a furniturelike rigidity. Sometimes we can become
present only through a struggle.

The presence of a person is felt as a "substance" that differs
profoundly from the sense of his presence when he is distracted and only partially present. When women, children,
or aged parents clamor for a man's presence, it is this kind
of substance they are clamoring for—not the arrival of a body
vibrating with rage or of attention attenuated into vague
inaccessibility. We men have great talent at parrying this
demand for presence. If simply denying our absence does not
work, we can be "too busy," or failing that, we can accuse
our mates, children, or parents of persecuting us or being
crazy. "You're always complaining that I'm not here. But
when I *am* here, you drive me crazy with more complaints
about my not being here. You need a shrink!"

Whether intentionally or unintentionally, when a man is
not present, he is committing an act of violence against himself
as well as others. He is creating distance from his own feelings
and dividing himself from others. With the growth of elec-
tronic substitutions for actual encounters and the use of chem-
ical substitutes to deny the suffering of ourselves and others,
the flight from suffering, from the personal, the intimate,
from emotion itself, has achieved a dangerous new dimension
in our time.

When a man is inattentive to his mate, even if he performs

a daily ritual of sex with her, she will feel his violence and be angry about his wandering attention. She might imagine that if she were different, he would be more present. He might even hint that if she *were* different—slimmer, sweeter-smelling, sexier, younger, more like his fantasy of a woman— he might offer more of himself. He is fooling himself. When a man is absent in this way, he is more invested in an image of what the world or his mate should be like than he is involved in the present. Lives are wasted in this process unless it can be acknowledged and revised.

When a man pits his idealized image of what life should be against the actual reality, the image always wins. The product of this competition between idealized image and actual person or reality is the splitting of presence by envy, the violent cleaving and rejection of the present by the preference for an idealized image. The image created by envy has no gaps or flaws because it is unreal, but by its measure, the present is always found wanting. When men are lost in envy, they lose their powers of speech as well as their capacity to be fully present in the flesh. This withdrawal into private imagery, into the violence of envy, is the core of male narcissism.

When men are lost in envy, even if they speak, even if they say, "I love you," the words are so diluted in substance that they lack resonance. Men may be said then to be talking words but not speaking the speech of persons. Shakespeare's Cleopatra points to this difference between talk and personal speech when she says of Antony, "He words me, girls." The difference is that words without substance create no trust and sustain no bonds. Speech—and the kind of behavior that flows from it—generates trust and continuity. The speech of a man of full presence fills the gap between persons, reduces the difference between them, and creates trust. Trust can be counterfeited by money or rhetoric but not for long, because trust is true capital, not inflated value. It is the substance of value itself.

The real substance of manhood is the creation of trust, in words and in action. The real substance of heroism is the expansion of trust beyond the circle of the immediate family, beyond the realm of friendship, and into a feeling of commonality with the groups on the very edges of society. Gandhi destroyed the myth that untouchables were different from other people, outside the realm of love. It is a truth we have succeeded in forgetting, and always to our tremendous loss as individuals and as a nation composed of many aliens who are mistrusted.

Love confers status and value on those persons we care deeply about. Heroism, the expansion of trust, confers status and value on strangers. Envy denies substance and value to everyone, oneself included. A man who is entrapped in envy is consumed by his own images. On the most fundamental levels imaginable, envy is toxic to trust, while love is the substance that creates trust.

To struggle against the absence of men is to struggle against violence and for trust. This book is conceived as a struggle against the absence of men, beginning with my own absence, my own guilt, my own painful discovery of the meaning of being present, and my evolving commitment to presence as a way of living that renews the substance of trust. The task of manhood today is to admit our absence, our guilty devotion to envy-created images, and to sacrifice those idols in the fire of our presence, our full response to real persons in the present. Burning the idols, experiencing the grief of giving up the false safety of our absence, is what creates the substance of manhood. Manhood is transforming absence into presence.

Presence is not accomplished once and for all. Achieving it requires constant renewal, because our dread of presence is profound, and the danger of seduction by envy and imaginary difference seems always at hand. But "If my life were different, I would . . ." is the substance of a lie. So is "If they were only different, I might . . ." Giving up the possibility of an appeal to "if," abandoning the false promise of the idealized images that assure our absence, is the way toward living fully in the present. Our presence is required now, unconditionally, not only by those who love us but for our own sanity.

Without other men to support us, we men tend to remain glued to mothers or wives, absent while present, terrified of being alone. The capacity to experience ourselves as separate from a nourishing woman is one vital step toward manhood; the capacity to speak to other men is the next. Feminists have rightly pointed out how pathetic men are in their speech to women, how, unless they can feel a perfectly accepting maternal presence, they withdraw into silence.[4] That is not speech but sucking the breast, being nourished at the most primitive level. There is better food than this.

To become men, we must speak to one another. I do not mean talk—about baseball, politics, cars—but to speak to another man about ourselves, our fears, our needs. For the silence of a man, beyond frivolous matters, is not benign but resentful, malignant, and punitive. Women and children dread the silence of fathers and husbands. Male muteness means "I don't need anyone. Leave me alone."

Speech is fundamental in our traditional religious understanding of how the human spirit reveals itself, and this should teach us something, whether we are believers or not. God speaks to Israel and expects a response. Jesus is the *word* of God, a symbol of compassionate speech to and from a mute humanity. The Bible tells us that moral maturation depends upon speech, upon our own social self-revelation of needs. And speech destroys idolatry, narcissism, our ever-available preoccupation with internal imagery. We must struggle to keep aware that silence is not strength but dread of self-disclosure, of vulnerability, and of the incapacity to respond.

My own profession, psychotherapy, has created a number of misconceptions about the ingredients of manhood and authority and the crucial necessity for them. Psychoanalysis was created by a rebellion against the authoritarian repression of impulses. Freud's own self-analysis focused largely on his father, and the movement he created has worked mightily to shrink the power of the tyrannical father. The core of psychoanalysis remains valid, the reinterpretation of the archaic, silent stories the infant tells itself, the insistence upon speech, and the gradual revision of those distorted stories. But life is no longer as simple as emotionally coming to terms with a dominant father.

Increasingly, we find ourselves dependent upon impersonal bureaucracies, which encourage passive rule-following, deny personal responsibility, and undermine the basis of *legitimate* personal authority—for our purposes, specifically of fatherhood and manhood. We are now suffering from an epidemic of family breakdown that is partly based in parental dread of asserting authority. It is an irony that psychotherapy must now learn to help rebuild the very structures of authority that it originally and progressively criticized as repressive and to reconstruct them on a new and more legitimate moral basis.

We live in a climate where the narcissism that breeds fantasy and emotional absence finds tremendous support. Increasingly, we lack powerful male figures, fathers who can help children in the hard process of healthy separation from their mothers. Too often the character structure that develops in the absence of a father has been denied the benefit of this process and is frozen at an infantile or juvenile level. An infantile character dreads both living and dying, confuses commitment or involvement with being swallowed by mother, jumbles separation and independence with abandonment and psychic death. This narcissistic character cannot use the father

or father image as the bridge away from mother and will be
defiant about dependence *and* independence. The reconsti-
tution of manhood, of fatherhood, of authority, is essential if
we are to limit this nightmare of child–mother fusion and
the lifelong childishness to which it sentences its participants.

Christopher Lasch's justifiably influential book, *The Culture
of Narcissism,* described a way of life that must die, a culture
of competitive individualism. Lasch showed how the pursuit
of individual happiness leads to the dead end of total self-
absorption, consequent numbness, and lack of meaning. He
argued that the narcissist has an impoverished inner life because he is uninterested in the past, in the future, or in others.

For Lasch, our society is narcissistic in a dual way. First,
many people with narcissistic personality types propel themselves to celebrity, living out the fantasy of narcissistic success,
the wish to be admired simply for being oneself. When people
become famous for being famous, the vital relationship between prestige and social productivity becomes unglued. But
our society does not simply exalt the narcissism of the few;
it encourages narcissism in everyone by undermining parental
authority, by emphasizing appearance rather than substance,
by encouraging dependence upon faceless bureaucracy, by
glorifying youth, and by making it taboo to grow up. Lasch
correctly suggests that the absence of limits—of fathers, of
authority—expands the terrors of infancy and makes it even
more difficult to become an adult.[5]

In addition to the challenges posed by the waning of family
authority, the task of attaining manhood today also has been
profoundly affected by the historical transformation of the
workplace. Technological revolution, combined with the long-
delayed progress of women in the work force, is eliminating
a traditional preserve of male pride and male bonding. From
this moment on, we men are going to need even more internal

security about our manhood, for we have been denied the old comforts and privileges of sex role divisions at work.

If manhood is to reassert itself as a term of honor, pride, and prestige, a name for a kind of courage and responsibility, then we can no longer afford to be ironic about such values. But first we must regain its credibility—a credibility that has been almost eroded by the revulsion against machismo and the awful history of male privilege—and imbue it with a new kind of speech between men, one that honestly acknowledges male impulses toward violence in the face of social changes at work and at home.

Manhood is a phase of the male life cycle, the phase of maximum power and responsibility. Adolescence and early adulthood are preparations for it, and its core is moral maturity. It is the center of the arch of a man's life; without it, men go from adolescence to senescence, from childhood to senility. Manhood is what we look forward to when we are powerless boys and what we look back on with pride when we are limping toward the grave. To be known as *a good man* is the highest compliment for a man. It is what men despair of achieving when depressed—in our careers, our family life, in our sexuality, in our values. Our idea of manhood is our motivation toward self-respect. And most of us could not be more aware that the old images of manhood need revision, especially those that now cause us shame.

As we revise the definition of manhood, we cannot simply adopt traditional versions of the man's role, accept some feminist versions of manhood as neuter personhood alone, or begin with manhood *now*, as if one could mold present men without regard to their traditions, their fathers, their heroes.

We need heroes. They are vital to social life; they incarnate the ideals of a culture, especially the protector and defender functions of manhood. The hero must be the shield of the vulnerable—the young, the ill, the aged. Our struggle to establish the value of the heroic as a goal for men today, one with deep roots in tradition, must be separated from the imagery of the romantic hero, usually male chauvinist and *revengeful,* which we developed to keep us safe from our fears about childhood dependency. Modern heroism must take a very different direction: the protection and extension of bonds of trust and the reduction of the differences that divide people.

We have seen how the traditional concept of man's role not only deprives men of their inner lives, of expressing needs and vulnerability, but also glorifies violence and simultaneously locates emotion in women even as it depreciates both emotion and women. Yet the dangers of our passively accepting some feminist critiques of manhood as *purely* chauvinist are less clear. Yes, we men must fight our brutal, denigrative conditioning in relation to women: our capacity to accept women as equal persons is still in a primitive stage. But we must also resist the easy temptation of overidentifying with a feminist critique of men, of turning against our fathers and, ultimately, rejecting our responsibilities. Renouncing our fathers can render us powerless to speak on our own behalf. Men cannot expect women who are in the process of first emerging from domination by fathers to have easily the capacity to appreciate them; women must fight their fight for equality. We may ally with them in their fight and support it, but our struggle is quite different.

Later, we shall be exploring how the history of the ideals of heroism and manhood is our treasure. We need to mine that tradition, not reject ourselves or our fathers in favor of neutral personhood. We need to engage in a true dialogue with feminism, not to react to it with angry resistance or guilty acceptance.

To become men, we need to know our fathers. I tried for

much of my own life to deny the gifts given to me by my father, and one particular memory distills for me the bitter-sweet residue of my ambivalence. When I was about ten, there was a softball game in a bungalow colony of the Catskill Mountains, fathers and sons playing with each other, not against each other. Our team was two runs down with two men on base. My father hit the winning three-run home run, but not only that: he hit the ball out of sight! In that symbolic moment, I was so proud of him that my heart nearly exploded. My father rumbled around third base into a field ringing with praise, in that moment joining himself and me to Joe Di-Maggio and Babe Ruth—to heroes. He opened a path of power for me by *doing what needed to be done*, publicly. I can still hear the crack of the bat connecting with the ball; even today, it is an unfailing source of voltage and emotion. The meaning was clear: A Shapiro can do what needs to be done. *I* can do what needs to be done.

But the gift was not so simple. I also grieve that this rel-atively distant identification with my father was the best of my entire childhood. We "worded" one another, but we did not speak to each other. We had no real connection until much later in life. In fact, I have not even spoken to him about this until recently. I still feel both pride and grief in this moment of identification with his prowess, and probably some lingering feeling of inadequacy (he always was a better hitter than I was). But mixed as this feeling of pride might be, it is precious, because I was often ashamed of my father.

My grandmother and my mother helped me to become ashamed of my father by devaluing what he did well and denigrating him for not being who they wished him to be—the same practice men engage in. Their criticism of him implicated me, for I was in their care, and I felt disloyal to him as well as ashamed of myself for desiring to rise by my father's fall. What I am trying to suggest is that female criticism of fathers, whether feminist or seductive, is no simple thing for us as men.

It is deceptive to try to be an innocent man, for none of us can be wholly innocent of depreciating women. Our fathers were not completely innocent either, but neither were the mothers, sisters, wives, or daughters who were victimized by male supremacist ideology and behavior. So let us shoulder our responsibilities. The sins of the fathers *are* visited upon the sons, even unto the fourth generation. Let us not deny this, but let it not blind us also to our inheritance. I am grateful to my father for the gift of my life. I am still engaged in the process of trying not to resent him for being who he is. I forgive him for not being all I needed him to be, and I forgive myself for wanting him to be more. I try to accept responsibility for who I am. This way of facing our fathers as equals, to be detailed in chapter 3, opens the possibility of manhood.

If it is never resolved, being competitive with fathers or brothers keeps us children. Although competition challenges men to rise above their ordinary selves, constant, relentless competitiveness only expresses dread and jealousy, not commitment to values. We must repudiate the compulsiveness and the emptiness of being competitive with everyone about everything at all times. To compete in this way is the opposite of the kind of heroism we need to cultivate if we are to restore the idea of manhood to the realm of repairing trust between men. It is a heroic act for a man to overcome his jealousy of a father, brother, or son. The jealous fear of being displaced or of not being good enough only obscures the purpose of mature activity, which is to create value by layering quality, tenderness, compassion, and vitality into one's experiences and relationships.

Overcoming our fears—of being engulfed by our mothers, of being rendered powerless by our fathers, of competition from brothers, of irretrievable loss—is a precondition of our realizing manhood. But first we must acknowledge that they exist. We are all vulnerable to these fears, and no one achieves perfect poise, but in the effort to acknowledge and overcome them is the manhood-making process. We men must take the heroic vow not to live dominated by fear nor to wear a mask of invulnerability. The pretense of strength only blinds us to our true emotions and saps the vital energy we need for the process of overcoming these fears. Only in truly over-coming our fears—rather than pretending that they don't exist—can we taste joy and the capacity for generosity and give true pleasure and comfort to others.

Until the world is more just and less violent, we will con-tinue to need heroic models. Erik Erikson's studies of Gandhi and Martin Luther recognized the need for heroism and are good antidotes to the tendency in psychoanalysis to reduce heroism to neurosis.[6] The psyche cannot become its own world, after all. Men need to be turned *toward* the world, not away from it. Psychotherapy must be able to prepare men for the world, not attempt to provide a substitute for it. Within such a context, those definitions of manhood and heroism that view the achievement of self-awareness as a goal in itself provide only one side of the equation.[7]

Kurosawa's film *Ikiru* provides a memorable illustration of the kind of heroism we shall be exploring. A Japanese clerk, a thoroughly ordinary man, is diagnosed as having terminal cancer. He vows to make his life meaningful, and determines to create a park for local children. Nothing—not his im-pending death, not his own timidity, not the apparently im-penetrable bureaucracy—can stop him from making that park. This assertion of the value of human effort that both spans and fills the gap of death and otherness—this is heroism. A man looks to *his own tasks,* undeflected by envy of others or by fear of their envy. Each man has his own world to care for, a task we can accomplish by acknowledging our fear and overcoming both it and the limits of our narrow self-concern. We are all terminal, after all, and we need our acts to have meaning in the face of death.

Heroism is not the lemminglike willingness to die on the battlefield or the blind bravura of following an idealized leader but the courage to *be* a leader, to intensify the meaning of human kinship. Many men, even you and I, can be heroic in our own particular worlds and areas of responsibility. But to act in such a way, we must have beliefs, values, knowledge, and courage. To overcome our desire to be children—to run, to hide, to deny, to avoid—we must not only be self-aware; we must allow our minds and hearts to be penetrated with the meaning of our actions, for ourselves and those we care for. As men, we need to learn first how to care for ourselves as imperfect, vulnerable, suffering persons; only then can we learn how to transcend egocentricity by identifying with the needs of others. A man is self-authorizing. Without being rigid, authoritarian, or totally self-sufficient, a man will initiate action, take responsibility for the decision and for the consequences. It doesn't mean he may not have doubts or misgivings or that he moves ahead with total confidence, but he is not looking for a father to obey, blame, or defy.

The fact that adult women are now expecting responsible, independent behavior from themselves as well as from men is wonderful for all of us, for there are so few adults in the world, of either sex. Traditionally, only a few men entered adulthood or manhood, traveling an easy pathway instead of risking the narrow ridge where questions end and responses must be given. *Now the path of adulthood is open to all of us who, instead of avoiding vulnerability to other persons, can respond to social need.*

Men are called upon to respond in a variety of directions:

toward parents, mates, siblings, children, and the community. No one can do this perfectly, but no man can avoid responding without encountering guilt. A man's name is called, and he must answer or face judgment by those who call his name and by himself. Responding to persons is not simple or easy, for even some of those who ask our aid may try to attack us or demean us. But those defenses are the dragons killed by the hero who cares enough to find the person under the fangs and claws.

What are women asking men for these days, when the number of divorces stands at one million plus per year? Women are asking men to recognize their equality as persons, to care about them as persons, and, above all, to speak, to be present. Silent men, absent men, are unresponsive to women because they are defending themselves against their vulnerability. A man cannot honestly love a woman without being open and vulnerable to her. A locked jaw is a locked heart, and women are wise not to trust locked jaws and locked hearts.

The need for males to be men is radical. In the self, the home, in the workplace, in the community, in international affairs, men are needed. Heroism is needed. We have defined heroism as the ability to cut the umbilical cord that binds us to passivity, to fantasizing, and to magical approaches to solving real problems. The sword of manhood is not made now of steel but of energy and intelligence, of light. Men do not need to *try* to please women, thus demeaning themselves. A man is enough for a woman, as a woman is enough for a man, but he must learn to speak, to be present.

The traditional virtues of manhood are good enough for us if we can but remember them and reinvent them for ourselves: to protect; to defend; to build; to be loyal; to be a link between generations; to uphold the piece of heaven depending on our efforts; to be disciplined and responsible; to give of ourselves with all our might, heart, and soul, reserving nothing; to be gentle to those weaker than ourselves and to emulate those finer than ourselves.

If we believe in these values, we have a way to live, a way to respect ourselves. A man's capacity to care, to need, to know, and to be involved is the making of the world. Every man is *responsible* to make his relation to the world. Sages have said that every word we speak, and every word we fail to speak, engenders a devil or an angel. Surely, then, a man is responsible for his speech, for how he lives, for those he loves, for *what* he loves, for his presence and his absence, for his violence, and for the use of his death as a sacrifice.

In the next chapter, we shall be looking at some of the ways we men have become frightened about manhood and at just how urgent it is that we acknowledge and overcome our fears.

2

THE REVOLT AGAINST MANHOOD

What is the source of our first suffering? It lies
in the fact that we hesitated to speak. It was born
in the moment when we accumulated silent things
within us.

GASTON BACHELARD

Evidence of our revolt against manhood seems to be everywhere. Before we look at its elements, let us look for a moment
at one another and at the effects of our unwillingness to
acknowledge our own feelings.

This book is addressed to silent men. It has a simple message. Your silence is hurting you, your loved ones, and the
community that gives you life.

The silence of men is the terror of the earth. The silent
man punishes his mother and father, who need his forgiveness. He punishes his mate, who needs his presence and his
reassurance. He punishes his brother, who awaits his word
to approach. He punishes his children, whose smiles hesitate
in the silence of his gaze. The silent leader creates mistrust
in his constituency, and the silent citizen curses his community
with noninvolvement. The silence of men is vengeful, a breed-
ing ground for revenge, envy, and resentment. It need not
be that way.

When men refuse to speak, they are fantasizing. When they

fantasize, they are children. Male silence is a form of immaturity, a denial of our vulnerability to social needs. The narcissistic lie of male invulnerability now threatens to unravel the whole social order.

Many of the agonizing divorces that take place each year would not occur if we men could speak our needs. Most of the crimes committed by juveniles would not occur if fathers audibly and demonstrably cared about their sons or if sons could speak their own needs. An extraordinary amount of the violence and injustice in the world is caused and perpetuated by male refusal to speak with opponents. Gandhi and Martin Luther King, Jr., refused this silent projection of inhumanity onto "the enemy"; they died as martyrs to a future when men will speak to others who are different but no less human.

Much of the testimony of feminists during the past two decades is a record of the injury and rage they have experienced in their relationships with silent fathers, brothers, husbands and sons. Male silence means: "Leave me alone"; "I don't care"; "I don't need you." We have noted that the silence is defensive, designed to protect men against being vulnerable to their own dependency needs. The silence proclaims the lie that men do not need others, and the lie undermines the mutual need that binds couples, families, friendships, and communities. It is true that silent men are also frightened, but that does not excuse the lie, the mistrust, or the damage caused by that self-protective silence, nor does it ease the pain inside men's hearts.

Barbara Ehrenreich[1] gives one feminist perspective on the recent history of the narcissistic male revolt against responsibility. It begins with the men of the 1950s marching into corporate life, marrying, parenting, and becoming breadwinners because they dread being seen as deviant, as homosexuals or failures, if they live differently from the norm.

Ehrenreich goes on to describe the emergence of disreputable Beats and the less unrespectable *Playboy* "philosophy" of the 1950s, each preaching its own brand of rebellion against conformist responsibility. Then men begin to agonize over their vulnerability to coronary illness from "stress," and Ehrenreich concludes that the male revolt against the breadwinner ethic developed *before* the feminist revival began.

Ehrenreich's childish men exercise furiously to protect their hearts, still willing to compete for money, prestige, and success but not necessarily to support others. The androgynous hippie rebellion of the sixties introduced the long-haired male and the new ideal of passivity that defied all previous masculine norms in the name of the right to consume one's own sensuous pleasures, avoiding the traps of money, ambition, power, and responsibility. The legacy of the sixties ushered in the popular psychology of "individual growth," further fostering a climate of tolerance for divorce and "doing one's own thing."

Men who envied the freedom of adolescents searched for a perpetual hedonistic "trip," rebelling against what they sensed was empty responsibility, an empty mask of masculine authority. It is as if, having lost the status and the honor of the role of sole breadwinner, men had determined to jettison dignity as well.

Feminists taught that one could not depend on men; one needed the government to guarantee financial equality and independence. Many women who saw their security only in traditional family life were furious at feminists for threatening their "right to be supported."

Ehrenreich is properly horrified by her own story of the collapse of the breadwinner ethic and with it "the notion of long-term male emotional responsibility toward women." She is ironic about the fact that men continue to expect nurturing from women in exchange for *less* support and no lessening of their depreciation of women as parasitic. She leaves us with a slender "hope" that in a "world without a father," without commitments, men can somehow become manly again.

There is much to heed in this bind of feminist analysis. We men need a positive, adult definition of manhood as the mature phase of our lives. We have long possessed an infantile definition of manhood as symbolized by the Ideal Father; we more recently have acquired an enraged feminist definition of manhood as pure Domination; we have a childish male version of manhood as Perpetual Fun; and we have an adolescent version of manhood as Defiance of Authority. But we have no recognized and useful definition of being an adult man.

In *What Do Women Want*, psychotherapists Luise Eichenbaum and Susie Orbach describe a familiar phenomenon:

> Women involved in relationships with men found that although they had made enormous changes, their men had not. Women's developing autonomy clearly forced certain issues out into the open for couples. Men were making behavioral adjustments to women's demands, but changes in couple relationships clearly required more than men doing the dishes and helping out with the kids.[2]

Women need the protective *and* the vulnerable sides of men. But most men have been perceiving newly assertive women as people who do not need their protection, as people too threatening to reveal themselves to. Instead of responding to their own needs and to women's authentic desires, we men have been withdrawing from the *display* of independence by women, spitefully leaving them plenty of independence but giving them no support, acting dumb about every lover's need for mutual dependence.

"Where have all the men gone?" ask many women. Into sportsland, through the looking glass, some say, never to return. "First there was Saturday football," said one woman who blames televised sports for her divorce, "then there was Sunday football, then all-day Sunday football, then Monday-night football, and now there are Thursday-night games and new football leagues playing almost all year. It's a very, very serious situation."[3] But is sportsland really an issue?

In 1978, Natalie Gittelson[4] reported that many men's response to the feminist movement was basically a withdrawal from manhood. She found men more interested in masturbation than in love. The men's liberation movement was preoccupied with rebellion against responsibility, something Gittelson called "unbecoming men." Increasingly, feminists like Gittelson have become uneasy about male regression from leadership, when what women seem to want and need is more male responsiveness, without domination.

The formation in 1983 of the National Organization of Men—and its publication of "A National Anti-Sexist Men's Organization"—confirms this trend toward a stance of male dumbness about the needs of women and children. Their brochure states:

> We believe that it is possible to *unlearn* much of the old-fashioned Male Role, and to live freer, happier, and much more fulfilling lives. It's not easy to do, but it can be done. We have formed a new national men's organization, which has as one of its basic goals to help ourselves and other men unlearn the "macho training" that has led to so many of men's problems.[5]

This group is full of rage and resentment, but, although rage is often the first step in a process of change, it alone cannot help men to achieve manhood. Male silence, the refusal of responsibility, and childish male liberation are aspects of a larger phenomenon of male regression.

One of the founding fathers of the United States, Thomas Paine, could *assume* the value of becoming a mature man when he struggled with American public opinion about taking responsibility for self-government. Paine wrote that filial respect was not owed to King George III as the "father" of the American people because he had violated that parental bond by becoming a tyrant. "To know whether it be the interest of the continent to be independent, we need only ask this easy, simple question: Is it the interest of a man to be a boy all his life?"[6] Paine lived in a time when he could assume that the values, privileges, and responsibilities of the mature man were self-evidently more appealing than the state of boyhood.

Now listen to a thirty-one-year-old current American hero, Jimmy Connors, tennis champion: "Mature is a bad word. I never want to grow up. I always want to stay the way I am." The *Time* article that quotes Connors also states that "Perpetual adolescence is the tennis player's manifesto."[7] One reads in the *New York Times Magazine* admiring feature stories of American heroes like baseball pitcher Tommy John, whose "eternal boyhood" may be the ideal dream of American men. In the timeless world of the green diamond, the author muses, boys can be men while magically remaining boys.[8]

Now that neither the "natural" progress from boy to man nor the social roles assumed for centuries has the power of legitimacy it once had, men ask defiantly, "Why *should* I grow up?"

Popular wisdom has it that all men are boys inside and that perhaps, as some have suggested, the only difference between them is the cost of their toys. But that is surely a very recent idea. The belief that youth is a state superior to manhood—to the extent that some men of forty envy their adolescent sons not their physical vitality or their freedom to be boyish but their very state of freedom from responsibility—is surely new.

The revolt against manhood—against authority, respon-

sibility, heroism—has many sources, and it has the most serious consequences. For it is a rebellion not only against
manhood's oppressive, male-machine, macho dimensions but
against maturation itself. The crisis of manhood we now face
is best understood as an epidemic of "puerility." Puerility has
been defined as "the attitude of a community whose behavior
is more immature than the state of its intellectual and critical
facilities would warrant, which instead of maturing the boy
into a man adapts his conduct to that of the adolescent age."[9]

The central aspect of the puerile is the confusion of seriousness with play. The trivial is treated with great importance,
while the serious is treated as if it were only part of play-
acting. As we consider the condition of men today, I will
highlight this *absence of seriousness,* this confusion of playtime
with the demands of responsibility. Considered as a code for
adultness, "male liberation" is an especially puerile notion,
akin to the *Playboy* "philosophy" in the poverty of its conception.

The basis of the *Playboy* ethos is roughly: "You won't get
me; I'm keeping it all and spending it on myself." A prospect
that evokes Huck Finn, dreading the wilderness and family
life but heading for Bloomingdale's. The *Playboy* ethos was
the first philosophy of Indoor Man; the playboy avoids both
nature and society, preferring to have fun in his "pad" with
a succession of ageless playmates.

Manhood's current disgrace reaches beyond the realm of
revolt against seriousness. Today's puerility includes more
critical matters. A study released by the House Select Com-
mittee on Children, Youth, and Families reports that 65 percent of divorced fathers do not pay support for their children.[10]
If one considers that this statistic does not include those abandoning fathers who do not bother to divorce, one can see that
a huge number of men are guilty of deserting their children.
When we add to this the number of men who stay with their

families and commit acts of violence against wives or children, we are left with a chilling view of the crisis.

My face hurts from trying to smile, listening to puerile men endlessly describe their tennis and golf activities. Have you heard men who are bored with ethical or political issues become passionate about the Little League? I recently met an ex-banker who retired at thirty-four to devote his life to sleeping late and having fun. He will not date a woman older than twenty-five.

Any ideology of manhood that is based purely on defiant revolt can lead only to the dead end of puerile self-interest, especially if it is a revolt against responsibility to support and protect the aged, women, and children, the essence of the task of manhood. Manhood must be *for*, not against.

Most of my own ideas about manhood were formed in my adolescence, before I knew myself. My proudest moments as an adolescent were the time I knocked a boy unconscious with one punch because he was taunting me in front of girls at a party, mocking me and insulting my "honor," and the time I returned to football practice the day after my eyelid was ripped open in scrimmage, requiring twelve stitches. At sixteen, I was clearly developing into a traditional warrior. Then I started to read—Steinbeck, Dos Passos, Richard Wright, Hemingway—and to develop a passion for championing the underdog. I longed to undergo an ordeal, an initiation into the powers of manhood and heroism.[11] I viewed manhood as killing someone to protect someone else. But I did not wish to remain a boy. At any cost, I wanted to "grow up," to become a *real man.*

As an adolescent, I was defiantly *against,* and especially against my father and brother. When I was sixteen and at the height of my mania for competition, I was totally absorbed in demonic heroism.[12] I wanted to be Beethoven, Alexander the Great, Rembrandt, Napoleon, King David, General Patton, Joe DiMaggio, the quarterback of the Detroit Lions. I was constantly on the lookout for great men, men who were *different* from the masses but who, preferably, led and served them. I wanted to be different, not like my father, a mere private in World War II, or my younger brother, forever wanting me to include him in my games.

The only question for me was what form my "greatness" might take. I liked to imagine saving my female teachers in burning buildings, but I liked equally to fantasize about over-throwing tyrants. Slave revolts seemed to offer marvelous opportunities for romantic martyrdom. It was crushing to me to realize that the United States would not aid the Hungarians in their rebellion: I was ready to go and fight.

I know now that many of my notions about manhood were childish rescue fantasies, adolescent visions of revenge and heroic defiance, fairy tales with muscles. And I know now that ideas about manhood that define themselves *against* others are puerile. Their true home is our adolescence, when our rebellion, our awareness of being different from others, of not being controlled, helps us to define a world that is wider than our family. But if the rebellious adolescent fails to grow up, he must remain forever a fantasist and a narcissist.

Hemingway's code of manhood, with its intense scorn for those who presumed to know the world without being players, is puerile. Hemingway must be there, the eyewitness, when the bull is killed, when the marlin strikes, when the infantry wades onto the beach at Normandy—as if being there were in itself a measure of manhood. He knew very well that the truth a man must master is the truth of violence, but unfor-tunately, as has been said of one British MP, he "immatured as he aged." The terse Hemingway style was a virtue in evoking events dramatically, but it also was a mask for an emotional impoverishment so severe that it kept him more than half in love with violence. He became addicted to violence. He never faced his own violence toward women, and he ended his life in a world of eternal play, a puerile man whose isolation and emptiness were unbearable.[13]

Hemingway, Emerson, Wolfe, Twain—all seemed to sound the same note of defiance against the soul-shriveling conspiracy of society when I read them as an adolescent. Surrounded by a much more feminized and corporate society than the one they railed against, I secretly prepared my Huck Finn soul for gestures of rebellion. The problem with my sophomoric heroic literary sensitivity was that it kept me narcissistically focused on myself in the theater of my imagination: "Real men" were a vanishing breed, I believed. Heroism was being stifled in men, who were being everywhere seduced into conformity by the promise of comfort and security.

Eventually I learned to enjoy women more than fighter planes, but I also learned to keep them at an emotional distance. The women who showed me how deep sexual love could go could never be either social companions or the true partners of my thoughts and feelings. I did not want to be "involved"— a tragedy that extended through two marriages. Year after year, I kept my distance, reserving myself for myself, starving myself of love, lost in fantasy, prolonging my adolescence.

The ideal of manhood that I struggled so hard to sustain was a puerile one. Still, the notion of manhood that I gained from Hemingway and the others had the possibility of *evolving* into something serious and mature. The children of parents who weathered the Depression and World War II had a sense of *seriousness*. There was still a belief that men were *protectors*.

A generation ago, men told stories of heroism. Today, men tell stories of victimization, about being abused by fathers, employers, wives, children, society. And it is all *one* story. I call it I.R.E.: "I" for the sense of injury, "R" for resentment,

and "E" for estrangement. For theirs is the story of enchant-
ment by Circe, of the transformation of men into subhumans
by the wish to be taken care of by an idealized mother who
turns into a witch.

The puerile seems to have triumphed. This kind of male
powerlessness is both a form of amnesia about the heroic
ancestry of manhood and an effort to magically conjure protective parents by acting immaturely. Immature men feel: "I
am being hurt and no one cares—not even me. I just withdraw into a state of silent, bitter judgment and let things fall
apart. I will not help. No one is worth it." Such an attitude
both expresses and creates despair about care: it is too hard
to care seriously about anything. It is a careless attitude,
and the essence of the puerile is carelessness about serious
things. But if men lose the sense of caring, the sense that
they are protecting something, they lose all sense of direction. Their lives have no meaning and their deaths have no
meaning.

It is difficult to grasp much less chart the range of present
male confusion and distress. An airline executive, bleary after
his fifth scotch, said to me, "You know what I think about
being a man? I think that seven things are expected of a man
today: to be a good provider, to be a good lover, to be a kind
father, to be social and a good conversationalist, to be a good
soldier—and did I say provider? How many is that? Is that
seven? Well, I just want to say, and I have said so at Rotary,
that if any man has done three out of the seven, that is damn
good. Because it's all just too much. That's what I think about
being a man. It's all just too much to ask."

In vino veritas, perhaps, but this is only the partial truth of
resentment. Many men feel this way, and some of the resentment has a mysterious, almost paranoid dimension: "They"
are using us and destroying us, and the enemy is unclear.
Someone is doing something to men.

Men have an infinite number of ways to express "do not count on me" to wives and children:

> They are silent.
> They pacify with counterfeit words: "Sure, I will . . ."
> They interrupt.
> They smirk.
> They lecture.
> They withdraw.
> They go to sleep.
> They watch TV.
> They say, "I'm trying."
> They promise to be good boys.
> They say "Yes, but . . ."
> They leave.

By giving double messages about their dependability, men hope to coerce women into "doing it all" and leaving them alone.

Many men today seem to be in a trance. They worry about money, aging, sexual potency, their images, security—but not about whether they are measuring up to their own ideal of manhood. The question rarely arises for today's man. It seems almost as if he has lost his sense of honor and has become shameless.

From the nature of this puerile lack of concern about the loss of manhood, courage, and readiness to deal with reality, I have sometimes despaired that the only activities that can awaken us from this trance are war, violent sports, and the magic of competitive business. Without the stimulus of violence or a manic fantasy of making a million dollars, men tend to withdraw into the kind of silent resentment we have described as based in narcissism.

There have certainly been other times in history when men were confused about their identity and when their self-mistrust bred more mistrust in women, and perhaps such crises of male identity are periodic functions of social change. But we are suffering this now, and we must try to respond to our era's male regression without idealizing the past, making war, using women as sacrifices to male insecurity, or creating Utopian fantasies.

For me, the most dangerous aspect of this male identity crisis is not any one particular symptom—i.e., falling birth rates, rising coronary rates, the expansion of the gay community, the anguish of maturing women about meeting a good man, or even critical unemployment among white-collar men—but the lack of serious response to a major cultural crisis.

The religious calendar and the traditional gender organization of behavior no longer direct a man's use of his time. What *is* the best use of a man's time? Puerile men try to totally control their own time. They withdraw into a video trance, resenting any intrusion. If the parent, mate, child, community, or employer claims their time, such men become passive and perform the minimum of what is being asked of them. They regress into resentment and feel *forced* to work, to be a parent, to make love.

There is only one way for men to break out of this polarized trap of resentment and loss of self, and this is through the moral discovery that a man belongs to the community that needs him in his fullest dimensions as a person. If he does not belong to such a community, he will be not a man but a whining infant, a puerile dreamer, no matter how big his paycheck, how crafty his tennis games, how skillful his sexual technique, how snuggly his fathering behavior. If such a community does not exist, it is a man's task to help create one.

Men who have no community to serve become infantile, become mere spectators. And there are many such men today:

They are "just looking, thanks." It is of such men that Germaine Greer has said, "I sleep with men. I don't expect anything else from them."

Some men never wake to seriousness. One woman I know tried for three years to get her husband to agree to feed, dress, and manage their three boys one morning a week so she could prepare for work more easily that day. He agreed, but he would oversleep, forget to buy food, misdress the children, direct the operation from bed, and so on, and then complain that she did not trust him to do the job *his* way. Confronted directly about whether or not he cared about her or the children, he would say, "Yes, but not at seven-thirty in the morning." This man complains that his wife nags him.

I have been presenting these various manifestations of puerility as instances of a general revolt against maturation, against the traditional concept of manhood as mastery and responsibility. But I have not yet asked *why*. Why puerility now? Surely it is not the true *desire* of men to be puerile, to be silent, to withdraw, nor is this massive social phenomenon merely the result of millions of individual decisions to remain childish.

No, there are powerful social forces acting on us men, acting to inhibit us, creating what Lasch called a "culture of narcissism." First, there is the breaking of the chain of generations, the loss of apprentice work, of the practice of personal mentors who transmit the ethos of manhood by example and story. There is also, as we have touched on only briefly so far, the widespread alienation that prevails between fathers and sons, as well as the social demotion of men through their loss of breadwinner status and gender prestige. As with anticolonial revolt, the critical onslaught against white male aggression has brought down legitimate authority along with domination and injustice. There is a general crisis of legitimate authority in personal and political relations. The code of honor among men that once depended upon class differences and gender differences has disintegrated, leaving men without guidance. And the advent of the nuclear age has created a numbing feeling about the actual adequacy of a man to protect his loved ones. It is difficult to invest in values one cannot protect.

All of these factors mean that the mix of motivation, reward, inhibition, guilt, and punishment has changed profoundly for men, dangerously favoring regression to the kind of adolescent behavior we have been illustrating. We have noted that while there are vital democratic social advantages to the revolt against white male dominance and although male rebellion against rigid masculine norms offers some welcome new behavioral flexibility, the loss of a guiding ideal of manhood has been socially catastrophic. Strong cultures honor youth, but they also insist that the young honor the cultural ideals of manhood and maturity; they do not fixate on adolescent forms of play without seriously threatening their own existence.

If we briefly survey just one arena of male regression, that of our relations with women, we can see how the constant factor of male dread of women, always active in male fantasy, has been reinforced by the climate of women's increasing power and male gender confusion and envy of women.

One friend of mine expressed his fear of women by telling me a story about his army buddy that dated from their postwar service in Germany. His friend, Mac, was on duty at a guard-post that was surrounded by a cyclone fence. Two German prostitutes beckoned to him, and he went over to the fence. One pointed to his penis and then to her mouth. It seemed a good idea at the time, and when his erect penis was firmly gripped by one of the women, the second took out a knife and told him to throw his wallet over the fence or she would castrate him. He believed her and paid the ransom.

"The difference between men then and now," said my friend, "is that Mac had a choice." The punchline was clear: now it is the wallet *and* the penis.

Or consider the story of Bill, a lawyer in a large New York City law firm. Sometimes he has to work late. Eleanor, his wife, attacks him for not caring about her or the children. His real lack of care, however, does not reside in his late hours but in his fear of confiding to her that she is making his plight worse by denigrating him at a time when he needs her understanding. He does not care enough about himself or his relationship to Eleanor to tell her that her childish inability to function unless he is there at exactly six p.m. is another part of their problem. Instead, he tries to pacify her by promising to come home early in the future. But in reality, he cuts her off, avoids her, and feels he cannot trust her.

Bill feels that, although Eleanor demands everything— time, sex, money—she is incapable of empathizing with him. He refuses to tell her that he works late because he is frightened to negotiate with his boss for better pay and fewer hours or that he fears losing his job, because she has shown fear and intolerance about any "weakness" in him. He would rather die than need her support—or rather, he views depending on her *as death*. He imagines that she would mutilate his pride. Hurt by her lack of appreciation of his efforts at work, he refuses to respond to her own fears of being alone and unloved, and he devotes more hours to jogging, landscaping—anything to avoid her. He will neither act protectively toward her nor show any vulnerability or need for her.

Bill feels, "I am alone; I am doing everything alone." He denies his pain and his need and continues, punitively and in an armored way, to do everything alone. He refuses to ask for anything, but he will condemn Eleanor for not understanding his silent needs. He has an idealized image of a wife, but Eleanor flunks his standards, and *he is glad*, because it means he does not have to struggle to change his own bitter silence. His envy is his childish glee in proving that "no one cares." Bill is too frightened to fight for love or trust. His unspoken feeling is: "If you don't want me the way I am, I will refuse to be with you. I will withdraw and withhold myself. I will come home still *later* and be with you even less." Enamored of his resentment and comfortable in the imagined safety of his monologue, he does not care enough to begin a real dialogue. The conflict with Eleanor is "too much hassle." He will work and silently curse her and all other women—though he might find momentary comfort with another woman as immature as he, a woman who seems to be making none of Eleanor's demands. Sometimes the Bills of this world even leave their Eleanors and remarry, only to find themselves confounded by the same dreadful circumstances they imagined they had escaped. They have changed their partners but not their understanding of what it means to be truly present, to act mutually.

In his envy, Bill is *competitive.* He feels he knows better than Eleanor how to behave, but he will not tell her he needs her, as an equal. He negates his own need and her gifts, denying his heart, undermining his own *self-trust* by refusing to speak, colluding in maintaining mistrust between Eleanor and himself by his silent refusal to make a better connection with her by *explaining* how he feels.

Like many men, Bill is resentfully conscious of feeling unloved but unaware of his own failure to make a wholehearted commitment to loving. Where would he find a model to teach him? Certainly not in the puerile psychotherapies of "growth." They would simply encourage him to leave, in which case he might retreat into misogyny or begin the same sad cycle with a new mate.

Jean, a woman who has struggled hard to overcome a submissive history, recently began to tell Frank, her husband, about her need to be valued more by him. When they first married twenty years ago, she had allowed herself to move into a house she had never liked because it was near her in-laws and convenient for him. Frank worked hard to earn money, but he left all household and social responsibility to her; he did not appreciate her work as in any way equivalent to his. When Jean became economically independent, she began to evaluate his behavior toward her. She felt that she deserved more time and attentiveness from him.

Frank could not comprehend Jean's request and kept saying that she was a romantic, that if she wanted more from him, *she* should give more and that he would respond. The dragon he needed to slay was the resentment he felt at any suggestion that he initiate more intimacy—lovemaking, socializing, or anything that might confer status on his wife. But this refusal to take the initiative in raising the heat of their relationship was costing him both the respect and love he wished to have. Many marriages die because men become withholding in their courtship behavior. They stop giving the gifts of time, energy, attention, and commitment, stop devoting priority to the marriage, which is a large part of what enables a woman in mid-life to be able to respond in a passionate way to a man. As people age and as they fear aging, as they lose parents and fear being alone, the need for commitment, intimacy, and support becomes even more pressing than before, and more essential to sexual love.

A man's commitment to a woman means two things. It means granting her his highest priority, ensuring that she knows that she and her needs come first with him. It also means maintaining continuous involvement with her and nurturing their relationship over time, rather than being a good boy to get sex and then withdrawing into narcissism. Commitment also involves the readiness to deal with the woman one loves *at her worst,* whether that means illness, awful in-

laws, harshness to one's children, insults, or being ignored.
Commitment means that one will not make a silent judgment
and withdraw, wishing the "loved" person dead, but that one
will risk conflict, again and again, to achieve the pleasure of
mutual attentiveness, a quality that is itself in need of con-
tinuing maintenance. The acceptance of ordeal by conflict *is*
caring.

Because most men lack a mature or even a heroic model
of such a way of loving in a relationship, they often resent
every step they take in the direction of seriously caring for a
woman. Those steps are now usually initiated by women,
who must cope with the puerile resentment of the men. Once
we men can devote ourselves to new values, we shall be truly
liberated—not to withdraw or flee but to enjoy the benefits
of the real intimacy and mutuality that are born of commitment and responsibility.

But now that male pride can no longer be sustained by the
roles of "provider and protector," how can we reinvent a male
code of honor? Men's traditional sense of purpose is rooted
in heroic myths of sacrificial service, but contemporary the-
orists snicker that damsels are no longer willing to be saved.
Some psychologists have said that "there are fewer and fewer
dragons around to slay (though perhaps more and more wind-
mills left to tilt at) in this highly technological, extremely
materialistic, impossibly egocentric age."[14] Fewer dragons?
There are more dragons: war, the pollution of our environment, unemployment, nuclear tyranny, the isolation of the
young and old, the erosion of democracy. One's immediate
community can provide enough real dragons to occupy more
than a few brave souls.

One precondition for our willingly assuming personal, responsible commitment is an awakening to the need for seriousness, to the necessity of suffering and experiencing guilt,
to the need for exercising judgment, and for the crucial ac-

quisition of speech. Male muteness and puerile resentment are devices to avoid suffering and guilt. We men often seek control and revenge, numbing feelings, in order to avoid accepting a reality that might demand personal commitment to a code of values. It is as if the awesome complexities of our age made the need for choice too overwhelming for only one person.

The technicians of the psyche are themselves hardly immune to losing a sense of moral responsibility, especially when they must deal with issues of violence. It is puerile and irresponsible to be seduced by technology of any kind, but we are constantly invited to treat serious issues of human suffering as if they were only fodder for the expertise of professionals.

When I first began to work as a family counselor, I had as clients a violent couple. Roger had just broken Ann's nose and had repeatedly bruised her badly, chiefly for behaving differently from the image of the wife he wanted. He felt victimized when she did something he opposed, and he imagined that his feelings of anger and oppression justified his violence. Actually, he denied committing any violence: he was sure his rage was a righteous rage and confident that he could persuade me he had done nothing wrong. Ann would just have to stop provoking him by being different from his idea of what she should be. Tragically, she agreed with him. She was sure that something was wrong with her. The punishment proved it: she was bad.

I took the "clinical" problem to the psychiatrist who was supervising my work, who regarded it as a long-term problem that required expertise in handling the phenomenon of sadomasochistic fusion. He smiled at the urgency of my desire to stop the violence, which he told me was "just part of the system." He was right about the difficulty of ungluing Roger and Ann, but he was dead wrong in his detached tolerance for her suffering. After seven years of being troubled about the logic of diagnosing victims on the basis of the violence that was being done to them and after listening carefully to a myriad of professional arguments that attempted to justify social immorality, I finally committed myself to making sure that men in my own community could no longer assault their wives with impunity.

Working with family court judges, the Volunteer Counseling Service, and many community and feminist groups, I created a program for violent men that confronted them with their responsibility—for their own violence and for its consequences. This is now a court-mandated program, backed up by a New York State law initiated by the New York State Commission on Domestic Violence.

The issue of responding to violence is a crucial one for manhood. Male liberationists have emphasized that violence really frightens men, and yet, they are also caught in the myth that violence is the primal root of masculinity. We men must discipline our violence and not be seduced by tough-guy myths. *But we are indeed less masculine if we avoid responding to violence that threatens the people and values we love and believe in.* Care is precisely this willingness to undergo conflict.

In the nineteenth century, exemplary heroism was displayed by unarmed British officers who had the courage to stand up under fire and thus to bind their men together so they did not break and run. Although anachronistic as a military tactic, the test by fire, confronting violence in all its forms, remains a test of manhood.

Again and again, we hear the "liberated" male voice complaining, "I don't *want* this world of ordeals, violence, feminists, loss, hard work, responsibilities, conflicts." The illusion that one can choose one's world is no better guide for men than the illusion that one can own one's time. The desire for our own worlds is a violent, narcissistic defense against our involvement in this world.

It is an irony that Freud, who unmasked the narcissistic defense as infantile, was himself confused about the nature of personal involvement in the world. Freud wrote in *The Future of an Illusion,* "Men cannot remain children forever; they must in the end go out into 'hostile life.' "[15] For Freud, religion is invented as a defense against childish helplessness, to compensate for the absence of a protective father. It is true that naive religious faith is a form of wish fulfillment. But Freud was wrong to suggest that religions like Judaism and Christianity serve only to protect men against suffering. On the contrary: they teach the positive dimension of suffering, which is an indispensable element of maturity.

Freud was a courageous man and a stoic. He had contempt for puerility in all its forms and was heroically committed to his work. But in his magisterial aloofness, he was not a good guide for men seeking a way toward responsible commitment to a community. He did not speak a language that endorsed the benefits of human suffering or human equality. He preferred a language of symptoms and an illusion of scientific research.

Freud himself remained violent, unable to comprehend his own vulnerability to his father's violence or to grasp how violent he was toward rivals, sons, or disciples. In a disturbingly intellectualized way, Freud denied both his own suffering and his own needs, as well as his own guilt. Although his life was in some ways tragic, and he endured great agony from his cancer, he refused to suffer his own vulnerability, preferring instead to keep an iron grip on his ego and his intellect. He was an heroic exemplar of the old code of *give much, ask for nothing.*

In fact, no one could give Freud much personally, only

allegiance or grist for his theoretical mill. *He* was the doctor and kept control always, never discovering that in suffering we find the power to need others and to let them be equal to our needs, to *be* our equals. Freud refused dialogue, which is the healing goal of psychotherapy (never the beginning, which is the patient's monologue and the silence of the therapist). Freud developed a language to decode dreams and desire and to explain how rage responds to absent love, but he himself was mute in the presence of presence.

Men who wish to remain boys because life is too violent remain full of a violent wish to control others. But neither wishing nor power nor puerile values can help us to face suffering, loss, and violence like men and to be responsible toward others.

If we cannot look to Freud as a good guide toward a life of dialogue, where can we look? One direction is back to the source of our religious heritage.

The lives of Moses and Jesus are lives of apparent *failure* to empower dialogue, like the life of Gandhi or like the philosopher Martin Buber's efforts to make of Israel a human community instead of another nation-state. Buber believed dialogue is the only proper way of life: being present, meeting the other in his or her concrete, specific otherness. For Buber, real failure is avoiding the demand for dialogue, refusing to enter into it. Where persons meet in the spirit of dialogue, meaning grows, as does the demand to respond fully. Buber says: "Man of today resists the scriptures because he cannot endure revelation. To endure revelation is to endure this moment full of possible decisions, to respond to and be responsible for every moment."[16]

The antithesis of puerility is responsibility. Boys strive for self-liberation and control of others. Men strive to acknowledge their fears so they can accept fuller and deeper responsibility. Responsibility means caring for the world around us in such a way that we give our all to protect it from violence and to steadily increase the presence of love and trust.

We have discussed some of the causes of the narcissism that encourages puerile behavior in men. But what are the origins of the flight from responsibility? Einstein's theory of relativity, the absence of absolutes in time, space, motion, matter, has been confused with moral relativism, the absence of *any* standard of evaluating values in a world without God. The concerns of modern literature have further undermined the nineteenth-century ideal of personal responsibility by substituting pawns of fate, class, the unconscious, and the antihero for the life of a moral person who expects his life to be judged on the basis of what he does and does not do. Crude Marxist notions of historical determinism further undermined the concept of the person as a moral agent.

The numbing of conscience that began with the slaughters of World War I unleashed the violence of injured nationalism. Ethnic *differences* were used as justifications for violence; class *differences* were used as justifications for violence. They produced a world of murderous innocents, the violent world we now face, in which no one is guilty—not the Palestinian or the Israeli terrorists, not the black militant terrorists, not feminist terrorists, not the men who break their wives' jaws for differing with them. This is the world we must come to be responsible for. Although we did not make it, we cannot avoid it. It is ours to nourish and change.

Years of murderous repression have produced a modern world that has been crucified by struggles for liberation. The wars of liberation by ethnic minorities have produced still *more* suffering minorities, more violent splitting; the struggles for liberation of oppressed classes have produced the struggle for liberation of the sexes—too often a liberation from living together that endures into hostile feuding that becomes the principal source of identity for the feuding parties. Violence is always the fault of the other. Healing violence, reducing the scope of violent splintering by difference, is a task for men now.

We have long known of the inhibiting effect that the corporation's hivelike hierarchy exercises on drones and indecisive middle-managers, but John Kenneth Galbraith has now raised the alarm about the erasure of independence and responsibility among the business world's top executives. "It is, of course, axiomatic that no responsible corporate executive expresses himself publicly in opposition to the decisions, purposes, social effect, political activities or malfeasances of his organization."[17] If men increasingly withdraw from all forms of family and community participation, replacing commitments and needs with acquiring more products, needing more services, and indulging in more drugs, placing our trust only in technology, we will just regress further into passivity.

When a man takes responsibility for violence and resolves to work for a world of *persons*, a moral world, his boyhood finally ends. With that commitment, none of the social pressures toward narcissism can stop a man from a moral turning away from egocentric fantasy and a turning toward selfhood.

Unless we men can grasp this story of responsibility, the story of a man's life, the meaninglessness of his life cannot be repaired. And the story of a man's life depends a great deal upon traditional stories of manhood as a kind of bank of virtues: without them, men are truly bankrupt. The story of a man's life is the story of the victory of purpose and meaning over chance, chaos, ignorance, and evil. It is the story of the active will breaking out of the bondage of passivity and delusion, making moral choices and commitments.

What I call puerile is the disruption of this true life story by the endless repetition of a story with a negative outcome, a story that celebrates that negative outcome as a triumph of spite. "I know what is going to happen, and it will be bad" is the story of the passive will, refusing to commit itself to action. The puerile revolt against manhood is a revolt against the bonds that sustain and enrich social life itself.

The value that I am arguing for as the source of all other assets is the increase of the substance, or presence, of reality, its very realness. Such terms sound mystical to those who cannot discriminate between embodied and disembodied speech. As schizoid ghosts, we talk words without substance, deluded by our own imagery, blind to our own real intentions and to the felt existence of other persons.

But evil is done by those who live in a state of unreality, by those who are ignorant. So teach Plato, Jesus, Buddha, the Sufis, the Zohar. This mystery has been revealed often, but the intolerance of the light of real presence keeps obscuring the truth. Love is one term for this presence. God is another. Truth is another. Radiance is another. Grace is another. Suffering is the mother of this understanding. The meaning of these words is a mystery only to men who are asleep. Good is what confers more reality on persons, and evil is what diminishes that reality.

Male armor diminishes reality. A French Catholic philosopher has said: "If things are really to exist for us, they have to penetrate within us . . . nothing can enter into us while armour protects us both from wounds and from the depths which they open up. All sin is an . . . attempt to bring back to the plane of unreality and painlessness an emotion which seeks to penetrate the depth. The law is inexorable: we lessen our own suffering to the extent that we weaken our inner direct communion with reality."[18] Men who remain unable to suffer remain puerile, exiled from the reality of human contact and from concern about the world they inherit.

Men in revolt against manhood share one characteristic: they are out of touch with their fathers, and whether they are submissive or rebellious, they have not become equal to their fathers. Injury, resentment, and estrangement also emerge in the form of the myth of the absent father, a matter to be discussed in the next chapter.

3

FATHERS AND SONS: TOWARD RECONCILIATION

I remember my father is alive
and it amazes me
because I have been living
as if I were alone in the world

from "Safely," by DAVID IGNATOW

Is there a new kind of father in the world, a nurturing father? Is there a revolution in paternity? Are fathers actually going to spend more than a few minutes a week with their children? Will they speak to them, person-to-person? Is it true that absentee fathers and absent-minded fathers are suddenly fighting for the privilege of parenting, zealously attending child-rearing workshops? Despite the highly publicized rhetoric of the "new fatherhood," the tradition of the absent, distant, silent father is still very much with us.

Writing about "the father" is a complex task, because the term embraces a multitude of faces—among them: daddy, dad, father, the patriarch, the ogre, the absent father, father figures, like priests and mentors, and God. The only *person* in this group of images is father, but father is the least well known, precisely because a father is not an image but a person playing a role.

We shall see that it is the absent father, what I call the

"internal father who does not care," a child's misinterpretation of fatherly distance, that licenses puerility.

Clarifying our imagery about fatherhood will make it possible for us to focus on reconciliation between real fathers and real sons through difficult meetings, hard words. Sometimes the very imagery that surrounds fatherhood makes it harder for sons to approach their fathers as persons. Approaching our fathers is the ordeal that helps sons to become men.

A son's name for his father is not neutral, because childish associations clustering around dad and daddy obscure the man himself. "Daddy" is a child's idealized perception of a protective father. "Dad" is an adolescent's more companionable view of a protective father. "Father" may become an adult's respectful, loving, and forgiving view of an imperfect person, a vision clarified both by having been able to let go of daddy and dad as well as by having become aware of the social distortions and expectations of the role of father.

To achieve independence and the ability to love, a man must separate himself somehow, anyhow—but always by a great struggle—from believing in the illusory promise that dad will, or should, take care of him. As long as a man makes an idol of his father, any gap in love or care feels like a betrayal. The son's resentment of that imagined betrayal keeps him puerile and inhibits his own capacity to love, to become a father himself. Sometimes a man can grow into a man only when his father dies; sometimes it is a father's absence or illness that releases the son's potential to mature. The expectation that father must always be there as a protector is the shield of boyhood, but it is the enemy of manhood.

The idea of father as protector begins in early childhood. The only consolation a boy has for his father's interruption of the intimacy with his "always-there" mother and for the shock of the fleshly betrayal of her purity is the image of his father as his protector against inner demons and natural and social threats. The son reluctantly surrenders the warmth of his mother's breast and the nourishing security it means for the promise that, if he leaves the nursery, his father will protect him in the valley of the shadows that lies in the world beyond.

Banishment, exile from mother's garden, is tolerable only if daddy's or grandpa's or God's eye is upon us. The terrible shock of realizing that *no one is there watching, protecting,* is what nerves a man's resolution to accept responsibility for himself and his world.

The development of manhood is composed of a series of realizations that love—adult love, responsible love—can grow only into the space that is opened by acknowledging the absence of the protective father.

Fathers, mentors, and father surrogates, like psychotherapists and priests, have the responsibility to educate males to the death of daddy as an ideal image and to the eventual death of father as a living person. In this way, sons can grow into the space vacated by the responsible protector. If sons fail to learn that the space is empty, that the role of father is *limited,* they will not be able to surrender the demand for unlimited protection that keeps them boys. And why should such a son ever wish to take on for himself the burdensome role of being an ideal father?

Few fathers these days become patriarchs. The patriarch is a man who has been able to extend his dominance and influence throughout the range of his entire family, sometimes in a way that is benevolent, and sometimes inhibiting. Most research on successful women suggests that the powerful, patriarchal type of father was a strong factor in having guided their self-confidence.[1]

Although the patriarch has been both idealized and attacked, he is today too rare a bird to evoke our concern. Most are eccentric individualists, as valuable and as scarce as American bald eagles. They are an endangered species and need protection. For our purposes, patriarchs are most important as *images* of godlike fathers, images that may become idols to children of mere mortal fathers.

The ogre is the bad father who, instead of being protective, is abandoning, punitive, or controlling. Unfortunately, cruel fathers are very real for many children. Perhaps three million fathers assault or sexually abuse their children each year.[2] Two million divorced fathers refuse to pay child support. Many of these men have been outraged by the divorce itself and by their limited access to their children; others are furious because their former wives have presented them to their children as monsters, and they feel powerless to overcome that image. Many divorced fathers do pay child support, but they use their children as helpless pawns in a vengeful struggle against their former wives. Ogres are fathers who inflict unnecessary suffering on their children and who are consequently regarded in a magnified way as BAD.

Sons who suffer from deprivation by daddy or from bad fathers feel they are themselves bad; they tend to fixate on longing for a good, protective father, someone to save them from their badness, a preoccupation that seriously interferes with their own development into men.

We have a new term now to describe the character of the abandoning or infanticidal father, "the Laius Complex." It is a term that developed when psychotherapists realized that Freud had skewed the Oedipus story: the myth is not simply about a regicidal and incestuous son but also about an infanticidal father.[3] Laius orders his son put to death. In fact, Sophocles' great drama *Oedipus Rex* is about our capacity to see *all* the violence in families, not just one side of it.

The Bible, too, may be read as a struggle to make men more responsible as fathers—less infanticidal, more aware of their jealousy, more willing to consider the claims of *all* their children. One of the Bible's basic themes is paternity.[4] God is the father who cares, and men are commanded to be more like him. God teaches men to be protective toward the members of their immediate families, toward their extended families, indeed, toward all the children of God. This jealous God values fidelity and loyalty. He is molding a new kind of family, one that is bonded not only by property but also by care, patriarchal but not infanticidal. This God needs the help of men, who often rebel against the tasks of manhood, especially against being compassionate fathers.

Infanticidal envy continues to afflict fathers. Many fathers are unable to overcome the envy they harbor for the son in the womb or for the son sucking at the breast. The child's first task is often to survive his father's envy—by smiling, by hiding, by any means possible. Moses, Jesus, and Oedipus all narrowly survive infanticidal rage.

The story of Gary gives us a contemporary portrait of a man who survived infanticidal rage by the narrowest of margins. Gary is a forty-year-old successful public relations executive. But he never feels safe, and the impression he makes is robotlike, as if even his emotions have been carefully programmed. Gary's father first showed paternal envy in his comments about Gary's puniness as a premature baby. His father regularly rebuked his mother when she showed love toward her new son. As he grew older, Gary's defense against this murderous envy took the form of separating himself from his mother and overidentifying with his father, depreciating her himself as disgusting, controlling, and invasive. His father's envy denied Gary the ability to be intimate and loving with women.

When Gary realized that he had allied himself with his father's attitude toward his mother and that his choice was dividing him not only from his mother but from his wife and daughter as well, his own perception stimulated a waking vision. He saw an open door leading to a garden, and he experienced the wonderful possibility of going into that lovely garden. But then a voice said, "Beware!" and he shrank back, frightened.

Freud's notion of castration anxiety is not adequate to express the self-inhibition that this vision represents. During therapy, Gary realized his tendency toward workaholism was an obedient response to his father's prohibition against enjoyment. Gary had solved the problem of his father's powerful envy by denying himself any pleasure—time, music, fun, love, recognition, confidence. As a means of pacifying the threat from his father's murderously envious tone of voice, he had distanced himself from close contact with anyone. He was confused about the value of anything he did, of anything he possessed, gave, or received.

Gary's terror of the garden is both a way of avoiding the snake of his father's envy and a device to punish himself for his own envy. His solution was self-exile.

The Garden of Eden is the formative myth of divided or neurotic consciousness. The myth is a condensation of all the levels of envy that assault the psyche, not simply man's envy of God but also God's of man, woman's of man and man's of woman, the creator's of creation and creation's of its creator, parent's of child and child's of parent. Envy deadens relationships by making distance between persons.

The envious father is also the distant father, and understanding the imagery of the distant father is vital for our purposes, because this is the father whom most of us have experienced. And despite the flurry of interest in "new fatherhood," this is the father most children will continue to experience. There is absolutely no evidence from any source to indicate that large numbers of men are spending more time with their children or that they plan to take paternity

leaves or are willing to undertake a major share of child-
rearing. Fatherhood is a role for most men, not a passionate,
central vocation. For most distant or absent fathers, it is sec-
ondary to career, marriage, and recreation.

Most fathers are unknown to their children because they
are physically absent much of the time and often absent-
minded toward their children when they are at home. Even
there they are otherwise engaged, fixing the car, raking leaves,
watching television, jogging, or paying bills. The resentment
that fathers so often project when they are at home is often
a sign of denied and hidden envy or jealousy, of the wish to
be emotionally absent.

A child must learn to deal with both the real and the
emotional absences of a father—the father's anger, envy or
emotional distance—and the child's own imagery about that
absence or distance. For most men struggle not with their
actual fathers but with their internalized images: the absent
father does not care; the angry father is an ogre.

The father who dies can never be perceived as a benevolent
figure if the child cuts him off when he dies, resenting the
death and concluding "I never had a father" as a way of
numbing the pain of loss. The father who "never was" becomes the absent father, the chilling father who does not care.
He is the product of a child's ingratitude and resentment.
But the dead father gave his child the gift of life and many
other genetic, psychological, and perhaps material gifts and
guidance. A son's reconnecting to his dead father, even late
in life, can cause profound psychological healing.

I have known three men who lost their fathers when they
were children. They were angry, bitter men who could not
enjoy their lives until they realized that they were carrying
terrible burdens of guilt.

One of the men lost his father when he was still an infant;
he had barely known him. When he was fifty, he finally

located his father's neglected gravesite and erected a stone; he was startled at the sense of inner peace that he experienced, and only then was he able to get out of debt and begin to live decently.

A second man lost his father at the time of his sixteenth birthday. The father had been a poor man, and my friend was ashamed of him, bitterly resentful of his death. He had become a wealthy insurance broker, but he was isolated, refusing to participate in any community activity. His only recreation was gambling. When he was forty, he experienced a crisis of guilt toward his father. It came upon him during the season of his father's death, just before Christmas. He embarked on a process of rediscovering his father whom he found had been a wise man, highly esteemed in his church. He rejoined his father's church, where he began to develop a social identity and a feeling of belonging for the first time since his father's death.

The third son was bereaved at age twelve. His father, a community leader and a successful entrepreneur, had died suddenly after a short illness. The son was unaware that his father was so ill and was unable to visit him before he died. Numbed by loss and guilt, the son dropped out of high school and continued to live a marginal life until he was thirty. At that time a series of dreams about his father propelled him to visit his grave for the first time since his death. He became depressed and then began to grieve for the little boy who had lost his father and for the real father he had lost. He remembered the games he had played with his father, remembered his voice, his touch, his laughter, and his pride in him, his only son. He remembered that his father had been brave, intimidated by no one. And this meek man, who avoided contact whenever he could, began to turn around and to face his life, struggling for the first time in years, persevering, feeling his father's spirit strong in him.

Paradoxically, fathers who have died may be more present as positive, guiding influences on their children than fathers who are physically present but who are experienced by their children as "never there." Any father is vulnerable to a child's judgment. Children lack discrimination: Daddy is either always there or never there.

What is *expected* from fathers? There are ideal expectations, based on childhood needs for protection, realistic role expectations, and those expectations that are keyed to the limitations of particular persons. The demand for the ideal father reinforces the child's internal myth of the absent father, the father who does not care.

One man, boiling with resentment, complained to me: "My father never cared about me. He refused to get me a bike when I was ten, and when I was twenty and needed money for college, he told me to collect garbage on a truck, and when I needed money to buy a house, he was grudging, and when I asked him to help me buy a car, he said no. The only thing he ever did for me was take me skiing, and that was only because *he* liked skiing. He preferred being with his friends to being with me, and I hated him for that. He was never home with me, and then, when my brother was born, *he* always got the best stuff, even if he didn't ask."

When I asked him if he ever considered that his father also had needs, he answered, "I'm the son: I have needs. He's the father: he's supposed to deal with my needs."

The commercial rhetoric of Father's Day is so pathetically hopeful about the Best Dad in the World and a Father Is Always There to Guide that one can only be embarrassed to give or receive such effusions. Here the remoteness of fathers is thrown into the highest relief by the sentiments intended to bridge the father–child gap. The sheer unreality of the language reflects the unreality of the substance in the trust between fathers and children. All conventions are ideal, of

course, but the conventional father of Father's Day is a uni-
corn. No one has ever seen him.

A son's demand for a *perfect* father, a person who is *always*
being daddy to him, is, of course, an impossible demand,
created by the radical vulnerability of the child. The real
father can never live up to these expectations; hence, in the
terms of the child's secret, unspoken myth of betrayal by
daddy, every father is *not there* and does *not love.* The absence
of paternal care, any gaps in paternal care, are transformed
into a neurotic litany, a bitter ritual of eternal paternal non-
return and rejection. The puerile man is the product of the
boy's uncorrected myth of the absent father. "No one cares"
is the adult rationalization of the immature son who fails to
seek for his real father.

For men of my generation, the myth of the father who
does not care feeds on the absence of fifteen million fathers
during World War II, and on the tremendous impact that
absence had on the wives left behind and—for our purposes—on the small boys who had to cope with their mothers'
overwhelming presence in their father's absence, becoming
the little men of the house. But even without the war separation, the world of work has increasingly separated father
from the home. The distant father, the breadwinner, rarely
becomes a truly visible person to his children. He is the silent
one, the mystery.

The absent father is brilliantly explored in William Wharton's novel *Dad.*[5] Here the protagonist, an artist, returns home
to help care for his distant and now sick father, to accept the
ordeal of fear, hospitalization, deterioration, and death. The
comic desperation of coping with his father's clinging chil-
dishly to a denigrative wife comes to a climax in a scene of
violent regression. After being told he has cancer, the father
rigidly assumes the fetal posture, hiding under the bed, def-
ecating all over himself. The son's devotion to his father

(witnessed by his own son, who also does not speak much to *his* father) enables the father to return briefly to life, newly determined to grow a beard and to keep himself separate from "Mom."

Slowly, Wharton reveals that this absent, silent carpenter who vanished into his garden so often had elaborated a complete, idealized world. He lived there, in the garden of his mind. This is a metaphor for so many men who withdraw from full participation in this world. As his father expresses more and more interest in living in the present and speaking up for himself instead of merging with his wife, the son realizes that he must stop splitting his own life between fantasizing and presenting a counterfeit presence and become more fully realized in his relationships with his actual family and friends. In pursuit of his father's shadow, he grasps his own substance.

The struggle for full presence is powered by willingness to get beyond our resentment at the absent father—whether he is dead or alive—no matter how ghostly he may be, no matter how critical or ornery, controlling or forbidding. Climbing that mountain of resentment, struggling with our own muteness, wrestling with the fetal father hiding under the bed in terror, we discover the reality of our own life in the demand that *we be* the caring person we demanded that our fathers be.

Instead of hiding in our childhood litany of complaints and deprivations, sons must come forward to do battle with the paternal silence, the hospitals, the bitter memories, the distance, raising our fathers up by our own caring to meet them, wherever they may be, among the living or the dead. By this agonized effort of personal will and need, we bring about our own maturation. By closing the gap between father and son, we close the gap between an ideal of care and its realization and between the kingdom of the spirit and this violent world.

If there are going to be new kinds of fathers, it will be at least partly because there are new kinds of sons, sons who have learned to speak to their fathers. But it is the distant father we confront today, and we should not expect miracles from our fathers tomorrow. Reconciliation with this distant, silent, absent father can be our most important act of self-assertion, an act of accepting a real person, letting go of our image of dad, and growing into manhood in the process.

How can a son actually repair decades of silent distance and mistrust between himself and his father? Before I present some examples of my own experience as a very imperfect model, I would like to frame them with some understanding I acquired by hindsight.

Long before I could enact it in my own life, I sensed the possibility of reconciliation in Homer's story of Odysseus and his son, Telemakhos. In *The Odyssey,* the goddess Athena addresses Telemakhos as he sets out on his quest for his long-absent heroic father:

> *You'll never be fainthearted or a fool,*
> *Telemakhos, if you have your father's spirit;*
> *he finished what he cared to say,*
> *and what he took in hand he brought to pass . . .*
> *The son is rare who measures with his father,*
> *And one in a thousand is a better man,*
> *but you will have the sap and wit*
> *and prudence—for you get that from Odysseus—*
> *to give you a fair chance of winning through.*

And when Telemakhos recognizes his father, who was in disguise, he exclaims:

> *I swear you were in rags and old,*
> *And here you stand like one of the immortals!*

But Odysseus refuses the idealization:

> *No god. Why take me for a god? No, no.*
> *I am that father whom your boyhood lacked*
> *And suffered pain for lack of. I am he.*[6]

Here is powerfully and beautifully articulated evidence that all sons idealize, devalue, and exile their fathers, and that all fathers are responsible for exiling themselves. Nevertheless, true perception and reconciliation are possible if the process is acknowledged and understood.

Odysseus himself, "Son of great Laertes," does not hope to find his way home without visiting the land of the dead to sacrifice to his mother and to find guidance from his father surrogate and mentor, Teiresias, who tells him how to endure and when and where to sacrifice to Poseidon, the jealous father. Thus men survive and find their own sons to be a source of power. This understanding of *lineages*, real and symbolic, is also crucial in the "tribal" mythology of the Bible. To be a "son of" Jacob, Moses, David, is to be a "member of" and to know the limits of membership, to know what one may not do and what one must do. Once God is dead and the commandment to Honor Thy Father is denigrated, there are no limits to narcissism, and there is no way home to the continuity of generations or the community of persons.

Neither the death of one's actual father nor the absence of a biological son excludes a man from this lineage of filial gratitude. We have fathers and sons of the spirit also, and that is also binding and offers membership to anyone prepared for sacrificial love. In reality, there is a childless "father," a mentor, waiting for every fatherless child.

Even if most fathers were not absent, men would require more than the support of our biological fathers to help us grow into manhood. But the devaluation of the father who is there, who has been there, makes the ground shaky underfoot; it makes men vulnerable to idealizing unknown fathers, idols.

The best remedy for idolatry, the passive worship of childish images, is a real relationship with a mentor—a teacher, a priest, a psychotherapist, an uncle, a neighbor. The mentor is a guide whose own identity leaves him free to seek the full development of his surrogate son. He does not say, like the father, "Do what I say" or "Be like me" but rather "Be like you, discover yourself."

Historically, our greatest mentors have been the religious teachers. They have bridged the gap between the need of the child in a man for daddy-dad-father and the need to release the child from spiritual infantile dependency.

Jesus calls God "Abba," Father, using the Hebrew family word. He taught gratitude. The Judaic Father was the incarnation of the community. Reverence for the father and for God, the Father, as the source of the good in the community is central to Judaism, the foundation of Torah. Jesus repersonalized the doing of God's will, re-created the caring Father as a living presence in the midst of a history of abandonment, slavery, and domination.

The "Abba experience" is central to Jesus's mission and teaching, and if it is delusional, so is the hope of care in the face of crucifixion. It is precisely the abandonment of one kind of hope, the illusion of immediate responsiveness by the idealized father, the undergoing of forsakenness, the despair unto death, the drinking of bitter gall, that gives birth to another kind of hope. Jesus understood his death as continuous with his life as a sacrificial offering, as a bond of care between the apparently absent father and his children.

The refusal of the disciples to accept suffering or to understand that loss is the way to redemption offers a crucial event for comprehending the puerile quality of men who take flight from manhood. All the male disciples flee from Jesus.

Not one follows him to the end. Their flight is from loss, death, suffering—from reality. This same flight is the core of male silence, denial of emotion, armor against experience.

Jesus crucified cries out: Father, Father, why hast thou forsaken me?

Forgiveness of this abandoning, controlling, infanticidal father is the Christian awakening of the spirit from being dominated by resentment for the absent protective father. On the other side of that resentment lies gratitude for being born, for the created world, and for the revelation that all persons are real and suffer, even fathers.

If the Old Testament is an effort to create a father who cares in this world of infanticidal families and history, then the New Testament is an effort to forgive both the failure of fathers to be ideal and the perversion of kingship into domination, and a call to begin again to create a living community. Our cultural fathers have been wiser than their sons, "culture heroes," such as Nietzsche and Kafka, who accuse the fathers but who dread the reality of human life, which Martin Buber called "the meeting."

Let us consider Kafka's letter to his father, an unmailed letter, a monologue. It begins:

> You asked me recently why I maintain that I am afraid of you. As usual, I was unable to think of any answer to your question, partly for the very reason that I am afraid of you ... And if I now try to give you an answer in writing, it will still be very incomplete, because even in writing this fear and its consequences hamper me in relation to you and because (anyway) the magnitude of the subject goes far beyond the scope of my memory and power of reasoning.[7]

This is how Kafka avoids the meeting with his father. He proceeds with great courage to face his childhood terror of his father's envy, judgment, and persecution, but he is also caught in it and in *guilt*. He is guilty not just because his father imbued him with feelings of inadequacy but because Kafka himself remains trapped within the scope of his own mind, not caring enough about himself or his father to risk speaking. Instead of overcoming his fear, he accuses, blames, and denigrates his father, who remains an alien stranger. Kafka flees from the vulnerability of a meeting, blind to the fact that his father is a suffering human too.

Is it not curious that the three heroes of existential modernism—Kafka, Nietzsche, and Kierkegaard—never married? Kafka realizes that fathering a family is the highest thing his father achieved and that by marrying he could achieve independence and equality with his father. But it is on this point that Kafka, the hero of modern introspective victimage, lies to himself and takes flight:

> There is a view according to which fear of marriage sometimes has its source in a fear that one's own children would sometime pay one out for the sins one has oneself committed against one's own parents. This, I believe, in my case has no very great significance. For my sense of guilt actually originates, of course, in you . . .[8]

Lost in the self-righteousness of his accusations, Kafka cannot comprehend either the arrogance of his judgment, his falseness, or his spiteful defiance of accepting responsibility for his own guilt. The puerile man blames his father for his life.

The arrogance of accusing the father, blaming him for our suffering, is, of course, the subject of the Book of Job. It is also the vulgar understanding of psychotherapy as "blaming the parents."

My own arrogance toward my father took a different form. I felt I was *better* than he was, and, like Kafka, I became his judge. My mother's announcement at my birth that "the king is born" could not have helped make me more modest. As

Freud remarked, the first-born favorite son of the mother feels like a conquistador. And if I were king, then who was my father? A mere pretender to manhood, according to my mother. But he looked pretty big to me, especially in his absence, for he was drafted into the army and transported across the Pacific Ocean when I was four years old.

Sadly, my mother perceived my birth as a blow against my father—the birth of the king, her own knight, her own idea, so far superior to his poor flesh. She did not know the existence or the dimension of her envy or its dreadful consequences. My father feared her envy and envied me in turn. And I envied my brother when he was born and usurped my special place near my mother.

There were many times in my life that I felt my father did not care for me, and always with numbing consequences. More often, I silently judged him to be not good enough— as breadwinner, as father, as citizen, as hero. My purpose is not to abase my own perception, because I know that my father envied me, and he *was* often emotionally absent and sometimes desperately punishing. But I am a man now, and I know something about how hard it is to be consistently caring. I know better now than to accuse, blame, or denigrate my father.

Instead, I will honor the care that was there, sustaining my life, and nurture my gratitude for that. Because the care *was* there; it was mixed with menace, to be sure, but it was there. My father cannot remember it himself very clearly, but I have letters to prove it and to renew the springs of my faith. This does not mean I have ceased to suffer the consequences of his chilling behavior. Even now, on some nights after being with him, I cannot sleep, gripped by the old childhood terror that no one cares about me and that nothing I do can make him warm or get the chill out of my heart. In the past, I have become an empty, feelingless zombie to protect myself, but I have learned now to reach out to others to retrieve my capacity to feel. Forgiving is a constant struggle.

In 1945, when I was five and my father was twenty-five, he wrote to me virtually every day from rat-infested Okinawa and from troopships and airplanes, letters full of drawings of trucks, showers, animals, guns, the trays the GIs used to eat from, rattraps, parachutes, and other wonders of the world beyond Brooklyn. My father made me a ring out of a nickel and a salt-shaker out of bamboo. When he won medals for sharpshooting, he sent them to me. His great gift, as I continue to realize when I reread his yellowing letters, was his sharing his intelligent wonder at the world with me, his sending these words and pictures *to me*.

This linkage to my absent father became a powerful presence inside me. It was the making of my mind. All my life, I have made writing and drawing my resource, a haven, a world my father gave to me, the best he had to give. As I sent back to my father my daily drawings and slanting words, contact was made across an ocean of space and time. Like so many men, my father felt safer making contact from afar, through written words and pictures, than he did *in person*, through speech and touch. But any contact is a form of love.

Some of my father's letters show his impatience and resentment. He was no saint. Some of the letters must have scared me, with the descriptions of the atmosphere of war, of his using explosives to blow things up, with his warning to me to be good to my mother. But I am more troubled today by reading my mother's letters to my father. How he could have endured them is remarkable to me. Most of them go like this one, dated March 13, 1945:

I need you so and I don't even know where you are. You've been gone a week now, but this is the loneliest, bitterest day I've ever had.

March 29

> If only I had you to run to now, perhaps it wouldn't be so bad . . . Today, my mother—and it sickens me to say it, accused me of stealing $25 from her years ago. That she has been mistrustful is nothing new, but to learn about this has been in her mind all along is unbearable.

Clearly, my mother was near the edge of hysterical collapse when my father was drafted. With few emotional resources of her own, my impossible self and my brother were too much for her to handle. On good days, she "almost" falls down the stairs but gets off with a sprain:

June 27

> Steve loves to make things for himself—like cheese and crackers and peanut butter—just as you do—having him around is like having you in a smaller form—but I need you . . .

October

> Sometimes it scares me—my feeling of complete dependence on you and your love. God forbid if anything ever happened to deprive me of it. I'll just want to die—my whole life is built around you.

October 6

> The other night when Stevie wanted you and we talked about where you were and what you were doing he complained because you were only a buck private . . . I think you ought to put it to the Captain—man to man.
>
> One thing this little trip of yours means is that Stevie will have to start school without you here . . .

October 18

> Pop isn't working just now, either the work is too hard or the pay is too small . . .

My mother was furious at her own father, but she never realized it. He was a silent, angry presence, far from the ideal protector she longed for. He liked *playing daddy,* bringing bagels and toys to the babies in the family, but he gave very little emotional or material sustenance to his family and must have felt very guilty about their poverty. He escaped into gambling. No one knew him, really, but my mother's unacknowledged fury at him came down like acid rain on my father, my brother, and me. Where was her promised ideal protector? What was this dreadful reality?

In the vacuum of my mother's selfhood and in the violence of the myth she nourished about her absent father, the serpent egg of envy grew. The man she wished for became the ideal man I wished to become, and so I became a sword blade cutting the flesh of my father, my brother, myself, and others.

For my mother, my father's absence was more vivid than anyone's presence could be. His actual presence could never be enough to fill the void in her. He was whiplashed between her idealized expectations that he make "everything" right and her inability to feel that anything real was ever enough. She envied anything my father did that was not done at her bidding:

October 4, 1945

> Stevie finally broke down and cried, "I want my daddy." He's been acting funny all day, but tonight when I called him up for supper, he didn't want any, and that's unusual—not even a chop. Well I kept it up, asking him what bothers him and I could see he felt very funny and finally cried, "I want my daddy." . . . Darling he misses you, but he can't talk about it. It's just there . . .
>
> *I* do find it *difficult* thinking of you as a teacher of 50 men but there's nothing you can't do, if you really try. Why, for my money, you'd be a wonderful president . . .

Here is the snake in the Garden of Eden. The real food of love is made inedible by envy. My own nurture was being poisoned by envy, and speech was turning into the silence of idealized demands. I am not grateful for my food, and my mother is not grateful for my father's letters or for his real gifts, and so I must suffer and be charged to fulfill my mother's need for a king, a president, a God. She is too needy herself to know how to comfort me in my need for my father, and I am learning not to reveal any need to her, my father, or anyone else for many years. She feels "no one is there," and I feel "no one is there." And my father, in his own fatherless state, also feels "no one is there." No one really cares the way daddy would care—that one who would deny us nothing. Luckily, he is not here to be put to that test and found wanting.

My mother's guilt-inflicting letters were poisoning my father. How could he cope with the angry need that was being masked as love? Never mind him; he must be strong *for her.* He feared her violence and never really addressed it, at least not in my presence. So I grew up thinking that my mother's violent, invasive, self-absorbed demands were love. How could I know that what filled me with dread and made my father wish to avoid her was not love. It took me a long time to forgive my mother for behaving as if no one could be good enough. Later in her life, she was able to take more responsibility for her own needs, and we repaired our relationship. Reflecting on my own manhood in the process of writing this book has meant saying good-bye again to her; she died six years ago.

At twenty-five, my mother was terrified of her responsibilities; she became desperate, punishing. Her letters are those of a victimized child playing grownup in the absence of her daddy. The living presence of her family was unreal compared to the absence of the absent father. My father endured her punishing anxiety and the similar anxiety of his mother. He did what most men do when confronted by female violence: he managed to survive and keep a presentable façade by vanishing whenever he could. To present his full presence was too great a burden for him: He withdrew.

When I was twenty, I went 3,000 miles west, trying to separate from my mother, marrying, and attending graduate school in Seattle. My father wrote to me regularly, and much to my surprise, on rereading the correspondence, the letters he wrote to me were warmer than the ones I wrote to him. I had no idea then, or even seven years later, during my psychotherapy, when I thought my father was a only gray shadow in the background, how important he was to me. I simply had no memory of that little boy, dressed in his father's hat, wearing an army jacket, drawing soldiers, and crying "I want my daddy."

My first efforts at reconciling with my father came after my trip west to the Pacific, unconsciously following my father's path. Having separated from him, I tried to turn and face him, but not as an equal.

In 1963, when I was twenty-three and my father was forty-three, I learned that he had colitis, and I wrote to him. Clearly, I was still working on my mother's project to turn this inferior person into an ideal father:

October 8, 1963

> Dear Pop—I found your last letter rather disturbing. It is obvious that you are becoming more and more concerned about guilt feelings; their origin, and their effect on your ability to enjoy yourself. This, in itself, is a healthy sign, for you can cure yourself only if you realize you are ill. I think you also realize that guilt is a kind of inverted aggression. You have had serious problems with your mother, with ma, with my brother and me. And you *are* at a critical age. What is worse, you have no occupation that would enable you to work off or sublimate your problems, and which would simultaneously make you feel that you were achieving something. I am not surprised that your stomach hurts.
>
> The question is, what are you going to do? I have two suggestions. First, I think it is silly for you to want for my

brother to learn enough psychology to help you. You can help yourself. There are many good books on psychosomatic ailments. Believe me, they can help you. More general works, like Freud's *Introductory Lectures,* can also help you to reduce inner tension by enabling you to understand how your mind works, and by showing you how "normal" your problems are. If you don't make an effort to understand yourself, you will *deserve* to suffer. Introspection *alone* is not enough. You need knowledge.

Second, you have got to spend your time "productively." You do not want merely a hobby, nor do you want simply a way to earn more money. Golf is not the answer, nor is real estate—that is ma's way of expressing herself.

Hasn't it ever occurred to you that perhaps part of your problem is that you are starving the side of yourself that has always, even if in small ways, tried to be creative?

It was a letter that hardly deserved the warmth and vulnerability of his reply:

October 13, 1963

Dear Steve:

I have read and reread your letter several times and it is simply beautiful. I am fortunate and full of great pride to have a son as intelligent and as perceptive as you indeed are. I do take your letter seriously and what you have spelled out is not new to me since I was made aware of my problem after our summer of 1957. I had been suffering with colitis for about 8 years and bouncing from doctor to doctor until one wonderful couple at the S.G.S. colony recommended me to Dr. Granet. As soon as we returned to the city, I saw this doctor, who after one visit recognized the psychosomatic aspect of my illness and he sent me on to a psychologist friend for a little reeducation. You may have seen the name Cinelli in the house somewhere, well, he has been responsible for saving my life, and I don't think this is any overstatement, since you yourself in your letter pointed out that it can be a matter of life and death.

After about three visits to Cinelli, my colitis disappeared dramatically, however the condition is never really gone as long as I backslide into periods of unawareness and I come up with various other symptoms which are signals of distress such as the pains in the stomach and breakouts on two of my fingers.

In searching backward, Cinelli came up with an interesting coincidence wherein, every time we moved, I had a reaction and symptoms of distress. Any inactivity and boredom on my part is strictly due to my own lack of initiative since there is certainly plenty of things to do and see in NYC.

I am glad that I can tell you these things and I hope it will ease your mind that I am not in too bad shape and that there is no cause for alarm on your end.

In my humorless lack of humility, I was preaching Nietzschean self-overcoming to my father. Not only was he patient with my arrogance; he even managed to find something good in my effort to care. He used to like to quote Mark Twain's lines: "When I was a boy of 14, my father was so ignorant, I could hardly stand to have the old man around. But when I got to be 21, I was astonished at how much he had learned in seven years."

At this time, my father tried to close the gap between us, but I would not allow it. I thought he was not good enough, but the reality was that I literally did not know then how to suffer any emotion or how to meet any person in loving contact, in dialogue.

Reconciliation with my father was not a single event; it is an ongoing dialogue, a process of assimilating the past, of continually trying to enjoy more mutual appreciation in the present. This is difficult, because my father is more intimate by letter than he is in person. He tends to speak short, concrete monologues, avoiding responding to what is said to him unless great energy is invested in getting him to participate in a dialogue. And I have had to travel a long way from my withdrawal from my mother's violent presence and from my father's emotional absence into my own personal presence and speech.

Today, if my father says, "Yesterday, I visited my grandchild," and I reply, "She seems almost old enough to visit for a weekend without her parents," he might well respond, "The Yankees won again." I feel violated by his interruptive discourse, dismissed, rejected, and competed with. But I also understand that this disturbance in his receptivity is a defense against "taking in" anything that he fears might then control him. It is a very common defense in us men, but its recipient feels that no one is there, listening or caring. I have struggled to accept this uneven quality in our relationship, although it is still sometimes numbing. But the important things are the *continuity* of our relationship and the possibility *at any moment* of mutual revelation through dialogue. He can depend upon me, and I can depend upon him, despite the sometimes brutal gaps in communication that often divide us.

Many times in the last ten years I have brought myself to tell my father about my feelings about him, each time getting closer to knowing him as a person—gradually shedding the images of him as a failed daddy and an incompetent dad, letting him be himself. It is a constant effort for me to try to let him live his life—remarrying, moving away—without being judged by me. And our reconciliation is vulnerable to sharp regression, because he is very withdrawn, and I am still open to being hurt by his emotional absence and am angrily demanding as a result. I am vulnerable, like him and all sons, to a return to childhood feelings. Here is an illustration of a recent experience with puerile, judgmental regression and recovery.

During a visit to my mother's grave, I saw no stones there, the traditional Jewish markers left by visitors to a gravesite.

I assumed that no one had been there in a long time. I became guilty and then enraged at my father, blaming him for not caring more. The old litany began: Probably he doesn't care about me either! Does he call? No. Does he visit? No. I have to take care of my mother's grave all alone, and I have to drive a long way to visit him. Why should *I* care if he doesn't care? I'd like to simply forget about him, to punish him.

I telephone him to ask him to meet me for dinner. He says the ninety-five-degree heat is too much for him; he can't travel in it. Just as I suspect—I must do it all. I tell him that I'll visit him tomorrow, planning to tell him how he's burdened me, this father who is never there and always going away. When I was a child, he was always away in the service or going to work, and now he's moving to Arizona, where he will travel routinely in hundred-degree heat.

The next day, I roar into my father's apartment, and he tries to kiss me and embrace me. Odd behavior for a man who does not care. I calm down a bit. He *is* glad to see me. He sees I'm upset and suggests some old-time Brooklyn Chinese food as helpful. Okay, but I don't think he cares about anyone, I tell him. He never visits the graves of my mother or his father, mother, brother. He wouldn't even visit mine.

My father says, "I was just about to prepare things so I can be cremated and not cause you any trouble."

I say, "That is not a gift, not needing me to care for you."

He admits that he never visits the graves of his dead family members and that he probably would not visit mine.

So I say, "If you don't need me and I don't need you, where is the quality of our being family? When you move to Arizona, will it be like I died? Why should I visit you? What will hold us together? You cut people off. I'm afraid you'll cut me off, and I'm afraid I'll cut you off. I can't trust you."

He listens. I see that he is pained. He still resents his parents, his brother, my mother. He cannot face their loss. He never knew his father—he was always away, working with his mother; his grandmother raised him. Everyone preferred his brother to him, just as my mother preferred her son to him. He had been resentfully silent about this for most of his life.

He protests that it is not true that he cannot be trusted. He endured his mother's craziness and kept her alive at his own cost, emotionally, after his father died. He endured my mother's abusiveness. He endured her dying of cancer. And when his brother was dying of leukemia, he had to deal with it alone; his mother refused to visit her dying son because his hemorrhages spoiled her image of him. He assures me that if I need him, he will be there. He says that I never asked for anything and neither did he, so we just didn't know. He praises me for helping him when Mother was dying. Tears fill his eyes.

I keep eating spareribs, still suspicious. He *did* do all these things, but he did them the wrong way, grudgingly, resentfully. An ideal father would have been more loving, more understanding.

"I never learned how to talk," my father says then. "My father never talked to me. My brother and I never spoke. You and I rarely talk, only when you push me to do it. I try to avoid talking about bad things, painful things, because I'm afraid it will make me sick. I'll get caught up in it, like when I was divorcing my second wife and I felt a mad dog had bitten me in the ass and wouldn't let go."

He's proud of his pen-pal business, built in his sixties. He's content with his new wife and his limited routines.

"I don't feel I can't trust you," he says, "and I'm sorry if you feel you can't trust me. But don't get cancer to test me."

I feel ashamed, not of speaking angrily to him but of falling back into imagining him as the absent father—again, and at my own great cost. Because when I lose myself in the myth of the absent father who doesn't care, I become raging, mute, childlike. And then I use the myth to excuse my own difficulty in caring with a whole heart for others.

Visiting my father was a sacrificial journey, like visiting my mother's grave. Both opened me to suffering. After suffering, I become alive, and I can see more clearly. I can see my father with compassion. As a child, he endured violence and neglect. As a father, he *was* critical, negative, complaining, grudging. He was distant; he scapegoated my brother, and he envied me. But he did not always run away. He was not ideally present nor was he absent.

"I'm willing to talk," he says. "I just never know I *need* to talk, so I can't start it. I think it's better to avoid certain things, but I guess that makes it harder to talk at all. I realize you can't talk to yourself."

My father is honest. I say, "I try hard to forgive you, Father, for some things you did and some things you didn't do, but sometimes I just forget who you are." He takes that in while reading the message from his fortune cookie. "Maybe you ought to see if you can't forgive your parents too," I say. "You sound so resentful about them."

He can't see himself talking to gravestones. He can't grasp that the stone is in his heart. "I know I missed your whole childhood," he says. "I can hardly remember things. But just remember, you are the apple of my eye." Now he is crying, and so am I.

My father is a sweet man. He does respond. He just cannot initiate. So when there is a gap, a silence, it is up to me to fill it. Not with guilt-inflicting rage about the absent father, but with telephone calls, visits, my speech, my feelings, my true presence. His absence is his burden. It cannot rob me of my presence. Only absence of faith in myself, failure of memory, mistrust, can rob me of my presence. My father's silence is a temptation to rage and an opportunity to speak. The choice is mine.

I realize his saying "You are the apple of my eye" is a miss, already an avoidance of contact. It is what he suffered, *not* being the special brother, that he is trying to offer me. *He* was denigrated when he was a boy by constant comparison with his brother. But I do not desire that apple of envy. I do not wish to be Cain or Abel, Jacob or Esau, Joseph or any of his brothers. My father does not fully understand how to love without making denigrative comparisons. He is imperfect, but he is good enough for me, an imperfect son.

The childish myth view of the absent father creates a climate of distortion and a terrible vulnerability to delusion in adult sons and daughters. If boys are to mature, they must give up nourishing the childhood absence of idealized daddy, endure their adult suffering of this absence, and reconcile with their fathers. If they persist in clinging to the illusion of the absent daddy as the betrayer—if there is no reconciliation—sons will vent their infantile violence on their fathers and on close others as a puerile way to avoid responsibility. A man who fails to undergo sacrificial suffering will be unable to love. As Plutarch wrote long ago, only worthless men use the license of childish neglect to justify poor characters.

And so my father's distance from me is finally not a deprivation, for it gives me the opportunity to use myself to reach out to him. The nature of reconciliation between father and son is a matter of mutual respect and of capacity for closeness when necessary or desired. Sometimes a good father will deliberately create distance.

A friend of mine has four sons. The oldest, twenty, was making his father uneasy by plying him with constant questions—what courses he should take in college, where to go if he spent a semester in Europe, what to major in, what jobs would be best. My friend was upset because he wants his son to be more independent, and yet he kept answering the questions and fostering still more dependency. We decided these were not real questions but efforts to stay dependent *and* rebellious, efforts to avoid independent decision-making. My friend made the father's decision—he created more distance between himself and his son by refusing to answer pseudo-questions. He told his son that he was responsible for his decisions on these matters. The son was angry at first but then moved into the gap created by his father's self-restraint, answering his own questions. A man's reserve need not be destructive.

Acts of fatherhood are acts that balance support and care against the need to set limits for childish dependency. They are acts of discrimination. Fathers must judge whether their children want or need what they are asking for and what the costs will be for themselves and their children if they say yes when they wish to say no, if they fail to set limits.

Fathers who are controlling fail to understand that they are raising children who must become separate individuals, not clones or wish-fulfillments. One enraged father could not understand why his daughter refused to speak to him after he had commanded her to divorce her husband. Many fathers fail to understand that their children are not extensions of their own needs. To be a good father one must sacrifice wishes and fantasies, letting go of the illusory child to love the actual child.

While I was in the process of struggling with the notion of absent, immature, and controlling fathers and reaching for a clear understanding of reconciliation, I called an old acquaintance, a priest. I wanted to discuss this book with him. "Don't you think," I asked him, "that there's a great lack of comprehension about suffering, forgiveness, and sacrifice among fathers in the contemporary world?" I was regressing again

to my absent-daddy myth, and I wanted the priest to add
fuel to my denigrative fire, although I didn't realize it at the
time. Instead of answering my pseudoquestion, he acted like
a mentor and gave me a *gift*. He told me about his own father,
a policeman, who had raised five children. "He worked very
hard to raise us as good Catholics and make sure we had a
better life than he did, an uneducated immigrant from Ire-
land."

My envy saw an opportunity to open the gap between
fathers and sons. "But don't you think it's different to raise
children with devotion than to do it in a rage, as so many
fathers do today?"

"Well," said the priest, "when he went out for night duty,
it was sometimes very cold." I appreciated his modest refusal
to denigrate his father.

Blake said, "To generalize is to be an idiot." There are no
"fathers and sons in general." Only specific, real fathers and
sons. What the priest was telling me was that we must find
a way to honor all kinds of sacrifice, to honor all kinds of
suffering. "Young priests today don't have the power priests
had when I was young," he told me. "Lay people simply do
not obey these days without question. So now priests have to
have patience, and they suffer a great deal—simply trying to
prepare for weddings, for instance. The people have so many
ideas about how they want it done. Some priests feel used,
just part of the decorations at the ceremony. When you have
power, you suffer one way, and when you don't, you suffer
another way."

He went on to tell me that the bishops who drafted the
policy paper against nuclear power politics were very courageous, because many conservatives in the Church accused
them of having "no balls" to fight the Russians. Then he
remembered a time when he was "the darling of the fire-
house," until he walked a picket line with blacks on a civil

rights issue. He had always believed that a priest ought to be exemplary, a second Christ, and believes that is what they tried to be in his childhood. What he finds troubling now is the fault-finding in the media and among the public that is used to undermine trust and to denigrate models of heroic or saintly behavior. He recently reread some of the *Lives of the Saints,* and he found that they were "too flawless." We have to find a way, we agreed, to allow priests to be "vessels of clay"—real vessels of the spirit, but made of clay, imperfect—without losing faith in their authority or their abilities.

The priest and I also agreed that past idealizations have contributed strongly to modern tendencies to denigrate and to delight in denigration, as if the discovery of Nixon's terrible fears and deceptions of Luther's lapse into anti-Semitism or a congressman's seduction of a congressional page gave us license to respect and honor no one.

The contemporary denigration of fatherhood and authority is compounded of the mythology of an absent, idealized daddy, a bitter clinging to feelings of betrayal and abandonment, a refusal to suffer the present situation, and an infantile readiness to rebel against one's own commitments. Fathers, priests, and leaders are also real men, and we must honor them for who they are, not denigrate them for who they are not.

Suffering the absence of the father is often the ordeal that makes the human soul capable of suffering and being healed. This is the process that is re-enacted in psychotherapy, in which the psychotherapist may be said to be absent except for once a week, when he is still not present enough to satisfy the demand for an ideal father. What psychotherapy usefully does is provide a screen on which the client can project the repetitive story that shows him where he is stuck. In the transference formed between the client and the therapist, we see how the client needs to go back to the points of deprivation and trauma, often needing to accuse and blame daddy for failures of sensitivity, support, and protection. The therapist is able to absorb the violence of those attacks empathetically but also to give feedback, so the client can learn that it is the child part of the self that feels betrayed by daddy and that perhaps this is not the whole story. The client is encouraged to review his experience with his real father so he can experience how different his relationship is now, not only with his father, but with himself. In this way, we learn slowly to change, to forgive, to let go of the past—by suffering it.

Very often, clients wish to kill their therapists in the same way they wished to kill daddy—for not being there when they needed him, for dying, for being distant and living his own life, for not giving enough, for setting limits. The core of psychotherapy is facing the violence of our own frustrated needs, suffering them as grief, surrendering the wish for an ideal daddy.

The myth of the absent father towers over contemporary life. The "absence" of the ideal father creates an illusion that there are no men, no heroes, no manhood. The refusal to suffer the ideal father's absence in a *sacrificial* way produces anger and self-hatred in men. Substitutes for the absent father are delusions—magic, technological mysticism, state power, corporate "family" myths, angrily dependent relationships with women, and all the false versions of the messiah or Utopia. There is no substitute for the suffering of the absent father that does not depend upon a lie.

We have noted that suffering the end of an illusion of perfect care is what enables a man to emerge into the gap of the absent father and to fill it up with his own presence. That is the essential movement of manhood or heroism, the filling of the void created by the absent father. It is the deaths of fathers that create the occasions for creativity in the sons and disciples. When Buddha and Jesus die, religions are born, made, created by men mourning their loss and replacing them by offering their own manhood—not without reluctance or the temptation to worship idols.

The "deathlike silence" of the analyst, like that of father refusing to answer questions directed at daddy, like the dead, or the silent God, poses the problem of reality, maturity, and judgment to the person seeking "cure." The patient or client actually is the analyst, and a frantic one, seeking constantly to seduce approval or to smash the silence, to avoid *suffering*. But only the pain of silence surfaces the real substance of the self in a state of judgment for its narcissistic comic opera of illusion, violence, flight, seduction, its absence of commitment to ethical action. Unless the patient can hear his empty talk echoing in the silence, he cannot learn the speech of the heart.

Freud's rule of silence for the analyst was impossibly difficult for him to follow himself. In fact, as he tells us in *The Interpretation of Dreams,* reflecting on his being "obliged to talk for ten or eleven hours every day. . . . It was I myself who was the nonstop speaker."[9] Freud's need to be there as a person was a reflection of his own dread of absence, which interfered with the suffering of his patients, with their discovery of their separateness. Instead of becoming silent, so his patient could achieve adulthood, Freud became the controlling father.

I recognize my own ambivalent relation to Freud, one of my dead fathers, one of my mentors. I recognize his awe-inspiring struggle with his own unconscious and his tenacious detective work, but I also have a realistic need to criticize his pretention to be a guide in emotional and social territory where he was not at home. In doing so, I must stay aware that there is also another element in my attitude toward Freud, an element I share with those other critics who seek not a balanced appreciation of his gifts to us but to express only rage at the absent father, at his failure to be perfect, to be the God who shows us the way.

In mythology, the hero was intermediary between the gods, the dead, and men. The hero was a spirit of the dead who possessed great powers to influence the living. The hero cult was a cult of the dead, related to the cult of the ancestor but larger in scope, and it was designed to protect a community against the demonic dimension of the unpacified dead. The hero was implored to ensure fertility of fields, flocks, and family but the cult later evolved from a local to a state cult. Sacrifice to the dead was felt to sustain the world, because it made a living link between the son and the father, especially the dead fathers.

Freud was able to show us imagery of sons killing the father, but he was not able to see the need to sacrifice to his father, to honor his father. In so doing, he sacrificed his own son and many of his disciples, cutting them off, without hope of repair or reconciliation—a true modern man.

Such divisiveness is a substitute for suffering loss, for making sacrifices, and for the repairing of bonds, the other name of God. But we cannot *expect* a man, even a great man like Freud, to have all the answers, to both tell us what to do and incarnate that doing. Men are imperfect, only partially able to realize either in speech or action their own best selves. To reconcile with our fathers, we must try to mirror the best in them, not the worst.

Freud did not have the guidance of the traditions of his fathers. Jewish mystics teach the mystery of what they call "God's Holy Name," and it is the assembling of the letters of this name that brings God down to earth. Each letter stands for a separate virtue. When enough people "invoke his name" by their godly speech and action and bind God to earth, a community of real persons becomes possible.

Unfortunately, in our muteness and our towers of computerized, technologized, psychologized Babel, we have forgotten not only the letters, but also how to speak. Even family and neighborly *talk* is under assault, let alone speech between persons; for many of us, "media," not speech, fills the gaps between persons. But the "media" is not the message: it is the jamming of the word made flesh.

I know the first letter of God's name. It is Trust. Without trust, we cannot speak, because we do not expect to be heard. In the void of this letter, trust, we create our first idol, violence. This first letter is hard to remember. I keep forgetting to speak, and I keep forgetting the reality of others, that they need to hear me speak, in order for them to feel enough trust and security to be able to speak. But it is clear to me that the power of even this single letter is very great. Trust enables us to speak to each other and to forgive each other. In the absence of dialogue, people become threatened, violent, and accusing.

It follows then that muteness or monologues between father and son, brothers, husband and wife, friends, son and mother, and all other relationships that require *dialogue* to sustain trust and continuity, contribute to the undermining of trust.

Any leader is a "father" of his group. He must keep his word to them, or he undercuts the whole matrix of group bonds. Similarly, the father who does not keep his word to his son undercuts his son's trust in *any* relationship, not just his trust in his father. But the son who denigrates his father participates in the destruction of his own trust. The son's task is to overcome and fill the gap created by the silence, exile, or judgment by the father, because his own power to trust depends upon that effort.

The son—Jesus, Telemakhos, Freud's son, I, you—must forgive the father for failing to be perfect. For as we come to realize in our turn, in our dealings with our own sons, it is difficult to speak even one syllable into the face of indif-

ference, rage, or judgment. If we do not forgive our fathers
for failing to be our ideal images of what they should be, we
cannot become fathers, because we ourselves would not wish
to suffer the burden of these idealized demands.

The essence of totalitarianism is the breaking of the bonds
between fathers and sons. Stalin's first Show Trial in 1929
featured a boy of twelve who denounced his father as a traitor
to the state and called for his execution. Hitler summoned
the youth of the state, knowing he could break the opposition
of all groups if he could succeed in breaking family bonds.
The denigration of fathers is the only basis of the idealization
of the state leader, and it is also the death of the heart and
of the living community of persons.

The classical world did not center its attention on Oedipus.
In fact, the Oedipus trilogy ends with reconciliation between
Oedipus, his children, and God. Homer does not stop his
work with the jealousy of Paris or the wrath of Achilles but
follows it through to the point of reconciliation between a
father and his son. We in the modern world stop with Oedipus, with the regicide and the incestuous son, because we
are now historically fixated by denigration of the fathers, of
authority, of the fantasized betrayal of our impossible childhood desires.

The modern—that is to say, fatherless and unreconciled—
world begins with the death of God, with the denigration of
all absolute moral values as illusions. In the absence of gratitude for our creation, envy and narcissism rage out of control.

Maternal narcissism demands demonic heroic achievements
from male children, motivating the male child to compete
with the father for affection and status. When women are
denied public function and equality in marriage, their envy
and their love turn toward the son, brewing a grandiose
dream. An absent father permits an intense, needy mother to
use her son as a dream partner, punishing the father through

the son.[10] Such a son feels as I felt: if I am not a hero, I am nothing. And so the hero becomes an exhibitionist, driven by the adoring-demanding mother. The family group is split by narcissistic competitiveness, which prevents cooperation. The family members become divided by jealousy, isolated. The heritage of our generation is this split family, these puerile sons, these envious women, these mute fathers.

The split marital bond is the curse of family life. Avoidance breeds more avoidance between the sexes. This avoidance was better channeled by clan cultures based on separate gender worlds than by our fragile nuclear family. Female envy combined with male flight splits families and psyches. It split my family and myself between an absent ideal world and a present devalued one.

We have seen how men react when women and children make violent, idealized demands upon them: by silently withdrawing. The move a man needs to learn is a *forward* one, one that will address emotional violence with his own real presence, but one that will also have the confidence to set limits to the unlimited demand for attention. My father never learned that move, but partially because he did not, I did. He was split from his father and his brother by jealousy. I have learned from him and his history how to value setting limits, refusing to withdraw in the face of punishing, guilt-inflicting emotional violence.

My own long road of development as a man began with dread of my mother: invasive, competitive, intrusive, and negative. My image of her as harpylike portrayed her offering milk in one breast and envy in the other. Once a dependent child, silent about emotion, trying to avoid my mother's desperately anxious demands, I tried to cling to my father's shadow, inventing words for him, drawing guns, awaiting his return, dreading snakes and spiders. I needed his protection. But now I need it no longer, armed as I am with my own power to set limits for fantasy. I need him only to be a real person, my father.

Reconciliation between fathers and sons begins the reassembly of all the scattered letters of the Holy Name. It helps us to repair our family and leads toward a responsibility for community life. Even though some of the "letters" in our lives may be missing, we must try to make words, to make connections to a wider family world.

What about our fathers' fathers? My grandfathers did not speak much. Isaac seemed to prefer gambling to tailoring and fathering. Aaron was a successful businessman, then a deli owner, then a landlord. His wife performed all of the domestic duties, even did all the everyday talking. He spoke only on the Sabbath, usually pointing out what a fool the rabbi was. The towering male figure of the family was his father, Rabbi Moses Ben Shapiro, who came to the United States in about 1907 with the mission of ensuring that American Jews kept living inside the boundaries of traditional orthodoxy. My family was excited about publishing his papers, until some were translated and seemed to reveal an excessive interest in the correct pricing of chickens. These men, especially the Rabbi, had an important influence on my sense of identity, although I never knew them as persons.

The man I admired most in my youth, unconsciously wounding my father in his most vulnerable place, was my uncle Seymour. He served in Italy during World War II, rose to major, looked dashing in his uniform, developed a poison-ivy serum, and earned a doctorate in chemistry after the war. He gave me books—Darwin and Freud—and a helmet, but he thought poetry was nonsense, that women were slackers, and that the New Deal only rewarded goofing off. He worked with zeal, a new kind of rabbi of chemistry. He was a puzzle, and when he died of leukemia, I was only twenty. His sons know little of their father, and I try to remind them of what kind of man he was.

My father was raised by his grandmother, I have described earlier how both his mother and father were absent, working. On neither side of my family was there significant community involvement, not even with the Jewish community. When our extended family fragmented, it became up to me to hold together the pieces of my family, to seek mentors outside the family, and to be a father and mentor to others.

Family is not enough to satisfy our need for membership and connection to the world, but reconciliation within the family helps us to make familylike affiliations in the wider world. We do not need to *invent* reconciliation, but simply to *remember* it and renovate ourselves. It is a gift from the fathers. A moral life flows from responsibilities to the future, springing from acts of our fathers in which obligations were conceived and debts assumed, linking the present, past, and future in such a way as to make of a human life a unity. Both Aristotle and the Bible have taught us that the highest good for the self as a social being is found in practicing responsibility in a specific, concrete community, beginning with respect for the fathers, for our heritage. The broken tree of my father's family is my family.

We inherit not the Garden of Eden but a violent world that needs us. Let us waste no time in resenting our fathers, because we need them in our work of construction and repair. It is dialogue with our fathers that keeps us facing toward the real world and the ordeal of rivalry, violence, envy, loss, and love that creates the heart of a man.

4

THE BOND OF BROTHERHOOD

> This is a family in which brothers have done the
> worst of things to brothers ... mothers use their
> children as sticks—each brother a rod with which
> to chastise the other.
>
> SALMAN RUSHDIE, *Shame*

> All the men ever born are also my brothers.
>
> WALT WHITMAN

No word in the English language is more loaded with tension,
irony, and hope than the word "brother." A brother is a
family role and a symbol of ideal male fellowship, embracing
not only friendship but also a form of democratic community.
Above all, brotherhood means sharing—sharing goods, affliction, and affection. Yet brother is also a synonym for betrayer. When black men warmly call each other "brother,"
white men envy their sense of shared identity, but they are
not yet prepared to line up with their own brothers. The
bond of brotherhood heals the souls of men, holds families
together, and is the spirit of communal cooperation. The
breaking of that bond means division in the psyche, the family,
and in society.

Paradoxically, the ideal of fraternity remains powerful, while
the family bond it symbolizes has become weak. Brothers
have become invisible to each other. The issue of brotherhood

today seems so negligible that conferences on "men's issues" often do not even include a discussion of it. The classic of family therapy, Nathan Ackerman's *The Psychodynamics of Family Life,* fails to include a serious examination of brotherhood.

Many people I know rarely speak about their brothers. When I researched the contemporary psychological literature on siblings, I found a good deal about twins but surprisingly little serious work about brothers.

The Freudian tradition has almost ignored the richness of sibling relationships in favor of a darker vision. Psychoanalytic literature tends to describe same-sex siblings as rivals for parental love and opposite-sex siblings as incestuous surrogates for parental love. Brotherhood is, to be sure, oppressed by jealousy and sexual competition; it is also an arena for emotional and social richness to flourish.

Some contemporary psychologists write as if people have a choice about the influence of sibling bonds, as if the relative strength of the bond of being a brother depended upon such variables as access to each other in childhood, common interests, or parental presence or absence.[1] While brothers certainly respond to each other differently at different stages of their lives, the true intensity of our ties to our brothers is hardly a matter of our own discretion; the bonds of brotherhood are not simply relationships in the social world but internalized bonds. We may deny our brothers socially, but we cannot minimize their effect on our identities.

Today, instead of being the pylon supporting the bridge of family and community life, brotherhood in America seems to many men a kind of elective or voluntary association. As for being our "brother's keeper," the idea would not even arise in conventional conversation. This is not true in other countries.

An Indian cabdriver in London told me that times were

very hard for him. He had to work two shifts, had to provide for his wife and children, of course, and also had to save money for his sister's dowry. And, naturally, he had to contribute to the upkeep of his mother and father in the Punjab; it grieved him that he could not afford to visit them.

All the time I listened to him, I was aware that this cabdriver was cheating me, driving very indirectly to my destination while working on my sympathy for a big tip. I did confront him with this at the end of his grievous tale, but what struck me most about his recitation of oppression by family needs was what motivated him to take on such responsibility. He was inspired not by sentiments that were recognizable as care but by a sense of obligation, obligation assumed because "if other Indians discovered I was not caring for my sister and my parents, they would not associate with me."

What he meant was that he could not move to Miami or get a green card or in any way succeed in this world without his network of overseas Indian friends, who would refuse to help him if he violated their code of manhood. Cheating an outsider like me is only part of business, but if he did not care for his family, he would be *dishonored*. The obligations of brothers and sons are very clear in a culture of extended families.

In our culture today, we are in the dark about the importance of our relationships to our own brothers, but what we do to our brothers is what we do to our own hearts. We men will often find in our relationships to women a dreamlike reflection of our behavior toward our brothers. And it is not only our hearts, our marriages, and our family lives that are shadowed by our brothers, but also our friendships, our involvement with community life, and our perspective on the world. Our brothers are larger figures than we realize, and reconciling with them is vital to improving the quality of social trust.

Kinship obligations limit individual freedom. They are often regarded now as a nuisance. Most of us cannot even imagine a social world centered in kinship obligations, especially one that demands reciprocal dependency between brothers. The narcissistic male ideal remains the solitary, self-sufficient individual striving for total dominance in his own little world of goods.

Fortunately, there are some men who stubbornly insist that men are brothers and that they ought to help each other. A friend of mine told me about a bloodletting at his firm, a major bank. Men he liked and had worked with for many years had to be "terminated"; they were, as the British say, redundant. He thought about the suffering of those men and their families, and then he proposed to a group of other executives that he would be willing to take a ten percent pay cut to keep some of those men working. Would they join him? They thought he was joking.

For most men, sacrifice is simply not an option. But not for all men. I have known men like my friend and others who work tirelessly and with true humility for their communities, begging door to door for the Boy Scouts, for hospitals, volunteer ambulance corps, and other social welfare causes, collecting nickels, dimes, even pennies. "Men who live only for themselves are animals," is what they say. These men believe that it is simply common sense to support the community that supports them. They have gratitude for what they have been able to do, and they know that no man is truly "self-made." The very life of a community depends upon fraternal trust, mutual aid.

Men like these keep the ideal of brotherhood alive in the thousands of fraternal organizations men join and support, from the Boy Scouts to the Rotary and veterans organizations.

As a boy, I watched movies of Apaches drawing blood from their own hands and pressing the hands of their white companions, making the white men their "blood brothers." I understood this then to mean permanent loyalty, a brotherhood of the spirit that was sealed in blood, a more important kind of brotherhood than my fleshly bond to my own brother. But today I know that we have no possibility of becoming fraternal in the spirit if we are fratricidal in our practical relations with our brothers of the flesh.

Aristotle's *Politics* teaches that fraternity is the chief good of the state. A community thrives on the spirit of fraternal cooperation. The Greek philosophers saw social life as a hierarchy of fraternities—family, community, city.[2] America became one nation by fighting a great fratricidal war, waging that war against secession and slavery, inspired not only by commerce but also by the belief that all men are brothers before the law. Brotherhood was also the rallying cry of those who struggled to form unions of workers, of all men fighting to improve their status.

Yet we live in a different age. Cain could be comfortable today. He would not be wandering with a mark on his brow. One common contemporary perspective would simply have it that Abel was interfering with his upward mobility: Away with him!

But the decline of brotherhood confronts us with more than the loss of fraternal support among individuals. It is not only male friendship that suffers from the decline of fraternal feelings but also the life of the community and, by extension, the life of the world. Where will we learn to share, if not with our brothers? Where will we learn equality? Where will we learn to say "we" instead of "I"?

Men who do not learn about fraternity in childhood might be able to share problems, enjoy sports and socializing, even sit naked together in hot tubs but still lack the capacity for friendship. For the quality of friendship is not derived from a relationship with one man; it belongs to a culture of shared values, of the willingness to sacrifice for common goals and to make lasting commitments. And where will friends learn the art of cooperation and the bond of loyalty if not with their brothers?

One friend of mine, who is very responsive to friends in trouble, told me that he was surprised to receive a call from a man he had not heard from in six years. But he was even more surprised to hear this man say, "I'm calling you because you are one of my two closest friends." Before my friend could even register his astonishment, the man said, "Well, my other friend was surprised to hear from me too, because we haven't seen each other for twelve years."

I do not know a better story to convey the isolation of men, the illusions they have about friendship, or the barrier of silence that divides them from contact. In fact, this man would never have called his "friends" at all if it had not been that he was feeling panic because he had just learned that his wife was divorcing him. Is this conceivable for a man who learned to depend upon his brothers as allies in childhood?

Cain is an ancient myth. Brotherhood was never easy, and it is simply not true, as many of us like to fantasize, that men once were able to be easily intimate or that brothers once were able to feel more brotherly. Let us not forget that the Greeks and Muslims promoted fraternity in order to halt fratricide.

What did exist in an earlier America were more formal, ritualized obligatory rules for both brotherhood and friendship and more economic dependency between brothers and friends. But the pressures of possessive individualism in a modern, urban, mobile society have undone most of our traditional associations. Now friendship and brotherhood are "made" relationships, like marriage. Today's bonds are often perceived as temporary kinds of investments; we cannot afford low-yield relationships. *That* is what is different.

I am not suggesting that friendship cannot exist without brotherhood. Obviously, sole children can learn to be friends and so can estranged brothers. But our experiences with our brothers are far more formative and powerful than is currently believed, both for our friendships, our work, and virtually all our other affiliations.

We men seek in friendship an ideal brother relationship, a world of play, mutual affection, and protection. The best kind of friend enables us to grow in self-esteem and status. He reaches down to help us up.

When I was a boy, I had this treasure: a friend who was three years my senior. I can see his face now as vividly as I ever could. It was my joy to follow him, stretching myself to run faster, to play harder, to understand his new words. He had blond, curly hair and looked to me like Apollo, and I would have performed any deed of daring to deserve first place in his heart. For two or three years I dashed to meet him after school in the park, escaping from home, from my mother's anxieties, from my younger brother's longing to play with me. I wanted only to be with Joel and the rest of our gang. We hugged, we kissed, we wrestled, we argued; no one could divide us.

And then one day he vanished from my life. He had found a girlfriend, and he liked being with her more than being with me. I was crushed. A girl! She couldn't hit, catch, tackle, run like the wind, fight. But he was deaf to entreaty. I could not grasp what had happened. All I knew was that he was my special friend, and I was no longer his special friend. I did not want his friendship if I had to share it as a subordinate. Subordination, being *second,* seemed worse than nothing.

Of course, I was second to Joel in prowess, but he was

older, bigger, and rejoiced when I gained on him. That was not being second. Second was what my brother was to me—that is, nothing, dirt. I felt in total eclipse. At the age of ten, I was unable to grasp that I was feeling what my brother must have felt tagging after me—rebuffed, denigrated, filled with self-loathing. When we feel rejected, we cannot hate the people we idealize, so we hate ourselves and our own needs. We are ashamed of our deepest selves and try to disown that shame and inflict it on others.

Brothers and friends play a crucial role in relation to our self-esteem and our shame. When they reject us, we descend into the hell of self-hate, shame, and revenge, and we mistrust even our power to care. Isolated men, men who lack brothers and friends, are never far from rage. Mistrust of our brothers and friends causes us to mistrust ourselves. On the other hand, the acceptance and love of our brothers and friends helps us to accept and love ourselves; it heals shame and self-hate. The bond of brotherhood is the healing bond of trust. The breaking of that bond releases demons in the psyche, the family, and the community.

I never wanted to have a younger brother. I wished only for an older sister or brother, for idealized protectors. When my younger brother was born, I was four. My cosmos disintegrated. I was no longer the sun, and I vowed vengeance.

It was incomprehensible that my parents could love me and yet be able to inflict this awful deprivation upon me. Faced with a choice between my idea of a world, one that revolved around my wishes, and the actual world, in which this little usurper peered lovingly, longingly into my eyes, I chose my own self-absorbed version. I did everything I could to deny the existence of my younger brother. It was not simply that I was ashamed of him for being weak, needy, poorly coordinated, a baby; I wanted to negate the very event of his birth itself, to erase his very being.

My envy of his birth, of my father's shocking intimate collaboration with my mother against my jealous wishes, starting the growth of this alien, was like the taste of gunmetal in my mouth. Toward my brother, my gaze was a knife. My word was blood, his blood. I did not know then that I was surrendering my own vision and speech to this rage.

When I was eight, I was forced on many occasions to babysit for my brother, and I remember his begging my mother not to hit me when she returned from shopping, after leaving him in my "care." I did not want to "watch" my brother, who was four; I wanted to play. She left. I was malevolent. His nose might be bleeding from an "accident," or his tooth might be chipped by the time she returned. She would beat me until I was black and blue and then force me to say I loved my brother. I would wish him dead. Even so, he would try to intercede for me, like an angel praying for the soul of a dead person before judgment. Often my brother would get hit himself in trying to shield me. It made no difference to me. The trouble was that he was there, present, alive, when he ought *not* to have been there. I did not wish to love him; I wished only to subtract him from the family: Four minus one = three. I did not know then that I was losing part of my freedom to feel and think.

A woman friend of mine used to fantasize when she was a child that her sister would grow up and be her maid. When her sister invented stories about her doll, my friend would invent stories about how her sister's doll died. But at least her stories of competition and rivalry accept the *birth* of her sibling, and that was what I would not do.

My childish death wish against my brother persisted into adolescence. The only times I responded to him were on those occasions when I used him to reinforce dominance or control. I remember when I was about ten my mother would buy us identical little boxes of Blue Ribbon potato chips. I would then "play" with my brother: The game, I told him, was to see if he could choke me to death by feeding me his potato chips. He liked that. He liked making me laugh. I wanted only to have everything for myself.

Because I envied my brother so, I competed with him endlessly; I could not learn to share with him. Equality was a mystery. There were only two positions in life—special and nothing—and I did not want the second.

Brother Thomas Merton has written very powerfully of his younger brother in his spiritual autobiography, *The Seven-Storey Mountain*: "I suppose it is usual for elder brothers, when they are still children, to feel themselves demeaned by the company of a brother four or five years younger, whom they regard as a baby...." Merton recalls seeing his five-year-old brother, John Paul, gazing at him from a distance as he played with his friends. If his brother approached, Thomas and his friends would stone him. He remembers John Paul.

> ...standing quite still, with his arms hanging down at his sides, and gazing in our direction, afraid to come any nearer on account of the stones, as insulted as he is saddened, and his eyes full of indignation and sorrow. And yet he does not go away.... The law written in his nature says that he must be with his elder brother, and do what he is doing and he cannot understand why this law of love is being so widely and unjustly violated in his case.
>
> Many times it was like that, and in a sense, this terrible situation is the pattern and prototype of all sin: The deliberate and formal will to reject disinterested love for us for the purely arbitrary reason that we simply do not want it.... Perhaps the inner motive is the fact of being loved ... reminded us that we all need love from others.... And we refuse love ... insofar as it seems in our own perverse imagination, to imply some obscure kind of humiliation.[3]

We turn away from love because of fear, envy, and shame.
Where does our fear come from? Every baby learns to dread
its own neediness and vulnerability, especially when parents
reject its emotional needs. The child then disowns its needs,
identifying with the parent, being ashamed of the baby's
longings. If a family member is imperfect and a source of
shame, we wish to keep ourselves apart from him—different,
superior, special. The helpless baby brother is repulsive because he seems weak and incompetent, vulnerable in a way
we cannot bear to feel or to show ourselves. Thus parents are
repulsive to us when they show low-status behavior, poor
dress, or anything we can interpret as ignorance of conventional behavior.

Our need to be "special" announces to all imperfect others:
"I am not like you." Terrified to be seen as vulnerable, the
insecure child inside us struts about in its mask of perfection,
awaiting the arrival of perfect others before deciding to love,
inflicting shame and humiliation on anyone who approaches
his divided heart.

The need to be above the pain in one's own heart makes
a false self. As long as we imagine that we can control our
self-presentation, manipulating others into giving us more
than we give back, we retain the myth that we are unique,
special, protected, invulnerable. This false self lies about the
pain of the human soul, about the essential self. It competes
with real emotional needs, seeking to make its own world
according to its own wishes.

The competitive idea, or envy, is the fantasy that we can
make a better world than the one that exists, not by accepting
the pain of our own humiliations, the insensitivities of others,
and working to alleviate them, but by magically denying
reality—especially the existence of baby brothers. We men
substitute our own wish for reality in order to avoid suffering
our own shame.

Thus, we may wish to subtract a brother, add an ideal father, divide a sister in half, trying to avoid involvement with our actual family and preferring one that is tailored to our own secret, controlling desires. The envious elder brother waits for his royal, ideal world, refusing to respond emotionally to his younger brother, refusing to share, acting only to assert superiority or difference, to exploit, to humiliate. "You are a baby, dependent, helpless, excluded, ridiculed: Don't contaminate me."

Parents often intensify envy and jealousy in siblings by forcing them to compete for attention and preference. Most parents are unconscious of the profound influence their feelings about their siblings have on their attitudes toward their spouses and their children. My father was a slighted second son who married a woman who was the second youngest of five children. My father and my mother both envied their older siblings. When I was born, I was exalted: I made *them* first-born. But I was also the target of their envy, the rival who could now be controlled, humiliated, belittled. When my brother was born, he became the embodiment of their shame as well as the vehicle of their childish vengeance.

The spoiled youngest, the "baby," often becomes a weapon parents use against older children. It is not so much that younger siblings who become parents are angry at the older children themselves but that, from the vantage point of their own childhoods, they identify with the youngest and see the elder children as "bad" parents or "bad" older siblings. Year by year, parents re-experience their own childhoods through the lives of their children, and when they are not careful to distinguish the child in them from the child in front of them, archaic needs for revenge strike through the screen of the present moment. Old scores are settled on new skin.

The most biting consequence of my parents' own childhood rivalries was their tendency to divide my brother and me as they had been emotionally divided from their siblings by being compared with them. Although my father rarely showed emotional pain, one story that he told again and again revealed the depth of his hurt at his mother's denigration of him by comparison with his brother. After his brother's death, when my father was handling all her affairs, she began grieving in his presence to a group of family members: "Once I had a son ..." "Once she had a son," my father would mutter to me, "Who am I, then? Shit?" How could he possibly compete with an idealized dead son?

When parents set one child against another by comparing them, the children become enemies, for only one can be good, special, or the winner at any given time. "Why can't you be like ..." is the most damaging attack on a child's security. My parents did not know how to feel true acceptance for either of us, because neither of them had ever felt accepted themselves. All they could do was compare who was good and bad, in or out, up or down. Even if I had been able to overcome my primary envy, I doubt that I could have made a successful alliance with my brother, a rival who could displace me at any moment.

Trying to be *first* all the time is a hopeless process, like running up a down escalator, but that is what it feels like to be a sibling in a family that lacks the power to express love in a clear, direct way. Comparisons are not gifts or feelings but ideas that cut flesh. When parents whisper, "You are our favorite," they make a child anxious, not secure. To a child, this means, "I've robbed my sibling of first place, but can I trust them not to whisper the same thing to him tomorrow?" A child needs to be "good enough," not "better than."

It was not surprising that, as a young adult, I imagined my brother to have no influence on my life. I shared a room with my brother for nearly ten years when I was a child. My most powerful feelings of living with another person were conditioned by the feelings I had toward him as a child: feelings of negation, shame, domination, and relentless competitiveness. Now I know that my relationship to him permeated my early relationships with women.

My first marriage was to a mute, shy, ashamed youngest child. She gazed at me with the same hurt expression I saw in my brother's eyes. But I rarely looked into her eyes, and I never asked her for anything. I used her, depreciated her, and cut her off. I devalued her not only as a woman but as the image of my brother. And like a younger sibling humbly clinging to an older one, hoping for the kind word that never comes, she accepted being devalued.

If I thought my experience were unique, I would keep silent. I offer the following story of my guilt as a brother as a sacrifice, because I know now how common it is, this "Cain Complex," and I offer it as part of my reparation to my brother, who suffered so much from my coldness and from the lie that he was not important, in himself or to me.

In 1967, my brother visited me in California. I was twenty-seven, a young professor of literature, a talking head frightened of being a person of flesh and blood, obsessed with status. R. D. Laing showed how the numb or schizoid person develops a "false self" in order to appease the social judges of its own inner numbness. I knew and admired *The Divided Self,* yet I myself remained divided, more concerned to seem to be someone important than to be who I was.[4]

One evening, I arrived home to find my brother sitting on my manicured lawn in front of my immaculate house. He did not look like the conventional hippie of the era; he looked shabbily dressed and exhausted. I knew but did not want to know that he was in great pain. Unsure of his welcome on this unannounced visit, he began to explain his presence.

"I had to come, hitchhiking, and I couldn't call because I had no money because I lost all my money in Las Vegas. I went there to rest after following Jack London's trail back to Oakland, where I picked lemons. My suitcase broke."

My wife invited him in. I'm not sure I would have. My impulse was to give him plane fare back to New York and to dispatch him there immediately, but I was too tired to drive to the airport.

After only one day of my brother's emotional chaos, I was ready to kill him. Jack London was my brother's hero, the self-sufficient, powerful man. The contradiction between my brother's heroic fantasy and his dependency made me frantic. His belongings were scattered all over my house, and his need for attention interrupted my scholarly privacy. Now I insisted that he leave immediately and rushed him to a bus, treating him with contempt and and wounding his feelings deeply.

There I was in California, the Egypt of the West. I felt like the Biblical Joseph, doing very well for myself in Egypt but betrayed by the appearance of my starving family. But clearly I was only imagining how well I was doing; no one who behaves this way toward a brother can really be doing well. I was only numb, emotionally and morally.

But absolutely no one in my circle of friends at the time believed that I had done anything to be ashamed of. Like marriage or friendship, fraternal bonds in California were fragile, momentary, dependent on temporary feelings. Such notions as obligation, suffering, sacrifice, or even decent courtesy could not prevail over my exaggerated shame about my fantasy about my brother as a different breed.

I was afraid that someone might see that I was not what I pretended to be. The humanist professor could not empathize with his brother, caring only about his market value in the status stock market. I did not realize that he haunted me and that the more I disowned him the more I was doomed to rescue *other* drowning brothers.

When I emotionally disinvested in my family, projecting

my feelings of shame onto them, I did so with the fantasy
that I could simply withdraw trust, loyalty, love, and energy
and later reinvest them in a new family that I alone would
choose. I did not realize then that in trying to maximize
interest on my investments, I was losing unrecoverable emotional capital. When I rejected my brother and sent him away,
my secret shame became even more deeply rooted, while my
feelings of trust, loyalty, love, and passion became stunted. I
did not know it, but I would pay dearly for the emotional
debts I had incurred to my brother.

When I reflect now about throwing my brother out when
he had come in search of me across the entire country, I grieve
for him and for myself. He did not deserve such insensitive
treatment. What could my wife have thought of me when
she witnessed how I treated my brother? How could she
continue to respect me? How would I greet *her* less-than-
ideal brothers when they showed up? How would I cope with
her neediness? Our marriage did not long survive this inci-
dent, though I doubt that either of us was aware of how
significant it was for us both at the time.

Breaking the bond of brotherhood is the prototype of sin.
With one fearful, angry action, I split myself, my family, my
marriage, and my self-trust. The denial of brotherhood has
a dreadful resonance. Did I realize, having negated my brother
a million times in fantasy and having eliminated him in fact
from my life, that I was branded with the mark of Cain, the
guilty older brother, doomed to be an exile? I had no idea
that my envy would be so costly or my guilt so great.

God warns Cain to struggle with the demons of envy and
jealousy, to master them. But Cain kills his brother and then
denies it. For that, he is cursed with his brother's blood. What
does it mean to be cursed? It means that unconscious guilt
is governing our psyche without our knowledge. My inability
to be compassionate and loving, to share with my brother,

was a lock on my heart, blocking me from marriage, friendship, and real devotion to community life. Instead of being
able to appreciate these real, limited goods, I burned with
zeal to avenge the humiliation of other, symbolic brothers.
Sometimes this kind of guilty substitution will enable us to
help others, but usually people who cannot help their own
brothers are too blind to truly appreciate symbolic brothers
or to truly serve their needs; we are capable only of trying
to use them in order to make ourselves righteous. Real politics
is a far more difficult art than the guilty zeal to "save" others.

Soon I would be forced to leave the academy because of
my compulsion to save my Third World brothers, to sacrifice
for them. What I would not give to my own brother, the
very recognition of his existence, I now demanded for the
Angolans. In a dreamlike, omnipotent way, I tried to do what
I would not do in a real and limited way: to respond to the
suffering of my brother. I spent my concern instead on the
needs of my brothers in Vietnam, Bangladesh, South Africa.
As we shall see, a long time was to pass until I learned just
how crucial it was to repair the broken bonds of trust between
my brother and me.

Younger brothers are not immune to the effects of envy,
as the following vignette will confirm. Nor are they so innocent. Their brothers envy them, and they are condemned
to be inhibited by that envy and to feel unequal, inferior.
Men who cannot accept or be accepted by their brothers
cannot easily have friends, because they cannot share.

Mark is a younger brother, a successful, fortyish audio
engineer. He is very productive but so driven about his activities at work and at home that he is unable to enjoy anything. If he pauses for a moment, he becomes uneasy. One
way he handles his uneasiness is to train for marathons.

Mark has been estranged from his older brother and has
no close friendships with men. He avoids referring to his

brother but expresses frustration about his inability to become close to anyone. One day he became depressed, which is unusual for him, and remarked idly that his brother had just gotten a job as a contractor in Saudi Arabia: "We never see each other anyway, so why should that upset me?" Nonetheless, he was upset. He was having difficulty waking up in the morning.

Although Mark remembered that his brother had once protected him from being afraid of drowning when their mother refused to accompany her sons to the swimming pool, his chief feeling about his brother was that his brother had rejected him. When they were children, Mark's brother would heap his own plate with food in order to deprive Mark of his share. Mark grew up feeling that he could never get enough. Sometimes he orders two meals and devours them voraciously. When he eats this way, he feels like a shark and is unable to communicate with anyone. He excludes his brother, before he himself is excluded; then, depersonalized by his own envy and ashamed of eating "his brother's share" of the food, Mark becomes numb.

Mark is afraid of his own strength, his own assertiveness, and ashamed of his emotional needs. Once, when he allowed himself to get really angry at his brother, he almost killed him. His fear that his brother might reject him is reflected in his marriage. He fears unrealistically that his wife will leave him. She is envious of his success, and he is defenseless against her envy, as if he were guilty of having stolen his achievements from someone. He cannot see how haunted his marriage is by the ghost of his brother's reflection. Mark suffers still from his brother's rejection, abandonment, and envy, and he will not be able to face any person honestly or ask anyone for emotional support, until he learns to face his brother.

Facing one's brother is often the most bitterly resisted and powerfully avoided task in a long-term psychotherapy. Many patients simply refuse to admit their need to see their siblings, whom they sometimes have not spoken to in years, blinding themselves instead to the costs in lost intimacy, lost trust, lost speech, and lost friendships. The estrangement costs us dearly. Younger brothers are barred from realizing their fullest potentials as long as they feel like "the younger one" or as long as they are still in thrall to the gaze, usually envious and denigrative of the threatened older brother. Estranged older siblings are inhibited in achieving their goals by a guilty fear of success, for achievement may unconsciously mean the death of their sibling rival or their own death at the hands of murderously envious siblings.

Envy and jealousy between brothers makes the most trouble when it is denied, when it is kept secret. Once acknowledged, jealousy loses its power. When brothers avoid facing feelings of envy, they cannot come face to face with any person, including themselves. It is very difficult to admit envy, for envy is a source of deep shame, an admission of rage and of feelings of inadequacy. Yet if brothers leave each other in this condition of emotional distance, they only condemn each other to other forms of emotional exile.

The failure to love one's brother, along with the feeling of not being loved by one's brother, makes dreadful distance seem "normal." Often, guilt and shame about a brother are so great that men do not even try to love again; neither women or other men seem worthy of their fragile sense of trust.

When I reflect on my history with women, I can see how powerfully my brother's emotional neediness stamped itself into my unconscious. Because he was so troubled I became fascinated by the need to rescue unstable people. But because I deadened myself to his need, I became dead emotionally.

When I was twenty-eight and suffering from my recent divorce, distressed about the Vietnam war, and pondering the right way to use my status as a professor, I became fascinated by one of my students, a brilliant and beautiful young woman who was subject to hallucinations and catatonic seizures. I was *curious.* Just as I had used my brother to get more potato chips, I thought I could use her to learn about the link between psychosis and the imagination. Thinking she was so helpless that it was safe to risk involvement, I let her touch my heart. She revolutionized my life.

One day she said to me, "Steve, are you alive?" "Oh, oh," I thought to myself, "here she goes. She's going to hallucinate that I'm a corpse or a zombie. Look out!" So I said, suppressing my rage, "Sure, I'm alive." "Are you really alive?" she asked. "Yes," I said impatiently, "feel my hand. It's alive." And then I nearly fainted from shock, for I realized that my hand was ice cold, like my voice. This "mad" young woman was not asking me anything; she was telling me something. She was telling me that I was not alive. And she was right. She could tell the difference between living people and dead people.

Here I was, teaching D. H. Lawrence, the Bible, Marx, Freud—and I did not know the difference between being alive and being dead. That was a revelation. My enlightener had compassion for me; I could hear it. She persuaded me to see her psychotherapist, and I went. She was the sister I never had, the shadow of my brother pleading with my mother not to hit me, interceding to save me from the death of my heart.

During my psychotherapy, I was able to change some of my attitudes. But my understanding of my affliction did not go deep enough. I could not grasp that one root of my narrow, frozen behavior was my competitive, envious attitude toward my brother. So when I married again, I did so without having resolved the competitive matrix of my feelings toward the person I lived with.

This time I married a woman who was a supercompetitive second daughter. Because she perceived me as her rival older sister (when she was not viewing me as her absent ideal father!), I could evoke nothing but competition from her. If I loved anything, she could not respond. She resented my achievements and imagined that her lack of empathy for me was only a minor issue. She mirrored the way I once acted toward those closest to me—relentlessly competitive and envious. Sadly I soon fell back upon my own envious sibling behavior. Lost in our regression to childhood, neither of us was able to maintain the relationship.

Millions of us marry the images of our siblings and lose their love in a tangle of competitive attitudes. One of the most common patterns among men is jealousy of a younger, baby sibling who gets "everything." Such a man may marry a woman, give to her, and then envy *her* for receiving such gifts; ashamed of his resentment, and not buying gifts for himself, he will speak not a word, silently raging against the baby who receives. He believes that to speak would be to become a baby himself. Silent jealousy of the sibling means injury, resentment, estrangement, a combination that is often more powerful than marital love.

After many years of mutual avoidance, cold letters, and colder phone calls, my brother and I started on the path of reconciliation. Why? For my own part, I became less deaf to his appeal for attention. I no longer believed that he belonged to an inferior species. Catastrophe educated me. Affliction has consistently been the only teacher strong enough to penetrate my illusion of control, self-sufficiency, and invulnerability. And it was a kidney stone that changed delusion into dawning knowledge of affliction for me. When you cannot stand, sit, or lie down without crying out in pain, you need someone—anyone. You do not specify differences of ideological correctness, of status, of manners. You just do not want to be alone at the edge of panic, in pain.

At this time, I began to learn about vulnerability. Then, when my brother startled me by saying, "Steve, if you punched me, I would be glad, because that would be some kind of attention," I could comprehend his pain. I had long since concluded that my brother would avoid any direct emotional confrontation with me. But I was wrong. My brother had rigidified into an accusing martyr, and he was not asking to repair our brotherhood, merely reminding me of my irredeemable guilt by his irredeemable victimization. But this time, I did not simply cut him off or turn away.

For the first time that I could remember, I needed my brother's help. I had recently returned East and was low on money. I needed to move. He offered to help me if I rented a van. Instead of behaving like a needy younger brother, he was behaving like a friend and ally. And I was not feeling so superior.

After my brother helped me to move my household to Nyack, New York, we sat and talked. I had a vision then of my brother that was like the scales falling from my eyes. He was sitting on the floor, rocking with laughter, a burly muscular, balding young man. And as he laughed, he began to sob. I have never in my life seen a soul in such agony as my brother in that moment.

For me, it was like seeing a metamorphosis, a gorilla turning into a man or Dr. Jekyll turning into Mr. Hyde. His body was rocking with hysterical laughter and with sobbing, and he began to hug himself, struggling to speak. "We are the same flesh, Steve, the same flesh."

I felt the breath knocked out of me, stunned by the depth of his vulnerability and by his agonized tenderness toward me. I began to cry too. "Yes, we are the same flesh," I said.

It seemed to me that it was my brother who was undergoing transformation, but it was my own stony perception that was becoming more human.

That was the moment my brother was born for me. For the first time, I accepted his existence in my heart. It had taken me thirty years.

My brother and I are still sometimes wary of each other, but I never deny our bond. When my mother was dying, we helped each other. When he was later in great confusion about a divorce, I helped him, or tried to. When he remarried and his daughter was born, I took her into my heart. We try not to let our father divide us when he resorts to getting us to compete for favorite-son status. There is no question today of the loyalty I feel to my brother, to our common past, our common future.

It is sometimes humiliation that opens the door to truth. Shattering the delusion of special protection attunes us to others, to empathy. Attentiveness flows not from difference from our brothers but from the sameness of our flesh in its agony.

During the sixties, when I thought I had special knowledge, I would not even condescend to speak with those who differed from me. I was immune to facts, knowledge, debate, logic, almost demonic in my delusion that only a revolution could establish brotherhood, as if by magic. But I certainly did not want brotherhood to include *my* brother. Brotherhood was an idealized unity that denied the reality of differences between the brothers. I had no idea of affliction then, or of vulnerability.

Times of affliction are times when we feel we cannot even stand up, much less function without support. When my mother was dying of cancer, my whole family was afflicted and grateful for any support. When I started divorce proceedings and my wife responded with a head-on car collision that nearly killed her, I again tasted the bitterness of affliction. Again I learned how I needed brothers and sisters. When we ourselves are in a state of affliction and shame, we are grateful that others do not treat *us* as a source of contamination but approach us in a spirit of common humanity that transcends the differences of personality. Unfortunately, all too often, once the vulnerability that opens us to experience has ended, most of our promises about reforming our lives to be more responsive to those who are suffering tend to evaporate into the euphoria of returning invulnerability and the renewed sense of being different from those who are afflicted. Our suffering must go deeper to educate us to brotherhood.

To be one with a brother makes it possible for us to be one spirit with a wider family of persons. But the vision of others as real, as suffering persons like ourselves, is not available to us if we continue to envy our siblings their birth, their gifts, or their difference from who we need them to be—or not be. Our shame of them, and of our own hidden violence, creates the need to emphasize differences that divide us. This division is our blindness. When our eyes open, we see only brothers like ourselves.

What I most resented about my brother after his birth was having to take care of him, to teach him. How ironic that those activities became the basis of my identity and my professional life as counselor, teacher, psychotherapist. How important it is for us to learn that our resentment conceals buried treasure.

Reconciliation with my brother has been one path out of the relentless competitiveness with which I was afflicted. What I now know is that having a brother did not diminish my share of parental love, as I had imagined. On the contrary, having a brother shielded me from part of the impact of my parents' tremendous difficulties. And it gave me an opportunity to act as a parent while I was still a child, accelerating my development. My brother's birth was a gift I did not know how to appreciate, the gift of human needs I might have responded to, the opportunity to appreciate differentness, the seed of love I almost killed in my rage to negate any deviation from my fantasy of a world that I wanted only to reflect my own childish desires. I am still trying to value fully the person my brother has become, and he is struggling to overcome his childhood mistrust of me.

Brotherly love can heal competitiveness of the kind I call envy, the kind of competitiveness that strives to have everything for oneself, that strives for domination, for sole possession of goods, whether they consist of the devotion of parents or of potato chips, status, achievement, power. Being a brother means recognizing the virtues of the truth that goods must be shared.

Brothers can promote equality in a very important way, not the fantasy equality of crude political theory, but the kind of equality that allows different spheres of prominence within a family framework of self-respect and mutual respect. By appreciating a brother's different skills and abilities, one gains security in one's own sphere. Instead of being first or nothing, let us sense the possibility of the stability in saying "we," "us," "our." And let us recognize the comforts of brotherhood: If a brother is important, a mother or father need not be all, and parental deaths become less devastating. And brotherhood protects us from destructively dependent relationships with our mates by reminding us of the wider world of essential associations—of friendship and civic opportunities—that lies beyond the arena of our immediate families.

Real brotherhood means establishing many centers of welcome, enjoying different kinds of goods, and engaging in different forms of love and association that promote self-respect. Brotherhood means respect for the equality of others as persons. Democracy can have no substance without training brothers for fraternity in family life. No one is more vulnerable to seduction by totalitarian father imagery than the brotherless, friendless social atom. No one is more vulnerable to fascist fantasies of controlling others than the "special child" of the parent who considers himself above his siblings and beyond judgment and guilt.

Brothers in the flesh can help us to build the trust we need to develop in establishing friendship and the spiritual brotherhood that is the real basis of community life. It can also teach us to have faith in a politics that is not corroded by cynicism. The repair of brotherhood is not a panacea, but if we wish to enrich male social life and to redeem our institutions and our world from mistrust, it is a good place to begin. Brothers who depreciate, cheat, or betray each other are unlikely to trust other people, even if they call them by names like "wife," "friend," "comrade," or "brethren."

Some of our happiest imagery portrays a world of "real" brothers, rejoicing together in times of gladness, supporting each other in times of affliction. Yet how hard it is for us to take even one step to close the gap that has been opened between brothers by envy and jealousy! Here indeed is work for a man: to close that gap, to speak the first word of reconciliation. To repair trust is holy, healing work; it heals more than the injured psyche and the torn family when brothers stand together, shoulder to shoulder.

Fraternity is more than a personal need. It is a political and social necessity. Freedom and equality are only murderous abstractions in a world that lacks concrete, mutual, emotional bonds of affection and loyalty between brothers. Without brotherhood in families, how can we ever find our way to the brotherhood of the spirit?

"Am I not a man and a brother?" Two hundred years ago,

this apparently simple question was adopted as a slogan by the Anti-Slavery Society of London. The power of the question's appeal is linked to the image of a black man in chains, one knee on the ground, hands raised up to heaven. Being a man, being an equal person, and being a brother are inseparably connected. We men need to work to realize the promise of brotherhood.

5

MEN AND WOMEN:
THE CRISIS OF MISTRUST

In summary, it may be said that the distribution
of roles between the sexes and the generations in
the United States has undergone a profound transformation, with a focus upon very young marriage,
early parenthood, large families, and emotional
self-sufficiency of each such unit, isolated in sub-
urbia, strenuously seeking a romantic realization
of a dream in a glamorized actuality rather than
a distant future. This turning in upon the home
for all satisfaction, with a decrease in friendship,
in community responsibility, in work and crea-
tiveness, seems to be a function of the uncertainty
about the future which is characteristic of this
generation.

MARGARET MEAD, *Male and Female*

The suburban fantasy of the perfect marriage in splendid
isolation was an offshoot of the building of highways and was
about as satisfying as the plastic food in the roadside restaurant
chains. All that is left of Margaret Mead's 1962 description
of romantic young marriage is its quality of uncertainty about
the future. Mistrust between men and women in America is
at the flood stage. For some, it seems like the end of the
world of marriage, the end of trust between men and women.

The erosion of trust between men and women is a result of the combination of some important contemporary social and psychological facts: the free play of male violence and male fantasy, the erosion of gender differences, the feminist challenge, and the degradation of love. The freedom to withdraw, to differ, to polarize, to divorce, has reached its limit. We men must now begin the process of repairing trust and restoring the value of love.

Divorce may free us from the shrouds we weave, but it also unravels our lives and impoverishes our histories. Most men and women quite properly gather up their cut and tangled balls of yarn and look for a new loom. What marriage makes is a shared world, a shared story, an endless conversation, an intricate tapestry linking private and public worlds. This shared world is precarious now, because it depends upon the voluntary participation of the mates. In traditional societies, marriage is the central, essential act, the social and cosmic ritual of world maintenance. The practice of arranged marriages survived because their meaning was social, not personal. "The love marriages" of our day leave individuals far more vulnerable to sudden feelings of total loss of meaning, alienation, numbness. Even the most well-motivated divorces assault us with great losses in meaning, painful gaps in our lives, the loss of trust.

The high divorce rates that prevail in America and the rest of the Western world do not mean that marriage is not important to those who divorce. On the contrary: people divorce because marriage has become so important that they have no tolerance for the imperfect marital arrangement they have contracted or for the imperfections of the person they once chose. The remarriage rate among the divorced is higher than the marriage rate for single people.[1] More than ever before, marriage is a refuge, a source of emotional support and meaning in a social world that increasingly alienates persons from traditional communities. But if it is perceived wholly as a refuge, it is a fragile institution indeed.

With the two women I have married, marriage offers far more than I could manage to elicit, not because of who they were but chiefly because of my own inability to invest myself fully. In spite of my marriage vows, I was unable to say "we" and "our"; instead, I wished to remain a totality, a world unto myself. I refused to need a wife. I spent both marriages waiting, still locked inside the pattern of dread of commitment that causes the cycle of marriage–divorce–remarriage to repeat itself without fulfillment.

Men are unmanned by dread and envy. We become men by learning to love, and it is by loving that a man gains a name and a social place, renewing the center of gravity in family life and recentering our wandering social cosmos of mistrust. Men need to suffer for their failures in loving and to learn from those failures, or they cannot outgrow the dread and envy that weaken trust between men and women. As we shall see, it is dread of aliveness that keeps men children, but it is envy that excludes them from giving or receiving love. Men mired in dread and envy are unable to speak with a human voice.

Men are socialized to control women as a way of trying to control their own dread of women. Study after study of male violence against spouses shows that all men view themselves as controllers of women, and this right to dominate and control may take the form of battering them to teach them lessons in compliance. Men who need to control women do not view them as persons but only as demeaned nourishers, bringers of food, and containers for dirt, violence, anxiety, and abuse. Battered women are the most victimized group of women who suffer from male dread.

Throughout history, men have denied their violence against women, and until the mid-seventies, when spouse abuse became a criminal offense, our culture conspired with the denial, content with blaming the victim. But denying violence does not alter its character. No man is responsible for the sexist programming he received in childhood, but we men are responsible for the consequences of our adult behavior. That is one paradox of human freedom.

The extraordinarily perceptive Henry Adams becomes curiously obtuse in his celebrated reflection on the lack of power of women in American culture, "The Dynamo and the Virgin." He writes that, in most cultures, the goddess has power, but "in America neither Venus nor Virgin ever had value as force—at most as sentiment. No American had ever been truly afraid of either."[2] The power of the Dynamo continues to grow, and the political and economic power of women is now growing, albeit slowly, but the power of women still shows its greatest magnitude in the extraordinary negative reaction it evokes: the phenomenon of male dread of women.

Sometimes the dread takes the form of a woman viewed as an octopus or as the snake-haired Medusa. An exhaustive study of American fantasy in children's comic books shows that these images constitute an ugly myth of woman viewed from the perspective of the early childhood dread of an engulfing mother.[3] But whenever insecure men feel threatened in their identities, we will encounter an impulse toward violence. And because romantic love threatens men's self-absorption, we men are often violent toward the women we enjoy or depend on.

Sexual violence surges out of the depths of men's early feelings of longing, betrayal, dread, and suppressed rage. The woman who awakens the depths of longing must prepare to do battle with possessiveness and jealousy. The more sexually exciting she is, the more she reminds us of our adored first betrayer, the absent mother. The more motherly she is, the more she reminds us of the child's perfect reverie and of lost paradise. Inside the heart of men lurks the angry boy as judge—punishing women no matter which way they turn.

We watch as if from a distance, suspecting the sweetness that lures us on toward the rocky surf, where we expect once again to witness only betrayal. Better not to need, better not to feel anything. But still it comes through—the touch of a tender woman, the fineness of a lip grazing one's ear—strong as dawn through clouds. Shall we risk the sun again, that awful opening? No, say dread and envy. Protect yourself. Stay distant.

Adultery and depression are both expressions of men's clinging to an idealized image of a woman as a source of rescue. As long as men divide themselves and wish for "another" woman, either actively seducing one or passively longing for the nurture that means the return of mom, they will remain in a partially infantile state of trance, clinging, but also dreading being engulfed. Caught in this dark corridor, they may awaken sometimes, but only to a squinting state of puerility, never fully awakening to responsibility, real pleasure, or full manhood.

A neurosis is a simple defense against dread that keeps a person oscillating in a state of unresolved ambivalence. When men dread engulfment or loss of identity, they must withhold themselves or run away to preserve their shaky identities. At that point, they confront the reverse dread of isolation and bounce back to cling to women. There, the dread of being trapped only makes them avoid full involvement, and they float in a state of empty, angry self-division.

A man in dread is a dreamer. He cannot bring commitment to a marriage or invest himself in it, because his dread prefers the illusion of fantasy to any real or living relationship. Dread sentences a man to wander powerlessly in the empty province that lies between narcissistic attachment to childhood fantasy and involvement with the present. Dread is fundamentally the dread of being born, being vulnerable. Most men who are caught in dread will deny they are frightened and invest themselves in a fantasy, leaving only a shell of themselves for others. The way out of this condition is first to admit the fright. By needing others, a man comes into contact with his own suffering self and takes the first shaky step toward manhood.

Men who are divided in the ways we have observed have the freedom to change. The power to love without fear is worth struggling for. But first we men must face our fears— of losing our freedom, of being controlled, of losing our identities, of being asked for more than we have to give, of vulnerability to loss and grief—of the tides of life itself.

The envious man says no to marriage, not merely from dread but also from envy. The envious man, single, married, or divorced, says no to a woman: I do not need you; you can never give me anything worth enough to me so that I will say, yes, yes, I will be born, forgive my mother, let go of feelings of injury, resentment, and estrangement, and open myself to the gifts I desire to have and to give. It is envy that says, *No, you are not good enough.* You do not deserve my love." But envy lies, and men who lie are ashamed and guilty.

The "helper" is a husband who says yes/no: Yes, I will give you a little; no, I will not accept responsibility.

A wonderfully comic illustration of the evolution of puerile man is "Man the Helper," an article written by Mary-Lou Weisman. She describes what happens when women ask men for "help" instead of parity, the sharing of responsibility. Male "helpers" come in various infantile forms, from the barely bipedal—"Where do you keep the ice cubes?"—to the more advanced "tell-me-if-you-need-anything" type, who uses his intelligence to avoid responsibility, to the more highly evolved species of specious helper, who puts the wash in the washer but "forgets" to transfer it to the dryer. "While he may be

competent as all get out at his job, as is she, he seems to pass
through the neolithic on his way home from work. . . . Civilization awaits the emergence of *Homo domesticus responsibilus.*"[4]

Man the Helper is dividing himself, holding back his capacity for full involvement, refusing responsibility; he may
become verbally abusive or violent if confronted about his
passivity, either denying that he knows what is required of
him or becoming enraged about being forced to do "too
much." The divided man is not often conscious of his dread
of being fully alive or of his envy of the woman he is withholding himself from. A depressed man will envy a woman's
animation and energy and will wish to use it and control it
for his own purposes. He will not share or join in his mate's
purposes. He grunts instead of speaking and is too tired to
listen to his wife's problems; he is even too tired to make
love, preferring the passivity of masturbating and the return
to the fetal trance, being sucked, sucking, fantasizing. This
kind of envy costs him his own selfhood and blocks the
fulfillment of marriage as mutual devotion.

Man the Helper, the puerile man, the man in the fetal
trance, does not desire to give anything to a woman; he will
only make minimal deals in order to get his wishes and to
control, or to maintain the illusion of controlling, the woman.
The divided man gives words or gestures, but they are counterfeit; his heart and his will are not in the words. He refuses
to give full value, and so he loses his own self in his defiant
game of giving less than his all. Injury, resentment, and estrangement remain enthroned in the heart of the man who
refuses to love.

The contemporary working-class man suffers from this
awful cycle of defiance even more than his white-collar coun-
terpart, because what he always perceived as his own particular power, the power of muscle, the power of the breadwinner,
has been diminished so profoundly. In *Joe the Engineer,* a

novel by Chuck Wachtel, we follow the experiences of a meter reader who can only fantasize an escapist future. We see the gap opening between the rigid, defiant blue-collar man and his awakening wife; Rosie wants to finish school, wants him to speak with her, wants to explore the world with him. She offers him the richer cosmos of a real marriage, but he refuses, lost in his envy of her growth and in his enraged sense that her change represents the personal betrayal of his fantasy.[5] It is a tragic description of the struggle we men face today.

The normal play of ambivalence that always characterized male–female antagonistic cooperation has become in the past two decades less fluid, more brittle, harder to repair. There are hopeful signs now of a new era of mending fences, especially since many feminists now recognize that some of their stories of independence need revision. Many women have found themselves liberated from oppressive marriages into the bitterness of wage slavery as the heads of poor, single-parent families, suffering humiliating losses of both status and leisure.

It has been harder than feminists thought to end male violence, to achieve income equality, to make a balance of career, marriage, and family obligations. The particular Pandora's box of idealized expectations that feminism opened has been hard to close. The mutual envy that had been kept in check by traditional gender differences between men and women has been wildly stimulated by two decades of unisex negation of any differences.

In one story I know, a man won custody of one of his three children after a bitter divorce and moved from New York to Florida. Six months later, when his other children traveled to Florida for their first visit with their father after the divorce, they had a nasty shock. Their father had not told them, but he had undergone a sex-change operation and simply arrived at the airport to meet them in a dress. He insisted that they now call him Mom. This man's punitive envy of his wife's power to create children devoured him.

When I heard this story, which may be apocryphal but is certainly true to the spirit of our time, I had a jolt of recognition. Those cheerful films like *Mr. Mom* and *Tootsie,* which show men learning through identification with women's roles, are only sugar coating for the bitter, competitive envy that now characterizes relationships between men and women.

The balance between a male and female world was sustained for thousands of years in all human societies by *gender,* by separate domains for men and women. That meant that men and women lived in different worlds. They used different language, different tools, dressed differently, behaved differently. They inhabited different spaces in the home and the community. Men and women met only at specific moments, but their labors harmonized. The separate worlds were not equal. In most cultures males were dominant, and femininity was a strategy to keep women passive and contained. But the end of gender division in the West, characterized by the modern organization of units of desexed labor in a unisex urban landscape, is certainly worsening women's circumstances, not improving them.

Equality between the sexes barely progresses, but the stripping away of the traditional gender protections for women goes on at an accelerating pace. Because men traditionally have expressed their love through their protectiveness toward women, the change inhibits even that source of generosity and male security. Neither fathers nor brothers nor husbands feel honorbound to protect women who are considered "equal" in a genderless social world, even though women are very far from having achieved economic or social status equal to men.

A world has been lost— the imperfect but highly seasoned

and stylized one of gender differences—but a new world has not been born. Divorce, sexual polarization, and growing confusion about how to treat members of the opposite sex who have not declared for homosexuality have created widespread irony about the value of marital relationships. Relationships between men and women have become characterized by mutual mistrust because of poaching across identity boundaries, because marriage is no longer eternal, no longer the joining of two stable, complementary tribal families.

Relationships based on sharing, genuine mutuality and reciprocity, on mutual respect, are rare and fragile because the foundations of support for those relationships—gender division, strong family bonds, containment of competition and envy by tradition—are eroding faster than individual honesty and "working on the relationship" can cope with.

How can women avoid stimulating envy in men? They cannot avoid it. They can only acknowledge the depreciation. It is the task of men to come to terms with their envy of women. The individual consumer is vulnerable to total envy and endless competitiveness, because he lacks everything of value to social life. He is empty. Consumer goods cannot replace kinship or marriage as a household partnership.

The man who lacks everything also denies he needs anyone. Households are disintegrating at the rate of one million per year. An angry man may tend to see the woman who goes to graduate school or who develops a career as the enemy of his security, but of course, she is merely responding to the same corrosive market forces that ended his role as sole breadwinner.

As a recent story about a fashion entrepreneur made clear, the more his business expanded, the less time he had to do "what he really wanted," to spend time with his family. The more successful he became, the more he had to fly to his ranch in Colorado to inspect his herds, race back to New

York, visit Italy to research new styles, running at a tempo that simply destroys the rhythms of relationships that cannot be computerized.

The envious man must control everything, be everywhere simultaneously, competing with the clock, his own age, with any relationships others have that interfere with his own schedule. If "his woman" is not stationary, his whole world can collapse. The woman is not there to love or share with or to conduct family social relations or to be a companion; she is there to contain the violence of the man's tempo, to hold the shell of his identity together, to remember who he is.

The burgeoning refusal by middle-class women to settle for this role has caused widespread feelings of betrayal among their corporate husbands and former husbands. A politically ambitious friend of mine has been told by his wife that if he runs for higher office, she will divorce him. This is not what he expected to hear. His present political tempo is too fast for family life; any acceleration will shatter their already fragile partnership. But how can she let him know that he lacks everything of value, and that is why he values only what he lacks?

Men are encouraged to seek higher status by investing themselves in faster rotations of capital, goods, offices. They seek control and, in pursuit of that illusion, lose kin, community, wives, children, values, souls—all.

William Leach's *True Love and Perfect Union: The Feminist Reform of Sex and Society* shows how nineteenth-century feminists tried to criticize the possessive individualism that was already subordinating family life to entrepreneurial ambition. According to Leach, the women were undermined by their own "liberalism," for the liberal tradition asserted the "right of the individual, unfettered by oppressive custom, prejudice, law, or public opinion to determine his or her own destiny."[6]

The possessive individual claimed that one had sole propri-
etorship of his or her own person or capabilities and owed
nothing to society for their development. Because freedom
was regarded as freedom from dependence on others and as
a function of the possession of wealth, society became an
exchange between sole proprietors. And because women re-
formers could not break through the assumptions of this
tradition, women lost on both sides. Men crushed by the
pressure of competitive individualism can take no comfort
from women who feel that gender differences are anachronistic, who repudiate the old form of the subordinate partner
in the household, and who are still in the process of discovering the bitter realities of the equal right to compete in the
marketplace.

So Adam and Eve, bereft now not only of the garden but
also of kinship communities based on gender, of romantic
illusions, and rapidly losing the security of households based
on partnerships sanctified by religion, come equally to the
conclusion that one can trust only money. The divorce set-
tlement becomes the real ritual of initiation into modern life.
The vow of mutual support becomes the examination of assets
before trial, before the bitter deal is made.

Having arrived at an impasse, can men and women learn
to grasp that the violence they channel toward each other in
their rage and envy at their own insecurity, their lack of
embeddedness in a community of mutual needs, can be overcome? Can we learn that having been stripped of layer after
layer of value, we need not be in collusion with this ever-
accelerating process of breaking bonds, severing connections,
numbing personal needs? My answer is yes, if we men can
learn again to suffer affliction, if we can be educated again
to value virtue.

Value is learned in suffering. When I spoke to a couple
who were going to be separated from one another for two

weeks for the first time in their marriage of twenty years, I asked them how they were going to handle this break. They stared blankly back at me. They were pretending that this woman's going to a teachers' conference in her parents' home city while her accountant husband stayed home alone was a nonevent, that nothing was happening. In fact, in a kinship-based community, nothing much would have been happening. The man would not have actually been alone. And in the nineteenth-century household partnership, there would have been no conference to draw her away; nor would she have dared to go outside the symbiotic form of this couple's marriage. But now she was making a giant step, and he was denying his need for her. In fact, he was pretending that he was relieved at her leaving: time for himself, no bickering, and the like. They were not even planning to spend their last evening together or to work out a schedule for keeping in touch by telephone.

Four days after she left, he became ill. Feeling frightened and isolated, he overmedicated himself and became still more ill and terrified, until he ended up in the hospital. Only then did he call his wife, who became furious with resentment that she had to shorten her trip because he was incapable of taking care of himself. He used her rage to reinforce his own feeling that he could never have asked her to make his needs more important than her business trip. Instead of confessing his fears or his need for her, he manipulated her guilt, pressuring her to return by acting like a helpless child.

This man failed himself in two ways. He failed to suffer the affliction of his fright of being left, and he failed in his *virtue* as a husband. Failing to care for himself, he failed to protect his wife's adulthood.

Neither the concept of suffering nor the notion of virtue had meaning for this man, because he had no model of being a husband to emulate. His goal in life had been not to love but to earn enough money to need no one. But his needs are educating him, and the pain of feeling bereft is now awakening him.

How many of us have been caught in the cycle of believing that *apartness* and fantasy are the reality of selfhood? I have often withheld whole dimensions of myself from a woman to avoid feeling dependent upon her attention, and then I have gladly denigrated her for confirming my angry suspicion that she lacked the capacity to understand me fully. With great relief, I have withdrawn on such occasions into my library, the labyrinth of my defense against my own nightmare of strangulation by the threatening, potentially engulfing woman.

My own wish for an ideal, beautiful mother has taken many forms. My fantasy grew in the impoverishment of real emotional warmth, in the absence of actual, spoken, understanding. As a boy, I resented my mother for interrupting my fantasy. What were her simple-minded ramblings compared to the aesthetic and intellectual pleasures of the BBC? I wolfed down her real steaks and chops dreaming of servants, silver, extraordinary state dinners. I resented any demand on my time or energy, any obligation to share my thoughts or feelings, but I did not realize the depth of my guilt and shame about my fantasies, one of which began with the destruction of my part of the world through an atomic bomb. Somehow I survived, along with tons of food and several women I fancied. That was my idea of love: repopulating the world in my own image.

When I was about seventeen, after several interrupted relationships with girls, I avoided sexual intercourse and retreated into my own world of masturbation. It was easy to find fault with the girls; the closer one came to my feelings, the more I tended to depreciate her. Any fault would do: Her breasts were too small or too big, she was too Jewish, she *wasn't* Jewish, her hair was too frizzy, she was too pretty for me to feel secure about her. And any could become the trigger for my withdrawal. I had no idea that I was incapable of love or that I preferred my fantasy to persons, that I was narcissistic. The feeling someone is "not good enough" cuts two ways.

All the women I knew as a child denigrated men brutally. Both my grandmothers, two aunts, and my mother constantly elaborated an epic myth of the failures, absences, and profound inadequacies of men. The money was not enough or the achievements or the sex. The men never stood up to the denigration; they either left or laughed at themselves. From an early age, I felt that to be near women meant to be vulnerable to being denigrated. I could not then perceive the cultural devaluation of women that caused so much of their bitterness and envy.

As I grew older, my attitude toward women remained wary and judgmental. I dreaded both having my own identity confused with my mother's intense, idealized fantasy of what men *should* be, and I dreaded revealing myself as less than that impossible ideal. I wanted to please my mother and be heroic, but I also wanted to punish women for hurting the men I loved. I judged them inferior in sensitivity to men because they laughed at men's feelings, especially when they were unemployed, down, or otherwise hurt.

Women seemed to be the voice of society: conform, succeed, buy us things, work hard, stop playing. I did not want to help them nor did I want to be like the men in my family— except for my unknown, idealized, unmarried uncle, a scientist, who gave me books. I wanted to be the star of my own fantasy world; I did not realize that my silent withdrawal from women and men was a form of depreciation so virulent that it made it impossible for me to love.

I often turned to literature to try to understand the wild

ambivalence in my feelings toward women, my oscillation from idealization to denigration, from needing a woman as a savior nurse to dreading the same woman as a threat to my freedom. What I sought from women was my own idealized version of what I thought they should be. What I came to resent about women was their own idealization of men. But if a woman behaved as if she might not allow me to control her, I simply abandoned her and withdrew into narcissistic fantasy.

My attitude toward women was violent: they were there to give nurture in the form of food and praise and to be receptacles for my rage, anxiety, dirty clothing and dishes. It was an attitude I was familiar with; I had seen it in my father.

In my fantasy, one image of a woman was as good as another—they could substitute for each other in masturbation fantasies, like bodies cut out of *Playboy* centerfolds. One mouth, one ear, one vagina was as good as another. All had defects, none was good enough.

Few of the women in my life took issue with my abusive behavior: they were too fearful of my capacity to coldly cut them off. In my turn, I steadily accumulated guilt from wishing I were elsewhere, wishing them dead, depreciating them, holding back emotion, using them as typists, cooks, nurses, and cleaning women. When the guilt became unbearable, I would find a way to feel victimized and run away, free at last to withdraw from the intolerable presence of a familiar person.

If women gave me what I wished, then I dreaded being stuck to them, needing them, being made helpless by my need for them. If they did not give me what I wished, I denigrated them. Either way, they got punished, and I was able to justify the distance I craved. I could withdraw and still remain faithful to the only reality I loved: my own fantasy. From this perspective—my own envy of any reality I could not absolutely control—marriage was the true betrayal, life was death, and selfhood meant the loss of the secret, private self.

Because actually living seemed so *ordinary* when compared to my manic, heroic fantasies, I denigrated living. I did not realize that reality lacked dimension only because I was numb to it, afraid to feel. I desired my illusion, not real presence but some inflated ideal of my mother's. When I entered psychotherapy, my first words were: "My mother would slit her throat for me."

Like all too many men, I was emotionally starving but defiant about the possibility of a change in my life. The famine was most evident in my marriages. For seven years during my twenties, I lay beside my wife and I spoke no word, asked for nothing. In psychotherapy, I learned to speak, and then, in my thirties, I spent more years in the desert, lying beside another wife I would not trust. Today when I despair, I have learned to turn to the woman beside me and to ask her to listen while the terrified child tumbles out of my mouth until my frozen heart grows warm. The horror of vulnerability is still with me, but my need is stronger than my envy. I never want to turn away again into the desert of silence.

What has changed for me is the willingness, shaky at times, to show, to share more of myself, risking denigration, if necessary. I have learned not to dread any image of a woman. It is true that my mate is a wonderful companion and emotionally alive and worth struggling for, but it is also true that she is often preoccupied or envious, as I sometimes am. When she is envious, she attacks my desire for her by gaining weight, hoping I will denigrate her so she can run away back into self-hate and her own fantasy of independence and being different. When we are most happy, she is most likely to say, "I hate who I am. I'm not good enough. I wish ..." That is her way of saying to me: "This woman you feel you have possessed and know, this is not me. You have nothing."

In the past, I simply would have cursed to myself and thought, "You *could* probably be a lot better, thinner, more productive, richer, younger, more worthy of me," while preparing my own flight. But today I try to survive the feeling of rejection and to close the gap between us by saying, "You are pushing me away." I know her distancing of me is not "personal," only her own dread of being controlled, her envy of needing a man. When gaps open, a real lover struggles to remake contact, to repair trust.

A sophisticated attorney once asked me, his psychotherapist, how he could trust his wife after their skins separated. He felt loved and secure as long as their bodies were in contact, but as soon as they were apart, he began to doubt her, eyeballing every woman who passed as a possible replacement. He insisted that he loved his wife, but what he understood love to be was only this shaky attachment.

Women and men both desire the stability and meaningful continuity of marriage, as do gay and lesbian couples. But what binds couples together? Desire and need, freely expressed, form the basis of mutual respect—the desire and the need for conversation, for emotional support, for companionship, for sex. Nest-building, or the shared devotion to making a home into a place of comfort and beauty and a family and social center, is also a great binding force. So is the capacity to express aggression, both inside and outside the relationship. If no aggression is expressed inside the couple relationship, it will stagnate in resentment. But if the couple is the only province in which one's anger and frustration dare be expressed, it will be overloaded to the point of disintegrative bitterness.

Another important bond between couples is a common "story" about the life to be shared. In a traditional society, the story of a marriage will be very clear, even axiomatic. It may be that a man and woman marry and have offspring to guarantee the fertility of the earth. It may be that the man and woman marry and have no children. As long as the stories harmonize, trust in the marriage is reinforced, but if the stories are incompatible, as they so often are today, every other strain in the relationship is magnified, and its very basis is called into question. When stories are incompatible—when the woman's scenario, for example, calls for child-rearing and dependency and the man's calls for freedom to roam—envy and dread will appear in the marriage's early stages. And unless the story is resolved, they will continue to breed mistrust.

Sometimes, modern couples agree on their story in the beginning but grow apart when the husband wants to retire to a golf kingdom just at the time his wife wants to begin a new life as an entrepreneur. Couples who agree on goals and values and are explicit about them secure their relationships from the danger of daily mood fluctuations. They know where they are going. But it is becoming more difficult for men and women to make their stories harmonize over long periods of time. It is a matter that needs our most serious attention.

We men have been pressured by the new scenarios constructed by the burgeoning of feminism. Sometimes the challenging rhetoric of independence and equality has made it difficult for men and women to find or even to invent a common story about their relationships and all too easy to discover and harbor sources of mistrust and friction. Sometimes the revisions that are required by women who are demanding more respect and freedom often cannot be contained by the original story that once bound the couple together.

Mutual respect depends upon equality of need and desire, not on sameness or on equal income or on the absurdity of the exact division of tasks. To love a person is to suffer and enjoy that person's realness—as distinct from one's idea of who that person should be.

For a man to love a real woman—as opposed to loving only an image of her—he must resist trying to become her ideal father, taking care of her, buying her everything; resist attempting to be the most romantic or most erotic lover, controlling her, or competing with her world. Instead, he must sacrifice his envy, his illusion, his dream of dominance, and desire her equality as a person; above all, he must regard her presence as a unique source of value. This is the basis of true desire. Although she will not be his sole source of love or support—only the most profound, because of the depth of sexual desire and the wealth of a common world—there can be no substitute for the beloved. For who else but a marital partner can support our personal, family, and communal responsibilities? If a man withdraws from this kind of love into fantasy, he is decreeing that all aspects of his life will suffer impoverishment.

Men may resent awakening to love and to mutual respect, stuck as we are in our addiction to dreaming, but that very struggle to love is what creates our manhood out of our childish fantasies. When a man loves a woman, he seeks a richer world for himself and for her.

I am twice divorced, but I believe that it is marital love that helps men most to make a coherent personal story and a rich social world. So I will marry again and try again to create and sustain a relationship durable enough to withstand the strains of emotional and social violence. Any marriage is more interesting and richer than any romance and far richer than any "singles" universe imaginable, for marriage is not only a continuous dialogue between two persons with rich histories but also the drama created by entire casts of characters from each family and social network.

Men are responsible for whom they love and for how they love, for the quality of their love. *The degradation of love* is the worst consequence of male immaturity. The degradation of love proceeds from the superficiality of a man's commitment to opening his heart to a woman, to the real dialogue of his own need responding to her need with full devotion.

"Why can't I have both?" screams the "minimalist" man in Peter Nichols's play *Passion Play,* who wants to keep his wife as his familiar companion while keeping her young friend as his sexual playmate. It is a scream that evokes Gunter Grass's fantasy in *The Flounder* about man's desire for a woman with three breasts. Even three breasts will not satisfy the puerile man.

It is our task to learn that nothing satisfies but a man's own wholehearted passion. It is an ideal we may sin against but not one we can do without. For without it, we are at sea, lost in sexual diversions and digressions. We do not know our story, our identity, or the true power of our devotion.

Our hearts alone can redeem us from the violence we do to ourselves and others. Our terror of needing the absent loved one creates an unreality of envy, denial, and competitive self-sufficiency. The imaginary *both,* the three-breasted ideal, the fetish, the armor, the refusal, the absence of emotional presence, the split we create by our puerile demand for both wife and mother, abolishes the possibility of commitment to any real person. The puerile man is divided—he is both here and not here. He wishes to be invulnerable to loss and suffering, but by his flight from emotion, he gains only numbness and growing despair.

Love is the expression of an integral self capable of unified devotion, secure against temptation, seduction, violation, violence, and deception. It is the bond of trust between different beings who love alike, and its power is the power of gravity, of stabilization. We are not referring here to the infantile ideal of the mother who always cares but to the heart that survives ordeals of temptation and is tempered to truth and radiance by sacrifice and devotion. Modern men have learned to denigrate this ideal only at their great cost.

The flight from being vulnerable and thus able to love is not simply immature but dangerous, dangerous not only to our personal lives but dangerous also in the public face it takes—the terrible worship of "invulnerable" forms of power. Without faith in love as reconciliation, we inflict our resulting violence and envy upon the world.

Male flight from vulnerability keeps a love relationship out of phase: "When you love me, I don't love you, and when I love you, you don't love me." Men and women sometimes care for one another, but cannot get "it" together, cannot seem to love each other in a continuous way.

Sometimes a man will court a woman very intensively, pursuing her, romancing her, loving her until he overcomes her indifference, only to find that her charms fade when she becomes interested in him. The smile, the voice, the breast, which had such fascination in absence, become stale, even dangerous, when available. The mystery here is a mystery about the difference between our attachment to imagery and our capacity to accept a living presence, the difference between desiring only our own desire and desiring a real person.

It is a cliché that marriage destroys love by institutionalizing it, by somehow changing the exciting chemistry of romance to boredom. But what truly disturbs the continuity of appreciation between lovers or mates is the unspoken need to withdraw to a secret place in the self where no one else is included. Sometimes this place is represented by a book, television, a garden; sometimes it is represented by a fantasy of another lover or by an actual affair; sometimes it reveals itself as alcoholism or workaholism. It is only when men wish to withdraw that they allow women to insult and avoid them; otherwise, they would insist on quality attention.

Love requires full involvement, making us vulnerable to the fate of another person without the possibility of withdrawing. Men still persist in the belief that love is going to be *given* to them in some easy way, as total support or continuous romance. The consumption of sex as a commodity is pleasurable and may temporarily be ego gratifying, but it also impoverishes the potential of the inner life. Sexual "objects" are substitutes, one for another. Love is specific, selecting one person and admitting that person into the depths of the self.

Time after time, in marriage counseling, I will ask couples whether they speak to each other during intercourse. The women cry and the men become angry and defensive: "Should I talk about the weather?" Lockjaw. Love cannot pass into such a man or from him into his wife. This man wants a blow job, he wants to be masturbated, he wants to discharge his tension, he wants to possess an erotic image. But he does not want to be touched emotionally. If sex is not transformed by love, by vulnerability, we are not even "cleaning our pipes." Because the hunger remains as does the resentment of feeling that we have been excluded from the feast, even as we go through the tense performance of intercourse.

Sometimes we glimpse the truth and set it aside. In order to love, we must go where we most fear to go—near our own wounded, armored hearts. Sustaining love means staying in the fire, enduring our vulnerability, and being willing to change.

Boys and males want to run; men stay in the fire, becoming alive and transcending their fear and envy of aliveness. Involvement and commitment are words of dread only to wounded or immature men who think they are synonyms for "trapped." To open the self allows the possibility of re-

newal and joy, not the draining of one's "vital fluids." Only
men and women who can experience mutual passion and risk
the melting of boundaries down to the core can sustain respect.
The willingness to be temporarily without boundaries is born
in the confidence of having a full self to return to—not a
counterfeit one based on fantasies and on the images of others.

Love begins with speaking personally. This makes it safe
to touch. If there is no speech, there will *be* only frightening
fantasy. Mute sex can substitute for these more personal, loving responses only in a very partial way, and mute sex restricts
lovemaking. Most women know this, but cannot speak it to
men who do not want to know it. I know a man who dreamed
he was having sex wearing a spacesuit, with only a small
opening for his penis.

Virginity means hoarding one's resources, waiting for life
to begin. Many men and women, single and married, are still
virgins, unpenetrated and unreleased, waiting for a mythical
right time to allow their passion to be awakened. Passion is
birth, knowledge of self and the beloved. And knowledge of
the beloved arises through dialogue. Women are not traps,
saviors, or persecutors. But how can men know this without
speech?

If we cannot speak during all stages of lovemaking, express
affection, hear tenderness, we will be lost in fantasies. When
a man speaks to a woman before sex, she loses her dreamlike
terror of invasion. The voice of love is a voice of gratitude.
If we do not hear this voice, we cannot open our hearts. And
often, sanely, our sexual "plumbing" will refuse to work,
having become frozen.

To refuse to be invested by love is to try to control the
risks of vulnerability. If we continue to refuse to risk vulnerability—to hurt feelings, to loss—what we really risk is
losing our sanity, being numb, violent, and dead. Love vi-
talizes the giver, and the deeper it goes, the more one is alive.

Love is prized for its radiant sensitivity, its resonance in every part of the self, its unifying power. Love confers energy and clarity. Our choices as men are to risk aliveness or to live a living death.

We can achieve and maintain a state of mistrustful defensiveness in marriage by simply clinging to injury, resentment, and estrangement. But to suffer vulnerability is to confront the inner world. There, in the self, both dread and rage constrict the silent heart, screaming "*No. Do not come close. I will not respond. I will hurt you. You will devour me.*" To speak is to dissolve such fantasies. Fantasy is a bond to the past. Speech is a link to others. "I love you." "Do you care about me?" "I have tender feelings for you." "I want to make love to you." "I need you." At some point in our lives we must open our mouths, or we will never make contact.

Sexual love is the cauldron of birth, melting the barriers against involvement, illuminating *responsiveness* as the meaning of aliveness. We can receive only what we give. The more passive we are, the less we participate in ourselves. Passivity erases consciousness of the other person as a person and desensitizes our touch as it makes us mute. Receptivity opens us simultaneously to the other as a person and to our own potential for sensing, speaking, knowing, giving, doing.

An experience of making love is the beginning of loving, but it is the rhythm of those experiences that creates emotional security. Between peaks of sexual passion, one is sustained by speech, by emotional contact, by trusting oneself and the living being inside oneself to care for and nurture the internalized lover by acts of kindness and tenderness. If a man can feel that life inside him, experience gratitude for it, he becomes invulnerable to seduction through the eye and protected against jealousy.

Gaps in the relationship between a man and a woman are inevitable. But continuity protects us from mistrust. Com-

mitment to loving over time helps us not to fall into momentary gaps and confuse them with the end of loving.

The fear of loving is the fear of being born, the fear of
being fully alive. It is love that integrates one as a person,
makes clear that we need the answering love of a person who
is fully present. One is incapable of receiving love if one does
not give it, because, in the most painful sense, one is not *there*
to receive it because one is closed, divided, absent, dreaming.

For the man who cannot love, who is ashamed to *show* his
connection with an imperfect woman to the world as his
choice, the world remains a place of fear and of judgment.
Manhood does not express itself by seduction and flight but
by the struggle to be fully present with and for a woman.
When a man makes his place in the world with a woman,
against the grain of his fantasy and despite the gaps in trust
created by his history, he renews the cosmos of trust.

6

TURNING FORTY: THE PASSION FOR SELF-RESPECT

> You cannot relax because every Monday morning in the San Jose *Mercury* there's another story about somebody who made it that hits you right as you're drinking your coffee. The only way to do your job is to work an 80-hour week. So your wife resents it and your family goes to pieces.
>
> ROBERT REINHOLD, "Life in
> High-Stress Silicon Valley Takes a Toll,"
> *The New York Times,* January 13, 1984

> In the middle of the journey of our life,
> I came to myself in a dark wood,
> where the right way was lost.
>
> DANTE, *Inferno,* Canto One

As men approach forty, they face the most serious crisis of their lives. Some will die; others will be numb, immobilized by unacknowledged shame and guilt; others will manage to overcome depression, find meaning in their past history, and live in harmony with their values. They will achieve personal identity.

The mid-life crisis is not a fiction. Research on the lives of creative men has shown increased death rates between thirty-five and thirty-nine.[1] Mid-life is the time to face the idea that we are not immortal, to acknowledge the existence of death, to accept the end of perfectionist illusions about ourselves and the world. In mid-life, we men must accept the ongoing struggle against violence in ourselves and others without giving up to despair. We must ask and answer the question: What is the best use of the time that remains in the span of my life?

To emerge from this struggle with mid-life depression is to gain three convictions: a passion for self-respect, a need to enrich the time that is left to us, and a need to love. For those men who fail to mature and who deny the normal progression of aging, time becomes an enemy. They dread mirrors, look anxiously at the traces of middle age in their wives, try to seduce young girls. But when men succeed in accepting the loss of youth, time becomes their medium. Any moment, any experience, may become an epiphany, a revelation, an opportunity to practice self-respect, creativity, love.

When I become depressed about how little I have achieved with my life, I sometimes remember the saying: "Life is a ceaseless preparation for something that never happens," and I become even more depressed. Sometimes I smile at what my friend Judge Howard Miller says: "Keep perspective. Why get upset about whether you are a speck or a dot?" Best of all is when I concentrate on responding fully to what is right in front of me. Then I have no time to waste in feeling ashamed. Men who weather the crisis mid-life presents will take full responsibility for every moment of their lives.

When we men turn forty, we ask terrible questions: What if I made—or make—the wrong choices about work, love, success, investments? What if . . . If only . . . Have I aimed too high or too low? Whose life am I living? My mother's expectations? My wife's? My neighbor's? If I die tomorrow, will I have used my life well?

This chapter reviews the lives of men in the middle of their journey, men who become lost in the woods, and men who find the path of manhood. To be lost is to sink into shame; to find the path is to achieve self-respect. At mid-life, the meaning of time changes, growing finite, more dense with significance. Men able to change can become successful in using themselves fully as men. Men who fail to change still feel like boys, even as their faces wrinkle into age. To mature, men must suffer, must endure terrible visions of the god of status, the god of death, the god of judgment. They must make choices that enable them to keep their self-respect alive. And after forging an identity, they must transcend that personal identity by identifying themselves with the ongoing life of their community.

When we weigh our lives, sensing for the first time that more lies behind us than ahead of us, we use various measures for evaluating our achievements: the people we know; the places we have visited; the women we have made love to; the money we have made. But even the best lists cannot protect us from suffering the visions of what might have been.

The men who are most vulnerable to disorientation at this middle stage of life are those who are uncertain about what they really love. Some men have been so dominated by the ethos of the individualist myth that they feel they must do everything alone, be totally independent. They so dread being needy that they lose touch with their needs. These men have confused independence with alienation. They have no concept of successfully navigating the hazards of separation, of the progress from childhood dependency to the mutual dependence of mature relationships with mates, family members, friends.

Other men remain so terrified of being alone that they remain larval, unaware of either their own powers or their civic responsibilities. They cling to women who despise them, as if their lives depend upon the sight and sound of their mother's scorn.

Whether shaky men are possessed by wives or by pride of independence, they are almost always unconscious of being programmed by fear—of abandonment, dependency, loss, needs, death. When men turn forty, repressed fears begin to surge up, breaking through the defenses we call a man's "personality," his mask. In mid-life, men must face the fears they have been avoiding or risk the dreadful prospect, or retrospect, of an unlived life, a life not chosen.

At the midpoint in our lives, we discover that neither work, wealth, status, fame, nor masks of youth can shield us from vulnerability to illness, age, and death, from the turning of the wheel of time that lowers our parents into the earth and casts shadows over our days, while raising those younger than ourselves into the full blaze of noon. We may rage against it, envy the young, and protest that we are not ready, even defiantly delude ourselves that we can begin again. But if we do, we not only lose the esteem of others but also suffer the most painful wound of all, the loss of our own self-respect. The loss of self-respect means the fracturing of our identity. It means that our past history, our present actions, values, and feelings, and the future we are planning, cannot cohere or integrate. And it means shame.

At around forty, men feel a change about what gives meaning to their work. Young men work out of necessity, to earn money; they also work to get *bigger,* to deny childhood feelings of powerlessness; and they work to be part of something that they feel is inherently meaningful, like a powerful organization or a respected profession. But once a man is past mid-life, if some degree of mastery or success has been achieved, money, bigness, and external sources of meaning become less satisfying. We need to become part of the life of our times.

Only in this way can our work keep its central importance as a source of self-respect and identity. In mid-life, we men can no longer lose ourselves in our work; we must find ourselves in our work.[2]

Existential philosophers tell us that it is the need for *authenticity* that becomes pressing in mid-life. To be authentic, we must close the gaps between what we think, how we feel, what we say, and what we do. The source of this pressure to integrate our values and our actions is the sense that time is limited.

The great temptations for men at mid-life are the boyish illusions of triumph—power, money, status, sex. Increasing personal domination of people; accumulating greater amounts of money or goods that promise to improve the quality of life; climbing ever higher in the hierarchy of status; seducing ever younger women—these are the lures that drive men out of their own hearts and minds and into a realm of endless competition that brings not growing self-respect but only increasing emptiness.

No submission by others, no multiplication of our incomes, no progress from Datsun to Rolls-Royce, no additional women having orgasms with us, no multiplication of the number of their orgasms can compensate us for the loss of identity we suffer by the distracted pursuit of illusion. And neither money, prestige, power, nor sexual excitement can shield us from guilt or shame and from the necessity of suffering. The crisis of mid-life is a crisis of defining values. Are we even aware of what they are? And if so, are we living them?

A recent report on American values revealed that more than fifty percent of the American public is "ambivalent" about embracing a totally self-centered way of life. Moral standards are still important, but eighty percent believe that their own need for sensation, novelty, and ego fulfillment takes precedence over the needs of other people.[3]

When goods are defined as "ego-fulfilling" in this self-centered, narcissistic, consumerist way, whether they are cars, diamonds, love affairs, or luxury vacations, they lose whatever power they might have had to nurture us. Men are social, not private beings, after all, and our most profound sources of good, like our most profound sources of hurt and deprivation, are social. The capacity to appreciate persons in a way that continually renews our feelings is blocked by consumerism. The insatiable desire for new things is rooted in our dread of death and loss and in the ensuing emotional numbness to which we succumb if we do not overcome the dread.

There is a story about a merchant who bought a genie that had the power to sense when a thing or creature was about to die. One day, the genie pointed to the merchant's old horse, whose leg had begun to shake. The man ran to the market and sold him, and when the horse died the next day, he was overjoyed with his profit. Next, the genie pointed to the old servant who had been the merchant's nurse. Off to market he ran and sold her the day before she died. The merchant was euphoric. Now he had power over time and death. Next, the genie pointed at his aging wife. He was just in time to divorce her and remarry before she died. Then the genie pointed at the merchant himself. "But, genie, what shall I do?" "Go and sell yourself now," said the genie.

The problem of such a merchant is not that he must die, but that his dread of loss and his envy prevented him from valuing his relationships while he was alive.

Men in mid-life must resolve their envy or fail to achieve gratitude, the gate to the renewal of life. Envy tries to control time itself. If men can forgive their parents for not having been perfect and for aging and dying, then men can be free to live. If men forgive the world its violence, men can enjoy the world. But in order to reach the point of forgiveness, we men must acknowledge that there is something to forgive and achieve the power to suffer it. If we do not suffer the wound of time, the loss of youth, how can we use time wisely? Unfortunately, nearly all of us arrive in mid-life unable to suffer, the power to suffer blocked by our feelings of injury, resentment, and estrangement.

According to W. R. Bion, the great English psychoanalyst, a man may "experience pain, but not suffering. . . . The *intensity* of the pain contributes to his fear of suffering pain. . . . Suffering pain involves respect for the fact of pain, his own or another's. This respect he does not have. . . . Pain is sexualized; it is, therefore, inflicted or accepted but is not suffered."[4] The numb man may say he suffers, but he does not know what suffering is. Men who imagine that power, status, wealth, or sex can save them from pain, can make them invulnerable, will become emotionally numb.

The inability to respect pain results in the inability to feel compassion or empathy, for it means that a person will be out of touch, both with his own *felt* values and with others' needs. So, respect for pain, as simple as this may sound, is fundamental to the whole structure of human reality. Life lived on the basis of denying pain is life spent in the illusion of invulnerability; it is actually life unlived, unfelt, like a story that is merely skimmed. Allowing pain to penetrate our deepest being and taking responsibility for that pain: that is suffering.

The pain I speak of here is the pain of the hurt child inside us, the pain of the loss of our childhood, the pain of realizing that no one—neither idealized parents nor ever new mates—can protect us from time, from the pain of our violent, envious, twisted hearts, the pain of acknowledging the pain we have carelessly inflicted on others, the pain of knowing we can do otherwise, the pain of admitting that we have no control over our own vulnerability to loss and death.

Men who are full of denied pain have the most trouble

learning that although there is a loss in mid-life, there is also gain. It is true that younger men may remind us of our slower physical responses. It is also true that they remind us of our increased capacity for other pleasures: being closer to mates and other loved ones, reflecting, savoring moments that once seemed expendable because we believed them to be in endless supply. If it is true that young women now rarely glance at us and smile or that they regard us as "safe" instead of sexually dangerous, so are we also free of the compulsion to be looked at and of the blinkered necessity to look only *at* women who provoke sexual glances. This means a marvelous enrichment of vision. Who would not give up a world of coy glances to know what William Blake meant by "seeing the world in a grain of sand"?

Unfortunately, many men still give up their own vision, sacrifice their hearts, minds, and souls to avoid facing change, loss, death.

One man I know, Ivan, was in a state of acute agitation when he turned forty. He had always feared traveling alone, but he never wanted his wife to accompany him. In twenty years of traveling to business meetings, he had made a practice of having a woman wherever he went; even a prostitute would do. He was not afraid of growing old, he insisted; he felt fine, strong as an ox. His problem, he thought, was that one of the women he habitually saw on his travels was becoming troublesome, insisting on more time with him. He resented her for it, but he did not want to lose her because she was an excellent sexual partner and also had extensive business contacts that helped him in his work. Actually, Ivan thought seriously about only three things: marketing his product, sex, and his son's tennis game.

Business was good, sex was great, and his son's tennis game was improving. But his children—the son sixteen, the daughter fourteen—were very angry at him, so angry that even his frequent gifts to them had failed to diminish the intensity of their feelings. Ivan believed they were angry at him simply because his wife was angry at him. She was angry at him for not being at home more, but that anger had gone on for twenty years, since they were first married. He hated returning home because she made his presence there intolerable with her nagging about his absences. When she accused him of having affairs on the road, he avoided her accusations by playing tennis with his son. Now her anger had worsened, for she was very ill. Five years ago, she had been diagnosed as having cancer. He had refused to alter his "lifestyle" then, and now that she might be dying, he was still refusing to change. He gave her everything money could buy, but he could not bear the sight of her.

In fact, Ivan could not imagine changing the way he lived. He liked almost everything about it and wanted only to remain free to enjoy himself. He sent money to his parents in Florida, but he never visited them and avoided phoning them. The thought of their old age depressed him; he did not like to hear any bad news. Life was to have fun, and it was too short to waste on "downers."

Ivan did not, could not, feel guilty. He was upset because his children were angry at him only because he could not convince them that he was a good guy and a good father. He often explained to them that, after their mother died, he would give them a new mother. They were shocked, and he was shocked that they were shocked.

If Ivan's children refused to accept the new mother he was planning to install, he intended to cut them off. He would have new children with his girlfriend. He liked new things— new cars, new tennis rackets, new suits, new shirts, new customers, new friends. He just wanted people to be happy and not hassle him. Ivan was not planning to grow old or die. He was determined to stay new, carefully preserved from life's difficulties. He had earned it by hard work, hadn't he?

Ivan perceived himself as a man who loved everyone, and he wanted everyone to like him. If his children refused to like him, something had to be wrong with them. Someone had to be wrong, and it could not be he, for he could not tolerate or even acknowledge that he had any feelings of guilt, loss, or sorrow. Ivan cannot suffer.

As a psychotherapist, I have worked intensively over the past thirteen years with thirty men who were experiencing mid-life, spending at least three years with some and up to nine years with others. None of these men, all of whom live and work in the New York metropolitan region, has acute psychiatric problems. They are Jewish, Protestant, and Catholic. Although they are not representative of the male population in any scientific sense, as a sample they are certainly representative of the image of the most successful upper-middle-class men produced by our urban-suburban culture. The median age of the group I am discussing is forty-four; the youngest man is thirty-one, the oldest is fifty-five. If they are successful and if they are not psychiatrically ill, what are they doing in psychotherapy?

In terms of professional qualifications, achievement, and income, this is an elite group. One-third have legal or medical degrees; another third have graduate degrees in administration, business, communications, or the arts, and the remaining third are highly successful in sales. Only three of the thirty men did not complete college. Only three of the men have annual incomes of less than $50,000, and ten earn more than $100,000. All enjoy considerable success in their own work and have a certain status. They take vacations, and they maintain comfortable homes, luxury cars, boats, and plenty of discretionary income. One has suffered bankruptcy; one resigned from a secure job; one retired; but money is otherwise not a problem for them. Among them, they have fathered seventy-six children. As a group, they have obeyed the rules of our culture and have achieved the promised rewards. So, what has gone wrong?

All have come to psychotherapy because, notwithstanding a little pressure from mates, they know something is wrong with their lives. Some have been motivated by a situational crisis: illness, a divorce, the death of a spouse, a problem with a child. But none has remained for these reasons. Of this group, the most common reason for staying in psychotherapy is ongoing difficulty in marriage. In fact, twenty-six of these thirty men were suffering from being glued to wives, potential wives, or ex-wives to-be whom they experienced as abusive, punishing, or demanding in ways that baffled the men. Two of the men are gay and suffering the same kind of problem of fusion with their mates. Two other men are divorced and withdrawn from any serious emotional involvement for fear of tumbling back into a sado-masochistic relationship of angry dependency.

Aside from a tendency to be fused to a mate, are there other common characteristics in these men? One prevails. None of the men was able to feel—or at least verbally express feeling—or to respond appropriately to the feelings or emotional needs expressed by other adults. Four men were able to sensitively empathize with their children; the rest were too angry and impatient.

These undercurrents of impatience and anger surged beneath all their concerns. They described everything in the same flat tone of voice: the weather, a father's death, a business deal, sex, a child's problem, a wife's anger, a vacation—all seemed items of equal weight. Again and again, the men would use a variety of functional terms to express how things were going. A good week meant that things were going smoothly or without crisis. A bad week meant that things were not going well, not working out. Sometimes a good week meant more income. But whether things went well or badly depended more on the mate than on any other single factor.

The men reflect the women, sometimes quoting them. "My wife says I have been really out of it this week. I don't even know what she means, but she never lets up, demanding that I talk to her. When I do talk to her, she says I'm just talking words. Not real talking. I don't know what she wants. Talking is talking. She says I'm hopeless. Am I hopeless?"

Although four of these men tended to be agitated, humorous, and apparently expressive, none of them could accurately identify his own feelings. They thought they were angry at their children or at their wives, when actually they were badly frightened and unable to ask for comfort. Clinically, all thirty men could be classified as schizoid and depressed, a description of how we men "normally" feel and behave in this culture. They work hard; they come home and go through the motions of taking care of household and parental tasks; they watch television; and they look for reflections in their mates for clues about how to feel. They think they love their wives. But they trust no one, not even themselves. They cannot grasp the story of a man's life as a process of repairing and maintaining trust.

Twelve of these men have lost their fathers. Five have fathers who are over seventy and dying. Ten have fathers who are weak and distant figures. Three have fathers who are alive, abusive, rejecting, overbearing, or invisible. Not a single one of these men had an adult alliance with his father when he began therapy.

Only one of these men had a friendship with a brother or sister that was based on mutual respect. Two had business partnerships with brothers who were denigrative and undermining. Only four claimed to have close male friends. Three of these claims will not bear close scrutiny, for the "close" friends were actually halves of couples seen socially and were never seen one-to-one; the fourth "friend" was a business partner who manipulated my client in a very confusing way. The overwhelming impression one has from the life histories of these thirty men is of isolation from close bonds, of profound underinvolvement with family and friends.

What about their political involvement or community affiliation of any kind? After all, the traditional image of men and women, quaintly expressed by Rebecca West, is that

> Idiocy is the female defect: intent on their private lives, women follow their fate through a darkness.... It is no worse than the male defect, which is lunacy: they are so obsessed by public affairs that they see the world as by moonlight, which shows the outlines of every object but not the details indicative of their nature.[5]

All signs are that women today are becoming less idiotic and more involved with issues of social policy and power. But are men still obsessed with politics to the point of lunacy? Was political discourse just a form of lapsed gender behavior, a kind of socially sanctioned withdrawal from the sphere of women, like discussing sports? Most of these thirty men resent *all* public events, family or civic, as if they were interruptions of some private game. Most engage in public life only for private gain, for contacts for business, without passion for the public good.

Two men are active in party politics and attend many political meetings. One man, as its chief executive officer, is wholly involved in his company and its activities. One belongs to Rotary and other business organizations. Four are involved with church or synagogue functions. One man is a volunteer fireman. Two men coach Little League. But actually, these ten separate involvements are spread over only seven men, and only five of them derive significant gratification from these political or community involvements. This means that nearly twenty-five of this group of thirty are *private men.* They are concerned with their own incomes, mates, children, and personal lives. Consequently, they are highly vulnerable to any loss or change in their private lives, especially in their marriages, the core of their identities. They are unhappy, yet they dread any kind of change.

All thirty men entered their maturity, their period of maximum productivity, with feelings of resentment, deprivation, and numbness. At a time in their lives when it is most urgent for them to know what they care about and to be devoted passionately to those values, they are still angry that no one is caring for *them,* but they are also speechless about it, silent and punitive. Most of the men are actually very powerful intellectually, socially, and in terms of their potential energy, but few of them perceive themselves as truly effective. Instead, they are haunted by fears of failure, loss, and abandonment. Often they feel like frightened children. They fantasize: one wishes for a million dollars, one wishes to fish all the time, one wishes to be back with his first girlfriend. They lack self-respect.

If I had asked these thirty men "What are people for?" their actions would have answered, "To avoid." All of them are avoiding someone or some feelings, and because they are avoiding, they are restless. Because they desire avoidance, they are ignorant of their own natures. They cannot hear their own voices. Their own pain is not real to them. What they are avoiding is *suffering* that pain.

Until these men learn to suffer, they will be unable to identify with their own lives, to choose them, relish them, enjoy them. They will be spectators at the feast, trapped in avoidance, isolated in their own egos. The hell that they believe lies in the dreaded claims on them from other people will actually be their own self-judgment—for withdrawing, for refusing to experience their own fear, guilt, and shame, for their inability to suffer and thus enter the real world. These men are all trying to answer the question "What is success?" But the last place they look is inside themselves. The saddest thing is that they cannot experience even the good that they do.

One man and his wife prepared a great Thanksgiving dinner for thirty people, family members and friends. The host spent most of the time in bed with a migraine headache. This man is absent, divided, threatened by presence, and so blocked emotionally that he regards the approach of people who love him as a danger. He fears his own leadership, his own success, the admiration of his family. He dreads the envy of others.

To guide this man and his brothers into fuller presence, richer involvement in the world, is to guide them into acknowledging their own violence and withdrawal. For as soon as they break through that numbness into feeling, into guilt, an opening occurs. They feel closer to themselves, and other people become more real. The walls of exclusion that bar them from free social movement become doorways, possibilities. This does not mean that it is easy to become a powerful man, only that the energy lost and wasted in repression and avoidance now becomes available to men for constructive work, for finding the keys to the doors.

If men lose their paths, it is not only because they are frightened, envious, blind, or numb; it is also because the path runs through thickets that are guarded by dragons and mined by subtle engineers. The road signs are in strange languages, and the pilgrim is often helped into a ditch and mocked when he falls. There are toll gates of race and status, drawbridges of malice, moats of indifference.

In spite of all ancient and contemporary prescriptions for it, there is no clear path of moral development. The main cliché of contemporary psychology is the metaphor of the "life cycle," treated as if life were a kind of easy escalator that leads from stage to stage. In fact, to achieve respect and self-respect, men have to fight their way through layers of dense resistance, against tremendously powerful feelings of childish dependency in themselves, against the stings of envy and jealousy from family and friends, and against social inertia, the hostile, labyrinthine castle of bureaucracy.

When I think of what I have had to survive to grow into a man, I marvel, and I also realize how privileged I have been. Tormented by unacknowledged fears of their own, both my mother and my father were infanticidal in their envy; my mother battered me many times, and my father withdrew. Then I became caught in what seemed to be endless and hopeless oscillation: if I achieved to please my mother, I would lose the love of my father; to pacify my father, I would have to be careful not to achieve too much and to guard against enjoying what success I could allow myself. Again and again, I have been tempted to withdraw from all human relationships.

Nor were the dangers to my life merely psychic. Even as a middle-class white, boyhood gang wars threatened to break my skull or maim me for life. Anti-Semitism did not mean only being horrified at hearing about how my European kin were incinerated; it meant murderous assault by older boys in Central Park. There were many invitations to die in my life. And envy from women has not always taken the most subtle forms—one attacked me with a corkscrew in a quite determined way.

Social envy works like a chemically inhibiting substance, poisoning initiative. Men must fight their way through hundreds of tests, thousands of insults, millions of steps, to achieve manhood. Male resentment is partially the result of stinging insults received in the past when they were little, poor, ill, or otherwise lacked status and confidence. But by the time a man is forty in a society like our own, if he is white and middle-class, he has had the opportunity to gain enough social power to set *limits* to insults, to insist on deference and respect. If he has accomplished this, he knows just how crucial it is to support the efforts of others who are struggling without his privileges of class and race.

If a man has failed in his primary task to take care of himself, at mid-life he will still be poisoned by insults from his parents, mate, children, siblings, friends, and community. He will suffer humiliation and will not be able to respond effectively. And if the passion for self-respect does not blaze up into determination, a man will deteriorate.

Setting limits is the basis of self-respect. If a man's need to please others, to prove he is a man, to measure up, to "show" others, is *unlimited,* he is still dreaming of protective parents, and he will remain *reactive* to others, full of self-hate and shame. There is no end to judgment by others. A self-respecting man is his own judge. Saying no to more money, a promotion, an opportunity for sex may be the only way to say yes to one's own need to do what is meaningful. The higher up men go on what our culture absurdly refers to as the "economic ladder," the more they realize the delusive nature of competitiveness as a means to meaningful action. It is a realization many lower-income men are denied.

A lot of nonsense has been written about status and class. Apologists for social inequality like to pretend that people are competing for status symbols instead of for the thing itself, as if status had no substance. Or writers will suggest that status competition is anachronistic now that the rich and powerful also wear jeans. Status competition is a highly serious form of conventionalized social war.

Those who are born to high status struggle to keep it, and to keep it from others, unless it is advantageous to share it. Those who have low status fight to raise it, because it is about survival, about access to money, power, goods, prestige, respect, and appreciation. Those who have little hope of raising their status suffer the violence and insult of serving others' needs every day in every way. It is very difficult for a man to preserve self-respect in conditions of low status.

The agony of black men, of Hispanic men, of underclass men everywhere is an agony of shame, of mirroring inside themselves the low esteem they see for themselves in the eyes of others. I first understood how great a man Gandhi was when I spoke to an untouchable in India. At fifty, this man could remember the humiliation of being regarded as dirt by higher castes. Gandhi told the untouchables they could expect little help from others; they must raise themselves.

This man went to school, left his village, drove a truck, then raised himself to a driver for a tourist bureau. I have never seen more dignity in a man than I saw in this one. Apologizing for his grammar, he explained that he had to support his six children and that driving in traffic made him too mentally strained to learn more, or he would have raised himself further. But no man could now freely insult him or his children. They will get more schooling and have fewer children and gain more respect. Caste is doomed in India, because men like this driver will no longer suffer untouchability, but that does not mean the end of class or status competition. Caste was one way to *diminish* status competition by freezing people into hereditary occupations.

Competition for status is constant among men, but it need not freeze into caste, class, racism or the deadly individualist form of "me against the world." The root of the word competition means "petitioning with," and it signifies a kind of companionship in striving. If men become total competitors, they cannot even have allies, much less find mentors or become mentors themselves. The most dreadful thing about the life of a man who is always competing is that no matter what prizes he wins he will find himself alone.

To feel alone at mid-life is to need to change. The social-status system is not about to change. It protects hierarchy, allocates prestige, rewards men who sacrifice to it. It has no mercy. To worship status alone is to be alone with social violence.

When Jesus said, "Render unto Caesar that which is Caesar's," he meant that sacrifice must be made to the reality of social hierarchy, but the heart and soul is not of that world. After forty, a man should know the difference between the social hierarchy and the heart, and he should know that what he loves will determine which province he lives in. If he loves only power, status, ego gratification, and luxury, and if he envies others their goods, he is barred by his own heart's desire from entering the living world.

To emerge from numbness into aliveness in mid-life, men need to be honest, to suffer their own pain, and to have guides to self-respecting behavior. The old term for self-respect is virtue. The virtuous man has presence and speech; he does not hide in shame.

After forty, men sense the cool shadow of death; then they ask themselves *why* they are living. Illusions now crumble, illusions about youthfulness, about money, about power. In earlier periods, when a man's life was shorter, the questions were often synchronized with the onset of actual deterioration, actual death at forty or fifty. Now the crisis we experience at mid-life gives us signals about change, loss, and the possibility of self-transformation. This is the time when men need to understand the history and meaning of their own lives, its beginning, middle, and end.

Plutarch confidently made his biographies moral patterns for his contemporaries to follow. He told stories of Greeks and Romans to emulate and Greeks and Romans to abhor. For centuries men read his works, seeking patterns of identity. Shakespeare studied his biographies, learning about nobility and baseness from them, about the classical ideal of virtue. And what is perhaps most startling in Plutarch's universe is his understanding of the difference between jealousy, the inspired emulation of good men, and envy, the resentful wanting that is purely negative. Plutarch has no doubt about progress in moral virtue:

> We must, therefore, believe we are making but little progress so long as the admiration we feel for successful men remains inert within us and does not of its own self stir us to imitation.
>   In fact, love for a person is not active unless there is some jealousy with it, nor is that commendation of virtue evident and efficacious which does not prod and prick us, and create in us not envy but an emulation after honorable things.

Plutarch speaks of his craving to merge his own identity in that of the good man.[6]

Although we contemporary men have a longer adolescence than our ancestors, and although the patterns of our early lives have coerced us toward puerility, we can confront our own lives. It helps to know good men to pattern ourselves after.

It is time for us to understand that material success only reinforces our illusions of staying safe, our terrible anxiety about loss and losing control. Plutarch was right. The practice of virtue is more important to manhood than all the numbers sought by contemporary men—in dollars; commodities; objects of status, including women; weapons for "defense." There is no greater reward than the secure possession of one's own character, one's soul, one's self-respect. Without it, we men have nothing.

My belief is that men are starving for community and social

involvements. In mid-life, we need to build something, to love, to use ourselves, yet we volunteer far less than women and impoverish ourselves by the egocentricity of our private consumption. My own community of Rockland County is not an easy place to practice democracy. Indeed, there is no easy place to practice democracy. Working for the public good is hard, stony business, like the fields of this county full of rocks, but it can be made into a garden by our own determination:

> It is not nice to garden anywhere. Everywhere there are violent winds . . . floods, droughts, record-setting freezes . . . there is no place, no garden where these terrible things do not drive gardeners mad.
> There are no green thumbs or black thumbs. There are only gardeners and non-gardeners. Gardeners are the ones who ruin after ruin get on with the high defiance of nature herself, creating in the very face of her chaos and tornados, the power of roses and the pride of irises. . . . Defiance is what makes gardeners.[7]

The kind of creative defiance that makes a gardener is very different from the adolescent defiance that desires to keep starting anew, that refuses continuity and commitment. The self-respecting gardener knows nature will disrupt and unmake everything he plans, but he continues to make and remake his garden, with love and determination. The puerile man defies the real limits of his power, and so he defiantly plants nothing. He has no time for clearing, fertilizing, planting, ripening, for he is too agitated to wait for harvests, too depressed to invest all that energy without an immediate reward.

Especially at mid-life, time is our medium; we cannot fight it, only unlock its secrets. If we choose to love others and to invest our energy in a living community, we will gain in substance and decelerate the speed at which time consumes us. For we will all be consumed and so will our gardens, but we can still love and nourish what we will lose. To be responsible for every moment, every relationship, offers us the opportunity to use our powers to create trust and extend trust and to repair injury. We can make any moment infinite by investing it with all the wealth of our own spirit. To do that is to feel not only self-respect but gratitude for the gift of life.

The passion for self-respect grows out of the kind of suffering we have been describing, out of allowing one's self to *experience* grief and anger over one's own history of pain. This suffering is a kind of molting of man's armor. Suffering is metamorphosis. Out of the passive shell, out of the silence, out of the numbness, emerges a determined man, vulnerable and therefore responsive, unable to hide, unwilling to be a drone, fertile, winged, and capable of powerful speech. The acceptance of the knowledge of death is a powerful activator of this self-transformation. A man who accepts the eventuality of his own death will not easily be diverted from his goals. A man who accepts this limit, of death, age, loss, can set limits for others. He does not cling to others or fantasize that others can save him, and he will not permit others to abuse him.

The imagery of death that terrifies men is, in fact, the child's imagery of birth, separation. Suffering birth, suffering separation, expands and enlarges the courage to face life and death. Let us not waste our lives postponing it. Suffering is the midwife of manhood, the experience that sets limits for illusion.

The paradox of manhood at mid-life is that we must use every bit of our energy to mold the bit of clay that we are into a vessel of personal form, but we must not be too proud of our difference from other clay pots because, as the Sufi poet says, "When you smash the jugs, the water is all one."[8] Those men who fail to achieve identity envy it and are mired in unacknowledged shame and guilt. And those who do suffer and achieve personal identity know it is poverty when compared to the wealth of spiritual identification with others. When we are able to set limits to the insatiable, competitive desire to please others, we will be able to use our gifts to their fullest, holding back nothing, making a whole identity by serving the people and the values we love. For the only values worth living for after mid-life are those which shine in the face of death.

7

HEROISM: TIME BLAZING WITH MEANING

> We offered the Trust to the heavens and the earth
> and the mountains, but they refused to undertake
> it, and were afraid of it. But man undertook it.
>
> KORAN, Chapter 33,
> Muhammad Zafrulla
> Khan translation

When men are boys, they dream of becoming heroes. Boys
learn through the stories of heroes about moral development—of manhood, of courage, loyalty, fortitude, sacrifice,
protection of the weak, defense of the truth. How many
hours I spent musing about Superman, aspiring to rescue and
protect someone from terrible danger! I felt there was something exalting about heroism, and I sensed that even reflecting on it heightened the experience of time. Heroism makes
time blaze with human meaning. Heroism is trust made
flesh.

As a boy, I imagined the hero to be a man of unusual
physical power. Later, I was sure a hero was a man of extraordinary valor or a genius or a saint. He was always larger
than life, and people followed him because of who he was.
My childish adoration of heroic charisma inspired me to try
to stretch myself and my powers. I believed the old Russian

proverb that a hero is a person who endures for "one moment more"—he studies later, walks farther, tries harder.

Narcissistic men, like egocentric boys, want simply "to shine," to be special. They cannot grasp the reality of authentic heroic radiance: the creation of trust. Because they have learned that there is no father for them to obey, blame, or deny, adult men learn to take care of themselves, to set limits for those who would exploit them, and to accept responsibility for their share of the world—their family, their work, their civic obligations. Most men live inside this circle of opportunities and obligations, and their lives are defined by enlightened self-interest, understood as comprehending the care of this circle, this network.

The hero is called to a larger sphere of action. Most of the men who become heroes do so not because they will it but because they are seized by the needs of their time, often against their wishes and their wills. These are the men who devote themselves to the world beyond themselves with a passionate sense of responsibility.

I believe every man is capable of becoming a hero, and I also believe that heroism inspires all of us. Heroism teaches us that one man, at one moment, can make a difference.

No hero perfectly embodies a moral or heroic code. Even an exemplary hero like Gandhi, who knew how to peel off layer after layer of self-delusion to arrive at the truth about men, can be found late in life leaning on beautiful young women and sleeping with them "for warmth" and to test his vows of chastity. No human man is without his contradictions or entirely free of egocentrism. But the personality quirks of heroes are not fundamental. What is essential is their way of taking responsibility for life or for death in such a way that they reinforce trust in human kinship.

Heroism is not a comfortable notion. Our society oscillates

between its need for heroes and its need to be free of heroes. Heroes close the gap between our ideals and our ordinary behavior. They demand of themselves and their followers a very high standard of integration of thought, speech, and action. Because most men allow themselves a comfortable gap between ideals and action, a hero in the neighborhood can stimulate guilt and envy as well as admiration and emulation. In some men, the drive to be heroic becomes megalomania, as it did with General Douglas MacArthur. There are some heroic narcissists and some narcissistic heroes. Macho heroism that denigrates women is sterile, but so is the cynicism that suggests that heroism is no longer possible.

The current predilection for nostalgia for the past, the effort to see the present through the past or through the fantasies of extraterrestrial life that are so popular today are calculated to avoid facing the violence of the present. The lure of the past or of the fantasized future is profound. How much easier to wish to live in the glorious age of Alexander the Great or in the heroic cosmos of the future than to live now, in the shadow of the bomb! How much more romantic to live in the age of chivalry—as a knight, of course—than to have to deal with the demanding women of our own day. But men who trumpet the ideals of knightly heroism today, whether they fight for Islam or crusade for the one true religion in Jerusalem or seek to purify the Reich of Jews, quickly become intoxicated by violence and greed. The seductiveness of flight from the present is powerful, but the need for the continuity of heroic models is legitimate.

Some ideals provide actual life patterns that can be lived; others are mere symbols of national or ethnic solidarity. Every nation seeks to create a pattern of heroes for its men to imitate, both in peace and in war. Sometimes propaganda is deliberately fabricated to inflame men to make war, to work heroically, or to endure sacrifices. A classic statement of opposition to the state's manipulation of the impulse to heroism was made by Benjamin Constant, criticizing Napoleon:

> A government imbued with the spirit of invasion and conquest is obliged to corrupt a section of its people . . . to create an instrument for the active carrying out of its designs . . . it will also have to confuse the minds, warp the judgment and undermine the principles of the rest of the people, so as to obtain that passive obedience and willingness to sacrifice which are essential to a regime of conquest.[1]

Yet unmasking the cynical manipulation of heroic ideals does not mean that ideals are *merely* ways to dupe men, preparing them for slaughter or exploitation. To manipulate cultural ideals is an act of betrayal of a people and its ideals, but it does not make the ideals themselves any less crucial to the people or the culture. Like parodying knighthood, unmasking ideology serves our need for balance. But such irony is not a general license for men to avoid striving to embody the virtues in those ideal codes; they are usually qualities that are vital not only for the presumed security of the state but also for the human virtue of personal integrity. The almost fervent denigration of idealism in our time has permitted cynicism to flourish and has created a virtual vacuum in values; it has encouraged men to regress and pursue self-absorbed "lifestyles" which deny our human responsibilities toward society and leave us childish and isolated.

Saints, martyrs, and heroes are all imperfect men in reality. Sometimes inspection of their actual lives reveals that they have behaved exactly opposite to what the legacy of myth suggests, but their humanly flawed behavior should not keep them from being exemplars of cultural ideals. In spite of their flaws, their myths inspire men to independent action and to the necessity for understanding that we do not exist as separate selves without connection to the larger fabric that binds us and gives us life. The codes of manhood reinforce *group* coherence and trust, often at the cost of individual sacrifice.

One speaks now of heroism with irony, with "a wink." Pulitzer prize–winning author Russell Baker has observed that we do not now dare to make real heroic films like *Gunga Din,* only parodies like *Raiders of the Lost Ark*.

Joe McGinniss's *Heroes* is another parody of the American hero. A bitter book, it consists of ironical, Hemingway-like vignettes describing meetings with famous men who turn out to be disillusioning as heroes. The Vietnam vet who killed 115 men and won the most medals, Father Daniel Berrigan, General William Westmoreland, the novelist William Styron—all are denigrated by McGinniss. After the death of Robert Kennedy, McGinniss protests that he cannot find a new hero. He equates the loss of illusions with the vanishing of heroes, as if illusion had to be the condition of heroism. In a superficial, dismissive way, McGinniss plays the game of there-are-no-heroes-anymore-because-of: Freud, television, Watergate, the list is endless. It is an easy game, as those who have played it themselves know, but it is a deadly one, for its effect is to absolve us of responsibility for everything but ourselves.

The tension between ideal and parody is probably a necessary tension, because the claims of individual and group life cannot remain in static harmony. Heroic idealism tends to become obsessional, demonic, and antagonistic to the need to return to the familiar forms of everyday life—to dinner, sex, play. But some group ideals, in their archetypal, recurring character, contain essential elements for the preservation of social life. Like mobilization of the army when a nation is threatened, heroic codes of manhood need mobilization when social life is threatened, as in the profound crisis of trust that we are facing today.

A man I know contracted cancer of the throat at age forty-two. He was terrified of dying but refused to give up his work or his family role; he refused to give in to panic. Step by step, he fought the disease, endured the surgery, struggled with the dread of illness that threatened to swamp his enjoyment of life. This man's behavior is heroic, not because he struggled to survive and succeeded in doing so, but because he struggled to survive as a full human being and because he grew in dignity and respect for other persons in his ordeal. He refused to be a passive victim of disease or anxiety, and he refused to victimize others or punish them because he was ill.

The *real* self is a social self, a self capable of sacrifice. The real person seeks fulfillment in being useful, in being consumed by life. But this self needs trust in a living community to express itself.

When trust in the moral community no longer exists (God is dead), two kinds of lives based on lies become dominant as antiheroic "lifestyles." The first is the lie that the individual ego can replace the spiritual bond of community life. The second lie is that hierarchy is the same as community. The first kind of lie produces the manic self-inflation of the isolated superman in various incarnations—the dictator, the isolated, romantic artist, the tyrannical entrepreneur, the champion. This kind of deification of the personal will enthrones narcissism. The only kind of sacrifice this narcissist can comprehend is the limitless sacrifices he demands from others.

Even more modest versions of the "private person" reveal how easily we can resort to self-deification. A friend of mine stated that he could not comprehend how any father could send his son to war, any war. Having been psychoanalyzed, he *knew* that such actions were infanticidal. Didn't God prohibit Abraham from sacrificing Isaac? My friend reserved the absolute right to judge his government and withdraw his son and his fortune from the community, if asked to sacrifice.

What good father wants his son to die in Vietnam or Nicaragua? Only an ideal community could command his allegiance, he said, and since none existed or was about to exist, he rested his case. This personalism is what the Greeks called "idiocy" and the Hebrews "blasphemy," because it destroys trust in community life. Because pervasive mistrust has so deprived our institutions of legitimacy, such personalism can masquerade in our culture as the unmasking of their hypocrisy. One who doubts can simply withhold. But withholding is the position of modern man, the moral individualist. As we shall see later, this attitude is not good enough to sustain community life.

The second kind of life that flourishes in the absence of a moral community is the illusory life of the corporate individual. Here, the lie is that care for human beings can be found at the center of the state or similar organizations of bureaucratic scale and composition. The constant assertion of care, the rhetoric of caring, is important to preserve the organization's legitimacy, but it is basically a lie. The true rulers of these bodies are money and the necessity to maintain and expand power; persons are invisible. National bureaucratic elites, like multinational corporations, rarely exist as true communities. They are the corporate forms of the moral individualist. For such entities, the only values are instrumental values, and the only reality is self-interest. Persons exist only to be *used*.

The supreme irony of World War II was not that the vanquished—Germany and Japan—emerged as superproductive cultures but that the United States destroyed the world of community values it was trying to protect by creating the monster state to fight the monster state. In this artificial, technical world, it is virtually impossible for one man to make a difference. In the real world of suffering, one man makes all the difference—between truth and falsehood, trust and

mistrust, spiritual life or death. The hero is the living repudiation of the lie of the individualist and the lie of the
corporate state.

Heroism demands an ordeal that goes beyond normal limits
and that creates new human connections. The American Apollo
space missions symbolize state power, not human will. It
makes a great difference to us whether a potential hero represents human vulnerability or state power. As the philosopher Simone Weil has observed, it is much easier to die
in Napoleon's cavalry charge, intoxicated by power and glory,
than to die—or to live—for the crucified truth, for the weakness of humanity.

We cannot allow the state to monopolize or manufacture
our heroes. As David K. Shipler has observed, in the Soviet
Union the World War is celebrated as the great "heroic time
of unity" and is used by the authorities to falsely explain the
present and to mask Stalin's brutality. The Russian people
are cynical about the state's manipulation of hero worship,
but they long for heroes:

> Under the state hierarchy's tough rules, many Russians have
> lost their heroes and their faith, their faith in their ideology
> and in their future. Some respond by retreating into their
> personal lives, neglecting the collectivism that is supposed to
> govern the country's social structure. Others idealize an irre-
> trievable past rooted in rural simplicity and moral purity, a
> search for Russianness.[2]

People of all nations yearn for heroes who symbolize and
inspire their ideal way of life. Nation states mobilize propaganda to manipulate that longing and make it serve the state.
But true heroism is too erratically individual, too humanly
social to be confined for long in state molds. Official rhetoric
cannot contain the paradoxical energy of heroes. Heroism
resists bureaucratization, propaganda, and public relations

campaigns. Moral heroism serves what is holy, not the power of social hierarchy masquerading as sacred. Heroism in the service of the sacred must be unmasked in the service of the holy.

We men must take sides on issues such as nuclear armaments or U.S. Latin American policy. Heroes will seek not to serve state power but to clarify moral choices. The secret history of the development of nuclear weapons illustrates the awful bondage of heroic scientists to the state. When J. Robert Oppenheimer realized that the work he was doing on the hydrogen bomb was more in service to the sacred (state power) than to the holy (world peace), he balked. The state is an idol, and those who speak for it often lie.

The heroes are the people among us who care passionately about the social needs of those around them in the present moment and who pledge themselves to do something about fulfilling those needs. Others have acute reality to them, like pain in their own bodies. The heroic truth is almost blindingly simple: that others are no different from ourselves.

Just as the state breeds tension, violence, and injustice, so does sheer rebellion against the state or other institutions in favor of some kind of individual pastoral fantasy breed only victimization and passivity. We have seen that "men's liberation" is one version of this fantasy. The language of the victim is based in the easy assumption that if only "they" would stop persecuting us, everything would be fine—utopian, in fact. The state says there are no victims: everything is fine. The professional rebel says: we are the only victims; victimization is our only identity, and we are innocent; "they" are to blame for everything. The denial of responsibility by sacred officials triggers puerile revolt in powerless individuals who want to escape the responsibility for violence. The hero seeks neither justification nor blame, but responsibility.

The core of the heroic act is facing violence, competition,

and loss. The hero's life is a sacrifice to the life of the group.

Joseph Campbell, in *The Hero with a Thousand Faces*, champions the mythic approach to the hero. He argues that the "standard path of the mythological adventure of the hero is the magnification of the formula represented in the rites of passage: separation—initiation—return."

Like most Jungians, Campbell becomes dangerously misleading about how retreat from the world can help us with violence in the soul or in society. "There is no such society any more as the gods once supported," Campbell tells us, and the old "mysteries have lost their force; their symbols no longer interest our psyche." He is certain that the hero must make it "possible for men and women to come to full human maturity," but he is vague about how the "hero-deed" can bring this about.

Campbell sees the contemporary crisis of values as:

> ... opposite to that of men in the comparatively stable periods of those great coordinating mythologies which now are known as lies. Then, all meaning was in the group, in the great anonymous forms, none in the self-expressive individual; today no meaning is in the group—none in the word; all is in the individual. But then the meaning is absolutely unconscious. One does not know toward what one moves.

For Campbell, the whole world must be transmuted, but not by conscious action:

> The whole thing is being worked out on another level, not only in the depths of every living psyche in the modern world, but also on those titanic battlefields into which the whole planet has lately been converted.[3]

Mythicizing the hero obscures the need for the hero to actively participate in real groups, make real choices. Campbell's rhetoric is so inflated that one hardly notices the absence of living men and women in a real political world. Gandhi and Martin Luther King, Jr., were not archetypes; they were shrewd political organizers in the service of the holy.

The hero, past, present, and future, serves his community as a barrier against panic. The hero kills death, or the fear of it, in himself and his companions. The crucial decisions of manhood are concerned with how to invest our caring, how to face the reality of death with a feeling that we have used every gift we own, that we have left nothing of value in ourselves for death, that we have invested all that is good in us in others.

In the previous chapter, we observed how manhood depends upon our accepting the prospect of death, of acknowledging the certainty of loss of everything we love, on the willingness to let go of the illusion that we can protect ourselves from the vulnerability to loss. We can attain the mastery of living, of full giving to ourselves and those we love, only when we are able to appreciate our mortality. Acknowledging the prospect of our deaths teaches us the end of procrastination, blame, and asking infantile questions about what to do with one's life. The hero knows he can use his life and his death to strengthen the bonds of trust.

If a man consciously sets out to be heroic, he will rapidly be exposed for being grandiose, puerile, romantic, and narcissistic. That fantasy of leaping into heroism is for adolescents. What a man must set out to do is to fulfill his responsibility; in the course of doing so, he will find that the opportunity to sacrifice opens before him like a chasm he cannot avoid. But the *demand* for heroes is a demand for blood. It means that violence is out of control somewhere in the social system.

Much of written history is a kind of exemplary biography, from Plutarch's *Lives of the Noble Greeks and Romans* to John F. Kennedy's *Profiles in Courage,* an effort to remember what is worth emulating in the way men have lived. Heroism has a special claim on our memory, because it is so centrally concerned with the survival of cultural ideals, even at the cost of the death of men who embody them. Heroes secure the values of the survivors.

One man who was inspired to heroism by a moment full of significance for him was Joseph Polowsky, who was a private with the advance patrol of the U.S. Army's 69th Infantry Division as it linked up with the Russian Army at the River Elbe, ending German resistance in World War II. Polowsky was so inspired by that moment of brotherhood, a moment of peace and reconciliation for him personally as well as historically—a linking of his Russian past and his American present—that he worked for the rest of his life to promote reconciliation between the Soviet Union and the United States, founding an organization for that purpose, visiting Khrushchev, arranging reunions of veterans, trying to extend the feeling of trust that had been established, to keep the spirit of that great moment of unity alive.

Like many heroes, Polowsky used his death to further the purpose he lived for. In October 1983, as he was dying, he obtained approval to be buried in Torgau, East Germany, near the Elbe, making his grave a monument to the linkage of peoples united by a common purpose, transcending differences by sacrificial acts of brotherhood. Joseph Polowsky was a taxi driver, a common man inspired by heroic purpose.[4]

Gandhi was a hero who set time ablaze by his own sense of purpose, using himself as a spark. In 1931, with a handful of followers, ridiculed by Nehru and other Indian nationalist leaders, Gandhi determined to march through villages to the sea, where he used the issue of making salt illegally to dramatize the need to defy the oppressiveness of the British Empire. So this small man with a soft voice, an accomplished lawyer dressed like the poorest peasant, a man who was already a symbol of national resistance to colonial rule, a symbol of freedom, human dignity, truth, and nonviolent struggle, began his march to the sea. As he walked from village to village, people came to see him. Some joined the march and others sprinkled the dusty, hot dirt roads with water and flowers. And the reporters came; the news went out all over India and all over the world. The march gained force like the sacred river of India, rushing toward the sea. The spirit of defiance embodied in that march of Gandhi's so unified national resistance to British rule that the end of colonialism became inevitable.[5]

No one who knew Gandhi doubted the tremendous power of his personality or his power to motivate people through the promise to give their lives meaning and dignity. By his own devotion to his purpose, he unified other persons and organized them to struggle. Gandhi's work of unifying his people, of reconciling the holy and the sacred, foundered only in the face of the historic division between Muslims and Hindus. That gap remained, to split India apart. His death was the sacrificial death of a martyr, the death that stuns us into realizing the vulnerability of all persons and our common suffering.

A hero is not simply a terrorist for the side that wins nor is a terrorist a hero for the side that loses. Gandhi had to break the link between India and Britain because British domination humiliated his people in their souls, made them feel passive about governing themselves. He minimized the violence of the separation as much as was humanly possible. He renewed the sanctity of human life, re-creating its value in a nation where only those close to the ruling British had value.

Love is the substance that holds a human world together as a *felt* human reality. Commerce, law, and custom are the shell of human reality, enabling social life to function. But people are not functions, they become human only through the meaningfulness of their relationships to one another. Time becomes more vivid, the present more real, as people come closer to their human essence. The substance of love or faith is like a secretion that is felt and experienced as an intensification of human presence. The hero is an intensifier of this human presence for his community. Heroism creates social meaning and purpose. The hero magnetizes many people, drawing them into a growing field of energy, clarifying their reason for living, working, sacrificing.

In most men, this substance is evanescent. It evaporates rapidly in the presence of silence, violence, gaps, envy between persons. The heroism of a man like Gandhi is the refusal to limit the expression of this substance only to family or familiar groups, even in the face of violence. Some men pursue heroism because of an inability to love those close to them. Moral heroism is an *extension* of love, not a substitute for it.

We cannot reinvent the substance of morality, manhood, or heroism in an idiom that is foreign to a people's tradition. But we can renew the morality inherent in the tradition by showing how the virtues can function again in specific communities of need. And unless we do that, we are waiting for war or catastrophe to do what moral exhortation cannot do: restore the meaning of sacrificial presence and practice in the face of violence. Must blood do what spirit fails to do—cement the social order? Or can we learn this new form of heroism that Gandhi tried to teach us? Can we translate Gandhi into an American idiom? Martin Luther King, Jr., is remembered now in an annual holiday as an exemplary hero for his courage in fighting for justice; not only did he remember Gandhi's example but he succeeded in translating it into a specifically American version.

It should be clear by now that my intention is not to idealize heroism or to stimulate hero worship or idolatry, but to show that heroism is always available to us through our traditions.

When men fail to make commitments and to sacrifice for them, they feel guilt-ridden, not good enough—not because they failed to be great heroes but because they failed to be themselves, failed to remember the traditions of their fathers.

The problem of heroism today in America is that much of the energy of male striving lacks meaningful social context. We need everyday heroes to confront the life-and-death responsibilities of a new era of biotechnology, heroes who will clarify the differences between computerized efficiency and human productivity. We need heroes to protect the aged and vulnerable, to heal racial discord, to stop family violence.

If I have attained manhood and acknowledged my fears and the prospect of my death, then I own my death. No man is poor if he owns his own death. It is the shame of our time that such knowledge has often been left only to terrorists and criminals. Sometimes a man like Dr. Barney Clark, suffering with his artificial heart, reminds us of the ownership of our death and the proper sacrificial use of it. But more often than not, men die as they have lived, unconscious of the meaning of their actions. The hero is the man most conscious of the value of using his death as a bond of trust for his group.

The historian Philippe Ariès has traced three eras in Western attitudes toward death.[6] First came the calm death; then the formal religious death. Our period is described as the period of *nothingness*, which began in the eighteenth century but was still modulated by traditional social forms. It is not until the twentieth century that the stark face of death as nothingness appears, death unmediated by traditional rituals or community membership, stripped of gender, of rituals, of myths. This is when the flight from death, the denial of death, produces the terror of death that rules modern life. The twentieth century is the century of death. Our century makes the destruction of the living earth thinkable because all the social bonds of trust that make death tame have been broken.

The *unbinding* of the bonds of family and community is proper to adolescence, not as total liberation from bonds but as a step toward the necessity for rebinding. The traditional psychology of virtue was repressive and did not allow for this progressive rebellion, which was grasped only in the mystical traditions. But much of modern psychology has allied itself to irresponsible, individualist rebellion, and it needs the balance of a revised classical moral theory before schism destroys all hope of trust.

The task of the hero is to counter the power of death to destroy social values by using his presence to negate absence, by mobilizing the fullness of his presence to protest injustice, by making connections between divided souls and groups. Service is wealth, not loss. Is this kind of heroism too difficult to aspire to as the social world becomes more alienated, more technical, as trust diminishes while human differences seem to grow? If it is, then we are lost.

Kinship accounting is simple. One owes a death to one's kin. Medieval church accounting is more complex; one owes the family dead Masses, remembrance, charity in their name, intercession for their souls in purgatory. This kind of moral social accounting ceases to link the living and the dead when death ceases to be the moment of redistribution of wealth in the eighteenth century. When accounting becomes separated from family and communal debt systems, from moral valuations, it becomes technical, merely efficient.

Wealth was once exchanged for the promise of eternal life; now people are exchanged for the power of social engineering. As technical time accelerates, it loses relational value. Time becomes an empty unit. Wealth was once a *loan from God;* an accounting was demanded. The will was once a moral obligation; one sent for a confessor and a notary.

The shift from facing death as eternity and judgment to facing death as nothingness has vastly increased the power of death to paralyze a person's sense of value. Now, even the fact of a will is less esteemed in a time of high taxation. What shall we now exchange for our debt to death in a world of value fluctuation? How can we return from the nightmare of relative values to the renewed trust in absolute social values? How shall we revive the determination to make the bonds between persons once again holy? How shall we redeem the despair of a generation that has broken so many bonds, spoken so many lies, been complicit in the murder of so many innocents?

How shall we even imagine the heroic responsibility of undertaking such a task? Human values can be renewed, if men become more serious about the life that is loaned to them for a short season and about the meaning that can be made only by closing the gaps of trust between persons and groups. Into the gaps we must go, man after man, until they close.

Values cannot be policed, computerized, or legislated; they can be made flesh only by heroic men and women. There can be no "science of limits" to protect us from barbarous technologized regression—or from the continuous process of struggle between freedom and limits. Just as angry rebellion cannot save us from what I have called the sacred, from the need to preserve continuity in our social traditions, so conservative rigidity cannot protect us from the need for holy, disorderly renewal and change. The hero serves both faces of God, the preserver and the destroyer. He breaks when he must, but he keeps what needs preserving, because what he serves is not any particular social form but value and meaning itself.

Heroism creates value in human life in the face of violence, loss, and the threat of meaningless disconnections within persons, between persons, and between groups. Sacrificial heroism creates social meaning.

Those who create idols to worship, especially political idols, generally become intoxicated by a delusion of power and immortality. The industrialized world incarnated real productive power in persons, personifications, heroes like Roosevelt and Churchill. After the World War, many of the decolonized nations created fathers of their nations out of sheer need for the heroic integration of their new states. But they fatally reversed the process of personification.

Instead of real power personifying itself in symbolic persons, personification itself became the source of power, and political power was built on illusion and rhetoric. Many of these new heroes were stars of their own state-controlled media, acquiring power without building foundations for legitimacy, without the ordeal of sacrifice. Instead of heroic identification with the collective, demagogues promote collective identification with the leader, an identification that often destroys the basis of community life in favor of the one-party state exalting its immortal leader.[7] The real hero is not a demagogue. Heroes who seek to become gods on earth pervert the story of the hero by turning into the monster instead of slaying the monster.

When the hero breaks the limits that confine the thought and action of the conventional person, he risks intoxication by mania or the demonic. Demonic heroism destroys social meaning, destroys trust. The task of the hero is to oppose the massive inertia of ignorance, dread of change, and ancestral ritual, to make new moves. Innovation and revolution in any sphere—arts, politics, science, religion—may readily become euphoric and, like Mao's cultural revolution, ultimately destructive to community life. The hero may be needed to start the motion of the wheel that has become mired in mud; the hero may also be needed to sacrifice himself to stop its inhuman acceleration.

The demonic myth of heroism, or the myth of regeneration through violence, is a response to the human denial of helplessness, of limitations, and of vulnerability, a response to the irrational, impatient, immediate demand for a savior. It obscures the actual value of heroism as a *real* protective social function.

Renewal through violence appears throughout history. The Roman Catholic Church declared holy war in the eleventh century as a crusade to redeem Jerusalem from the Muslims. The crusading Christian justification of violence and war was based not only on the political need to kill idolators but also on a promise of individual expiation of sin, and it became a myth of collective expiation of sin. The crusade is a mirror image of the Islamic jihad.

The myth of regeneration through violence arose in America as the first colonists saw the opportunity to regenerate their fortunes, their freedom, and their power through violence—the destruction of the Indians, the enslavement of the blacks, and the violation of the land.[8] The myth of regeneration through violence is a structuring metaphor of the American experience, but it is hardly unique to America. The most striking quality of life in the new world was the lack of social restraints on human behavior, the possibility of imposing power on virgin, unsocialized nature. This regeneration through violence was also enacted by colonists in Latin America and Africa.

Early joiners of the Nazi party in Germany were similarly motivated by demonic heroic striving—by individual violence, revenge for past humiliations, and an ideology of domination. The ideology of violence relieved the guilt of psychopathic feelings in this group of humiliated men, many of whom were orphans, and many of whom had been raised in poverty following World War I. The irresponsible Weimar climate of scapegoating and vilification of realistic leaders called for violence as a solution to the "social sickness" and led, step by step, from unlimited verbal violence to unlimited violent behavior.[9] The virtue of destroying the pagan enemy, whether the heathen Indian, the idolatrous Muslim, or the Bolshevik, becomes the myth of regeneration through violence and generates varying forms of paranoid activist politics. For in killing "the enemy," we deny and destroy a part of ourselves, and we undermine trust in human kinship.

The paranoid hero is one who accrues power by violence and who placates invisible powers by his sacrifice of others. He kills those who threaten his group; he incorporates their powers to further protect his group; he sacrifices others to gain immunity for his group. In a word, he becomes a savior through blood. From the head-hunting and charm-hunting of primitive societies to the holocausts of Hitler and Hiroshima, the dynamic is the same: the illusion of a heroic victory over evil by a traffic in pure power. And the aim is the same: purity, goodness, righteousness—immunity from death through violence inflicted on others.

Demonic heroism creates divisions: us and them. Sacrificial heroism creates inclusions: all people are brothers and sisters.

To comprehend how urgently we need a code of inclusive heroism, we need a long perspective. Peter Brown's book *The Cult of the Saints* redeems a very important moment in human history from distortion. To our modern sensibilities, the cult of the saints in late antiquity has seemed a repulsive period, involving reverence for bones and hysteria about miracles. In fact, as Brown shows, the cult of saints was established by bishops who were struggling to create viable communities of Christians in the void created by the breakdown of social order.

The saints were used to heal divisions, to join heaven and earth. They protected the sacred status hierarchy of the community, which still reflected the language of Roman urban and aristocratic society, without excluding the holy, the newer groups, including women and monks, from participation. The processions that followed the relics of the saints involved the whole Christian community and created a safe social space where all could attend in the merciful presence of a human being who linked all to all. A saint's tomb was a place of justice and healing for the social group as a whole, including those who may have killed the saint. The stone buildings that enclosed relics of the saints were *public*. The rich could not reserve those holy bones for themselves, nor could barbarians simply return them to nature, burning them on mountaintops.

By creating new social space around the saints' tombs, the bishops increased their own power, but they also reduced the violence of the wealthy and continued the process of socializing nature, imposing urban social order upon wild places and pagan shrines. Reverence for the saints created a way for persons to escape the constricting obligations of kinship and village and to travel in a new, expanded orbit of social exchange. Like the later cult of nationalism, the cult of the saints provided a way to reconcile individual assertion and the need for social integration. It faced upward and downward, inward and outward. It released people from old obligations but bound them to new ones.[10] The hero, the saint, tries to create or to protect this marriage of the energy of the holy and the order of the sacred.

The mature wisdom of the Greeks about the tension between change and social order is the same as that of Confucianism, Buddhism, Judaism, Hinduism, Islam, and Christianity. One cannot force fate. One must play one's role, neither passive nor manic, doing what is socially needed with the skills one has developed, suffering the historical situation either by being consumed as a sacrifice to public life or by being ignored, living in a rehearsal for a drama that is not produced. Either way, readiness is called for. Some heroes are those who are called, who live in the moment of difference. Their fortune is their misfortune. Others choose their fate, consciously confronting the demons of violence in their time.

Survivors of the utopian social engineering of Hitler, Stalin, and Mao may not feel that the demonic will to revolution and order can be anything but psychotic or evil. They will be wrong. That same demon drives scientific and artistic creativity. That same ambivalent demon created atomic energy and split Teller and Oppenheimer, as well as the atom. It also split the Soviet physicist, Sakharov. Oppenheimer and Sakharov are heroes who refused demonic intoxication and who became martyrs.

Wisdom is reflective. After catastrophe, we learn. But only for a generation. Then the cry, "Never again!" is lost in the general amnesia that permeates the present. Heroism cannot be accumulated or stored, only remembered through example and remade in every epoch. It requires constant renewal and readiness.

One powerful play in recent seasons is Peter Shaffer's *Good*. It is about a man, an intellectual, a professor, who is hollow. He is flattered and seduced into becoming a Nazi. There is no value he is willing to sacrifice for—not friendship, not humanity, not love. This *refusal to sacrifice for the common good* is the core of the soul of the male who fails to achieve manhood. The refusal to be vulnerable to our kin and to the needs of our friends opens the way to personal despair, social disintegration, and dictatorship.

Manhood, democratic manhood, is precisely the barrier to autocracy. The American democratic cultural tradition, from Jefferson to Thoreau to Saul Bellow, is an effort to activate democratic models of self-respecting manhood. It calls for men who will defend values they are responsible for to people they are responsible to. It is a corrupt tradition, corrupted by violence, the murder of Indians and blacks, racism, sexism, inequality, and militarism, but it is the tradition of our fathers, and we must look to it for guidance, as well as transform it.

I have sought to demonstrate that heroism is a *universal* value. Violence is always present in human groups, threatening to fragment the self, threatening to split the group, threatening to invade another group. The hero voluntarily undergoes an ordeal to overcome his own violence, calms the violence of others, counters the power of death to destroy meaning, strives for justice, and values both the single person and the sacred order of the group.

The hero never submits passively to sacred order. Indeed, it is the friction of his asserting the values of both the personal and the social, the old and the new, us and them, that makes time blaze with meaning, illuminating the drama of their collision in the human soul. The hero tries to protect both change *and* social order against violence. He opposes the schism of "us and them." That is why he is so often the victim of violence from his "own" side. Gandhi was killed by a Hindu, not by a Muslim.

The crucial questions for a man are: Can I stand up and speak for what I believe? Can I bridge this gap between people? Can I halt the spread of panic and violence? Can my love or care hold these people together? Heroic manhood has been held so precious because it is the foundation of the meaningful social world.

We are now undergoing a crisis in values that resembles the nineteenth-century crisis of the death of God. It is the death of Progress as a notion of global rational social development. Technological development is so unequal, so confined to a few metropolitan areas, that it threatens the idea that humankind is one species. In a few centers—the United States, Europe, Japan, Korea, the Soviet Union—the accelerating tempo of research in biotechnology and information science is changing our concept of the limits of human control over nature. Space research and genetic-engineering discoveries promise and threaten not simply to expand human potential but to change its ecosystem. Since the development of the atomic bomb, some ethically sensitive scientists have foreseen this crisis of technical domination of the human world.

The physicist Freeman Dyson believes that only the "cult of evanescence," the poetic appreciation of life by a mortal, and thereby ethical, humanity, "holds in check our tendency to unify and homogenize and obliterate nature's diversity with our technology. It holds in check our tendency to unify and homogenize ourselves. It keeps us forever humble before the universe's prodigality."[11]

Dyson's "cult of evanescence" echoes what I mean when I say that heroism penetrates the present and makes time stand still. But his sense of the containment of a demonically expanding technology is aesthetic, and the heroic sense is ethical or religious: it is extreme attention turning into sacrificial action. The present becomes eternal when love for it is total, burning with the power of the sun, ablaze with what mystics feel as God's love for man. But mysticism is not enough. The hero must act to make a human difference, to turn mistrust into trust, estrangement into kinship.

Heroism is the hope of a breakthrough into meaning in the darkest hour. The despair men often feel at being locked into powerless egos reflects both a psychic numbness and a lack of hope that one man can make a human difference to a social life dominated by technology, wealth, and power concentrated in a distant, unresponsive hierarchy. The psychic breakthrough of the hero is into his own purpose as a human truth, a crystal of trust, as eternity. When men break through time, through their sacred differences, time then slows and begins to blaze.

Heroic virtues must be keyed to specific contemporary practices and circumstances. What virtues are essential to an era of rapid technological and social change? The virtues required are: courage to face change, reverence for the need for continuity, the capacity to face loss, the will to sacrifice, the capacity to identify with others, the creative use of our moral resources to sustain human meaning in new situations, and the responsibility to protect people disoriented by change.

There are always new monsters for heroes to slay. As historical time accelerates to the new rhythm of technical change, our need to remember heroes grows stronger, our need to feel time pulse with meaning grows greater, our need to feel the presence of eternity grows greater.

Life reduced to "information flow" is the final desacralization of nature. This new, dehumanized point of view creates the potential for a technical cosmology that does violence to every traditional "natural" value. We human beings hate gaps, especially gaps between the familiar and the unknown. Cosmologies are only ways of convincing ourselves that there is no gap between our experiences and our beliefs. Bereft of traditional religious cosmology, deprived now by biotechnology and robotics of even the "comforts" of the now traditional theory of organic evolution, we face a sterile, computerized cosmos. Human values must be defended against such a cosmos. Pharaoh massacred children, and Hitler massacred Jews, homosexuals, and millions of "others." The murderous logic of a technical cosmos threatens every human bond and value. As violence expands, the need for heroism becomes greater in all areas of social life.

When I was a boy, I thought that the hero was the man who was most different from others. Narcissism exalts this sense of being different. Now I know that the hero is the man who sacrifices his difference from others, undergoing voluntarily what those who are most vulnerable to violence undergo, whether they are blacks, Jews, women, or untouchables. Heroism abolishes otherness between persons and fills the empty technical cosmos with the substance of human kinship: trust.

VIOLENCE OR SACRIFICE

The false God turns suffering into violence; the true God turns violence into suffering.

SIMONE WEIL

Violence is a health issue. Bombing and urban crime are dangerous to life and limb in obvious ways. Family violence is not so obvious. But in 1982, the Surgeon General of the United States declared that family violence had become one of the most serious health issues our country faces. As a *New York Times* editorial states:

> In 1982 the National Center on Child Abuse and Neglect reported that "... the actual number of children abused and neglected annually in the U.S. is at least 1,000,000." Estimates on the number of women beaten yearly by their husbands range from two to six million. At least half a million Americans over 65 are abused by members of their families. Getting caught in family disputes is the cause of 20 percent of all police deaths on duty and 40 percent of injuries.
>
> Concern about the problem is hardly new, though it has yet to produce serious Federal commitment to a response. In 1976 the White House held its first Conference on Domestic Violence. In 1979 a Federal Office of Domestic Violence was established, but Congress nonfunded it out of existence two years later.
>
> In 1980 Congress debated the Act to Prevent Domestic Violence, proposing $15 million for community programs, to be

matched by states. Conservative opponents, who saw shelters
for battered wives as anti-family, killed it. Many Federal programs to help family violence projects have suffered substantial
funding cuts recently.[1]

Is violence normal? Shall we tolerate it in ourselves, in our
families, in our political life? What can we do about it? Can
we even grasp its full impact on us? Are we ready to see it?
Can we bear it?

As director of an agency founded to prevent the abuse and
neglect of children, I say that whatever the *stated* policy of
national, state, and local governments, the actual policy is
infanticidal. This fact is masked by euphemisms about hand-
icapped, underprivileged, unemployed children; some die in
the flesh, others in the spirit.

Those of us who work with children and families often
feel that it is our failure that so many die or become locked
into vicious circles of self-destructive and destructive behavior.
It is not our failure or our fault, but it is our responsibility
to speak. I sympathize with every judge, every social worker,
every teacher, every child-care worker because each is given
a terrible double message: Protect the developmental rights
of all children, but let many die. Do we still lack the social
will to make the sacrifices necessary to protect the lives of all
children?

Infanticide is attacked in the Bible. Jeremiah thunders against
Tophet, the high place, the altars where parents "burn their
sons and daughters in the fire," sacrificing them to gain favor
from the gods by their blood. But infanticide was practiced
openly until recently in the Western world.[2] Second daughters
did not often live to receive dowries. As a population-control
device, as a form of social control, as "home economics," as
a way to achieve magical goals, infanticide was felt to be a
necessity.

Surely abortions are preferable to the lives of terror and despair that many American children lead. Some are battered to death. Others are raped. Most are subjected to repeated acts of neglect and rejection that cause them to wither in mind and spirit. They develop learning disabilities and drop out of school—a euphemism for death. They become delinquent—a euphemism for death. They become drug- or alcohol-addicted—a euphemism for death. They run away—a euphemism for death. They become pregnant at fourteen—a euphemism for death. They become permanently unemployed and unemployable—a euphemism for death. Is there human life after birth for these children? Is it time for men to oppose the slaughter of sixteen-year-olds?

In mordant moments, working with the counseling service staff to try to undo in a few weeks the damage done to children by fifteen years of abuse by deprived, ignorant parents, neglectful schools, and budget-conscious communities—in those moments, I recall the solution to the problem of starving Irish children that was proposed by the satirist Jonathan Swift: "Eat them." Perhaps it would be kinder to say to these children, "We need your protein" rather than to say, "We don't need you at all." Because that is the message we are giving to perhaps one-third of our children. It is a "die" message.

Children internalize the violence between their parents as well as the violence that is directed at them. It can stunt their physical growth and inhibit their power to learn. It can cause them to hate themselves and feel they are ugly and bad and ought to die.

As the power of violence grows in our culture, it assumes more impersonal forms. Just as the machine gun replaced the aimed arrow, so the depersonalized parent replaced the extended family. The power of death grows as the power of communities diminishes. And as the power of death grows, the need for men as mentors and heroes grows. Just as violence destroys the bonds of trust, so manhood seeks to repair those bonds, by caring about human pain, about truth, about kinship.

Civilized societies have outlawed ritual human sacrifice, cannibalism, torture, and slavery. But human sacrifice is condoned in the form of domestic violence. Wherever justice cannot reach in a society to constrain violence, there will be sacrificial victims—mainly women and children. The main task of social institutions is to protect a community against chaos and violence. Historically, the justice system functions to end a vicious circle of feuding and revenge. The state reserves the right to extract revenge for murder. But murderous vengeance is hidden in every man's heart. And as justice reaches imperfectly into the home, so does it reach imperfectly into the hearts of men.

It is possible to focus on violent crime, murder or rape, and to deplore it, or to focus on arms sales and to deplore that, or to focus on racial violence and to deplore that. But it is very difficult to admit or to grasp the total dimension of violence in an entire culture, especially when that culture is one's own. A foreign correspondent returning to America writes:

> The cities of America seem inured to violence—to rape and murder, to the physical abuse of children and the beating of spouses—on a scale unimaginable in Vienna or Paris or Stockholm (or, for that matter, in Moscow or Prague). People seem to accept it as inevitable and develop a kind of stockade mentality to deal with it.[3]

Are American cities more violent than Hong Kong, Calcutta, Berlin, Cairo, Teheran, Rio de Janeiro, or Tokyo? It depends on which kind of male violence one is looking at. When we face the truth of any society, we confront male violence in some form. Should it console us to read in the *History of Violence in America* that: "Group protest and violence is episodic in the history of most organized political communities and chronic in many. No country in the modern world has been free of violence for as much as a generation"?[4]

The Bible, Homer, the Mahabharata, Heraclitus, Machiavelli, Hobbes, Marx, Darwin, and Freud describe reality as strife, as social violence. Does that give us license to deny that violence is our responsibility? We attribute it to others only at the cost of our true selves.

To deny violence encourages its dominion under other names—patriotism, revolution, maintaining social order, revenge, punishing sinners, defending the sanctity of family life. The problem is to adequately and concretely embody violence in order to make it more difficult to deny its presence, especially for men in their years of maximum social responsibility.

Paradoxically, many men enjoy violence as a form of entertainment. It sells newspapers. It is the main feature of television news. It pervades television programming. It spices our regular diet of mass media sports, especially football, hockey, and soccer. Pornographic films, magazines, and literature thrive on eroticized violence against women. But to enjoy violence in this way, men must regard it as aesthetic, as unreal, as a kind of anomaly, something apart from real life.

Because men inflict the most violence—in war, in political conflicts, in the streets, at home—it is men who must be responsible for reducing violence. Women have recently shown great heroism in exposing and confronting male violence, especially in raising our awareness about child abuse, wife abuse, and rape. We need not look far to understand that it is mainly men who deny, own, sell, profit by, and mystify violence.

One of the motivations of this book has been artist Nancy Buchanan's great work, *Fallout from the Nuclear Family*. The work was a tribute to her father, a famous physicist who lost his genius, his wife, his daughters, his soul, and finally his life because he identified primarily with his corporate status and with the growth of military technology. He failed to sacrifice his narcissism, and so he became a victimizer of his family and a sacrificial victim himself to the depersonalized world he helped to make.

The main emotional source of violence is pain or terror that is denied and turned to rage. Puerile men mindlessly deaden themselves and those around them, passively accepting violence or actively committing violence. Violent men will welcome the violence of others, like thunder following lightning. Men who mature spiritually are conscious of their responsibility to protect human life from violence. I am a man who remembers being a narcissistic child who lulled himself to sleep by wishing for an atomic bomb to devastate his enemies. Dr. Strangelove is no stranger to me. I have tried to describe earlier the many years I spent denying my own violence, dreading it, acting it out as intellectualized criticism of others, being powerless to identify with any victim of violence, feeling helpless about the possibility of my own capacity to effectively stop violence.

I know now that to know pain is to be capable of suffering, and to suffer is to be capable of empathy with others. To be capable of empathy is to sacrifice one's own self-will, one's own narcissism, for a social good that is valued more than one's desire to be superior to others, different.

Men who avoid identifying with their own pain devalue it and project it upon others who are then devalued. The paradigm of violence is the denial of humanity, of kinship to others, denying the value of their human differences. The double bind of the victim of projective violence is this: the black, Jew, Muslim, Asian, woman, or homosexual is told, "You are not like me, you cannot be like me, but your difference from me is a measure of your subhumanity and my license to abuse you." One measure of manhood is how we behave toward those who are different from us—the others, the enemies, women, the poor, the rich, the aged, the young, homosexuals, heterosexuals, the aliens.

To become aware of our own violence is to realize that sacrifice is its antidote. We have seen that the essence of violence is estrangement and that the task of a man is to overcome estrangement from self and others. The essence of voluntary sacrifice is empathetic identification, love. The mystery of spiritual heroism is the transformation of murderous estrangement, of the dread of invasion by strangers, into loving identification with those strangers, who turn out to have familiar human faces.

In what follows, I am referring to three faces of violence. First, I mean physical violence, the overt acts of violence that kill, maim, oppress, harass, suppress, and humiliate human beings. Second, I mean political violence, the process that causes structural inequality to persist in communities. Victims of inequality suffer early death, hunger, malnutrition, disease, and social insults that mutilate the soul. The third form of violence projects envy of the differentness of others, stigmatizing those others to justify physical and political acts of violence.

Every society continues to inflict brutal injuries on groups that are considered as "other" by the dominant men who rule. Sometimes violence is the only force that holds a group together. Even human speech is then sacrificed to power, and violence is done to language itself, destroying its function as the communication of meaning.

We have noted how easy it is to justify violence by an appeal to one's own victimization as a person or an aggrieved group. The revolution of rising expectations has made people and nations impatient to accumulate material wealth, often at the expense of others rather than by their own efforts. Sacrifice, the historic counterforce to violence, has become seriously weakened by religion's loss of status in the modern world. Today, sacrifice is incomprehensible to many men; it has become a synonym for masochism, irrational superstition, unprofitable behavior. Today the voice of violence is loud, while the voice of sacrifice is almost silent.

The massive presence of violence today and the very multiplicity of its provinces, both situational and personal, contribute to the feeling that perhaps dealing with violence is best left to experts in counterterrorism, criminal insanity, and ballistics. Or the cool professionals of "conflict management." The responsibility for violence rests with every man, because it is we men who inflict our rage on others. Responsibility for social trust rests with every man.

Contemporary "offender" theory recognizes six types of people who are prone to violence:

1. Normal people subjected to extreme provocation;
2. Groups dedicated to violent "lifestyles," such as murderers, terrorists, or military fanatics;
3. Organically impaired persons;
4. Overcontrolled offenders in prisons;
5. Persons characterized by high motivation for aggression or revenge;
6. Instrumentally motivated offenders, who use violence as a means to other ends, such as thieves, or husbands who batter wives to achieve their sexual submission.[5]

Such theories are interesting, but they fail to illuminate the realms of emotional violence, of violence that is stimulated by social injustice, or of every man's tendency to retreat into the violence of narcissistic fantasy.

Men who are insensitive to their own violence, harbored
secretly in such hidden forms as punitive silence, are unlikely
to be sensitive to those forms of violence that are often con-
cealed, such as child neglect or structural social injustice. It
is for this reason that I am arguing for the broadest possible
understanding of male violence and for taking the broadest
possible personal responsibility for it. Male violence must be
exposed as violence, whether it is found in fantasy, emotion,
language, acted out in families, labeled criminal, seen as part
of the "normal" social structure, or regarded as politically
"justified." Underlying every kind of violence is pain. The
painful consequences of violence obscure the painful origins.
To become a man who knows pain is to understand and to
be able to take responsibility for violence.

The rationalizations for violence are seductive. One political
scientist offers perhaps the most obvious justification when
he asserts that "certain grim facts of inequality" make it
impossible for any moral doctrine to effectively counter the
argument justifying violence on behalf of those who are deprived of the elements of human life. The fact is that the
difference in simple life expectancy between the elite and the
impoverished is *forty years*—a "species-like difference."[6] But
to conclude that these awful facts justify violence is to confuse
logic and pain. Human suffering resists quantification.

Even the struggle to create a language that is morally sen-
sitizing rather than morally numbing to violence has been
undermined, particularly in recent years, by the polarized
monologues at the United Nations. In 1974, UNESCO adopted
a resolution stating that "a peace founded on injustice and
violation of human rights cannot last and leads inevitably to
violence." But if only an ideal state of justice can end violence,
that violates the last-resort concept of "the legitimate revolt
against the tyrant."[7] The UNESCO position is pernicious
because it *encourages* violence, and in so doing, it validates

the insane logic that violence is necessary to eliminate the enemy, the enemy's difference from us, the social injustice caused by the enemy.

It is the history of human ethics that teaches us that violence is a technique of last resort. When all efforts to achieve justice fail, only then may violence be considered. Violence is properly regarded as a failure of human politics, of diplomacy, of dialogue, of law, of humanity—not an instrument to be readily used by the state, by rebels, by vigilantes, by terrorists, by criminals. Although the state is founded on its monopoly of violence, the use of violence by the state must be judged not only by the principle of justice but also qualitatively and quantitatively by the principle of the sanctity of human life.

No rational or moral discourse is possible in an unjust and murderous regime that sees itself as innocent of all violence and is horrified by the violence of "terrorists" opposing its rule, nor among terrorists who deny their own violence by pointing at the violence of the state, as if that justified any mayhem committed in the name of future social justice.

Benjamin Franklin said it was wonderful to be a "rational" man because one could find a reason for anything one does. The terrorist principle that violence may be unleashed justly against a state that fails to be ideally just is a rationalization for committing violence. No state and no person may reasonably be expected to conform to an ideal. Such an expectation is inherently violent and inherently intolerant of the differences and contradictions that are unavoidable in human social life. The proper work for man is not to unleash violence but to set limits for it.

Monologues about who justly may do what or have what occur in a moral vacuum. We have lost a shared definition of who deserves what in a community that defines goods as social bonds rather than as commodities. Even people who adhere to traditional conceptions of virtue in their "private" or church/community lives find themselves using political discourse in which "right" is what is most useful for those who have power. If politics is war by other means, and law expresses class interests, and moral discourse is propaganda, we are threatened by violence not only to our possessions and our persons but also to our values, our hearts, and our language.

As political animals, persons, and members of states, men are dignified by making choices about violence. As moral human beings, we must judge between violent options. We are often deprived of that opportunity by our leaders—even in a democracy. The most momentous decisions about violence in our time, like the decision by President Truman to drop the atomic bomb on Hiroshima in 1945 and the decision by President Truman not to drop the atomic bomb on Korea, China, and the Soviet Union in 1952, were taken in undemocratic secrecy. Violence loves to hide.

As a teacher, I have had an exasperating experience trying to teach highly intelligent graduate students of social work that violence is a central health and mental health issue in human social life. The fact that their daily work puts them in contact with the effects of violence—child abuse, rape, poverty, spouse abuse with deadly weapons, violent acts of juveniles—only strengthened their impression that these acts of violence were individual anomalies. Like psychiatrists, social workers are generally surprised to learn that they might be targets of client violence or might be perceived as representing a violent social order.

Psychiatrists were interviewed about violent patients.[8] Their surprise about the levels of violence they face is itself surprising. While it is true that an inexperienced psychotherapist may unintentionally provoke violence by pressuring a client prematurely to face explosive material, it is disturbing that mental health practitioners imagine they can avoid handling violence. Violent fantasy, with its suppressed rage, *is the medium* of psychotherapy. It is the primary task of psychotherapy to face, clarify, and transform violence.

The successful transformation of violence depends on five capabilities: recognizing violence in fantasy, feeling, and potential action; setting limits for violence; tolerating the rage that surges against the limits, without retaliating in kind; maintaining empathy for the pain that underlies the violence; and practicing deference or respect for the person. (Deference includes listening, conferring value on the violent person through the quality of one's attention, one's presence.)

How could I teach students to manage violence in their clients if they wished to deny its very existence? Violence is a response to threat and pain. Hearing about violence and pain produces anxiety. One must expect from listeners not simply denial but *layers* of resistance. So I prepared to deal with the discounting of everyday experience by following up with five armor-piercing educational projectiles.

First, I described to my students how Freud demonstrated the pervasiveness of violence in fantasy. Not only do children wish their parents dead but parents also have infanticidal wishes. I used writings by the psychoanalyst Melanie Klein to show the students how "normal" the basic anxieties of children are, how the dread of abandonment by a protective parent gives rise to rage and paranoid thinking.[9]

Second, I offered a model of childhood symbiosis, showing how human beings are born ultra-dependent on parents and highly vulnerable to separation fears. These fears motivate children to identify with their parents, while denying anxieties about separation or loss.[10] The child's tendency to imagine violence and to act it out arises from a life-threatening dread of abandonment. Then I told them of the equal and opposite dread that also causes violent fantasy.

Because of the shakiness of a child's separateness, or ego boundaries, he or she also dreads unity, terrified at the possibility of becoming consumed by the parent or the group. So the urge to violence may be motivated by terror of either distance *or* closeness, I explained. Terror hurts. Neurosis is a painful oscillation between these two poles of violence, caused by dreading loss of self *in* the parent or dreading loss of self by being abandoned *by* the parent. To withdraw, to isolate one's self, is one defense; to cling is the other defense. Both are violent.

The students denied this model of child development. Of course, they admitted, the children they worked with were violent in thought and action, but they were *different*. Normal childhood was and ought to be happy. *Their* childhoods had been happy. They remembered being happy.

I tried a third approach. I brought in newspapers and magazines. What about Vietnam? What about Lebanon? Why were there so many splits and factions? Why were people killing each other in Uganda, Argentina, Somalia? How about all the wars since 1945? It was reported in 1968 that there were more than fifty wars in the "postwar" period. Fifty wars in twenty years![11] How about the Holocaust? What about the relentless threat of violence against underclasses, ethnic groups, women? Their eyes glazed over.

Not fair. History was out of bounds. Their geography was not keen. This class was supposed to be about *individual development*, as in Erik Erikson—about stages of healthy, individual development in normal, ideal phases, in an environment that fosters growth. Why was I besmirching it with these concerns about "different" people?

How could I be saying that real environments, real families, real stratified communities inhibit growth, restrict personal development, mold a personality into defensive armor, a mask to protect against envy, jealousy, deprivation, and insult? Why was I being so *depressing*? Maybe the South Bronx wasn't an environment that encouraged human growth. But this was Westchester. Well, maybe women weren't exactly encouraged to grow to their full potential. But that was all changing now.

Not one to be discouraged by resistances, I prepared my fourth presentation: experiential learning. No books, no foreign, "different" authors, no references to olden days or faraway places. I will bring the violence into the room, I vowed. The "Bion Group" is a very sophisticated learning instrument developed by the English psychoanalyst W. R. Bion in 1944.[12] He discovered that if the leader of a therapeutic group starkly told the group that he would now be silent, making the group's task to study its own process, the group would experience both the primary anxiety of an infant as well as the violence involved in the formation of any social group hierarchy.

I explained that the group's task was to observe its own actions, and then I became silent. Each student reacted to the terror of silence in a group without a leader and then proceeded to act out all the conformations predicted by the Bion model. The classes idealized my teaching to try to seduce me into returning and speaking. When I remained silent, they became frustrated, violent. They rebelled by denying they had a task. Several left the room, enraged; some formed competitive pairs, excluding their classmates; some tried to reform the group as a dependency hierarchy by appointing a new leader. But all the illegitimate "siblings" who tried to assume the leader's role were quickly ridiculed, attacked, and killed off by competition within the group. Each group sought a scapegoat to vent its anger on, a substitute for me. Everything worked beautifully according to the model, but the class was so angry at me for inflicting the silence on them that few students could grasp what had happened.

Some did agree that they were terrified by the social vacuum created by my silence and felt dread of speaking into the hostility generated by everyone's anxiety about what to do. A few of the students saw the analogy with the infant's dependency upon the parent; they were terrified by the parental absence, as well as by the gluey, hostile unity of a silent group. Other students saw the analogy with the problems of social order in the absence of a legitimate ruler. But violent? Were they really violent? Did they really want to *kill me*?

My fifth approach to the task of demonstrating the centrality of violence in human social life depended upon social theory. I would show the students their own behavior reflected in social theory. We read René Girard's *Violence and the Sacred*,[13] which proposed that the very existence of humanity is due primarily to the operation of sacrificial violence. The invention by religion of a mechanism of substituting a surrogate victim, or a symbolic victim, for the uncontrolled rage of the group makes group life possible.

When leaderless, the classes immediately channeled their rage at being betrayed by the leader's absence and silence into a quest for a scapegoat, a surrogate victim. Alas, I was more impressed by student numbness than they were by my attempts to awaken their comprehension.

The scapegoat was originally a person made alien or an animal, which was symbolically loaded with communal violence, communal sin, and then killed. As a religious ritual, this sacrifice cleansed the community.

Today, scapegoats, usually women, children, the aged— the vulnerable, the different—continue to suffer for communal violence, although the religious forms have long since failed to constructively channel this violence into ritual. Scapegoating has become a substitute for politics in many communities.

The truth about human society is that there is always a

potential for violence, because the pain of floating anxiety turns into hostility. Violence is the disease of any group's inner system, and it is also falsely perceived as the "cure" for that disease when it is externalized onto outsiders. In the past, our best option has been to ritualize violence into a pattern of legitimized sacrifice. The "mystery" of religious sacrifice conceals the safe ritual purging or containment of communal violence through symbolization. Animal sacrifice, Greek tragedy, crucifixion of a surrogate protects the social whole. What religions accomplished by inventing a sacrificial victim, men must now redo by gaining control of their own violence and learning to sacrifice their narcissism to protect the group.

Violence is law-founding as well as law-breaking. Cultures are established by acts of unitive or regenerative violence, by the murder and exile of those who are different. The group that is united by its own self-legitimizing violence, whether invaders or revolutionaries, stratifies itself, re-creating the tension between those who are the same and those who are different. Inequality establishes the basis for a new round of unifying violence, either from the top down or from the bottom up.

The dynamic of violence remains fundamentally the same in persons and in groups. Group unity, fusion, become oppressive to the individuals' emotional and social needs to have separate identities. When group members begin to differentiate themselves, it wounds unity. Culture must cultivate tolerance for *both unity and separation*, security and freedom, avoiding the potential for violence that lies at either pole.

The task of moral manhood, of heroism, of leadership, is to preserve and expand human appreciation of differences within the unity of one reality. The human soul is one. God is one. Although we may be mutilated physically, emotionally, and socially in our efforts to assert our human difference or our human oneness, we must not retaliate violently. For our own wholeness and for the survival of society, men must sacrifice egotism to paradox. Differentness is holy; unity is sacred.

Totalitarian social systems seek to freeze the violence of schism by a violence of total social control. Anarchic societies, like tribal societies that fail to achieve nationhood, are splintered by the assertions of differentness. Many African nations suffer from tribal wars, from allegedly unresolvable differentness. Differentness and unity can be lost in the demonic, the violent, or they can be poised and survive in life-giving tension.

Violence is so basic, so fundamental to social life that it may define the identity of a group, as it does in feuding sects. When a group is structured by a feud, as many groups still are, avenging the death of a kinsman is the unifying principle of social action. The injured group owes its dead kinsman a debt of a death; kinship means vengeance. The feuding groups need each other to keep their own boundaries; periodic, reciprocal acts of public violence are essential to group identity.

A more sophisticated, symbolic form of the feud is the rivalry between athletic teams; a more tragic form is the pattern of war between Muslim and Christian sects in Lebanon. The reciprocal violence of the feud governs group relationships and group identity when better systems for channeling violence within the group either break down or fail to evolve.

The containment of violence by social ritual is never very secure. The U.S. soldiers who fought in Vietnam were not able to "purify" themselves upon returning home to "the world" after their descent into hell; the nation was not united enough to conduct them home through the ritual recognition of their sacrificial violence. So the violence contaminated them personally, and it continues to contaminate our culture. Violent unity is precarious; it precludes honest dialogue between equals who oppose each other.

When France tried to annex Algeria, to make her one with France, the Algerian "difference" prevailed. So enraged were the French colonial generals at efforts to end ritual scapegoating of the Arabs that they almost invaded France and caused a civil war. When President Reagan acts as if the Caribbean nations are part of the United States, we also face a problem of what I call "allowable differentness."

Human groups oscillate between two threatening poles; whether a family, a tribal group, or a nation. The pole of fusion, with its threat of the loss of individual difference, and the pole of separation, with its threat of the different individual depriving the group of unity, demand constant modulation. Men must manage this violence about difference.

Men must also combat the control of access to goods, which we call injustice. In the family, the violence of injustice still takes a typical form. The man controls the money and refuses to consult his mate about its use, wielding it to control her behavior, to make her anxious, to buy her responsiveness. He destroys dialogue by denying her equality and even her voice: he simply makes announcements and acts. Women trapped in such marriages feel the constant erosion of self-respect, as if they are prostitutes, servants, slaves. Men who care about human dignity will relinquish violent control, choosing to sustain the relationship through dialogue with an equal. Deference is the most human way to reduce violence. It depends on the voluntary sacrifice of one's own power and control and on recognizing the status of others. But deference is impossible in the absence of dialogue.

Men have only four moral political responses to violence. They may engage in violence to sustain the unity of a group, as President Lincoln did when he refused to permit the secession of the South from the Union. They may engage in the religious or theatrical symbolization of violence to diminish violence, remembering Jerusalem's destruction, or Christ's crucifixion. They may engage in actions of last-resort revolutionary violence, as in the American war of independence from Great Britain. They may reform social inequality through entering a dialogue of respectful equals. *What men may never do, as moral men, is to avoid or to deny their responsibility for justice, for social trust.*

The responsibility for justice may never be safely delegated and "professionalized." Citizens may not leave the task of ensuring justice to politicians, armies, police, or social scientists, for all such groups tend to legitimize their own violence.

The most important example of the evolution of dialogue into social reform to diminish violence is the action of democratic parliaments. Another kind of "speaking together" to reduce violence is counseling. The Safer Foundation,[14] established by an ex-priest, Gus Wilhelmy, is a prisoner-rehabilitation group which accepts that almost seventy percent of crimes are committed by veteran, repeating offenders. Unless they are specifically assisted in joining the community, the terror of social alienation forces offenders back into the forms of violence they have engaged in before. The Safer group absorbs the violence of ex-convicts and helps them to live, not only as surviving individuals but as contributing members of the communities. But programs like this work only if individuals volunteer time and energy to respect and struggle with the mistrust of ex-convicts, to help them to experience care and the mutuality of true community life.

We have seen that life remains infanticidal. Despite our knowledge that the first four years of a child's life are critically formative, as a society we underinvest in that period of a child's life. We neither educate parents nor furnish day care, and we drastically undervalue and underpay child-care workers. Investment in children is simply unprofitable compared to, say, armaments.[15] But the price we actually pay is incalculable.

The psychologist Robert Jay Lifton has struggled valiantly for many years with victims of violence. In his work with the survivors of Hiroshima and with Vietnam veterans, Lifton has expanded our knowledge of people who have internalized death, who have become deadened, who cannot feel, who are numb.[16]

Why is it so difficult to dramatize the reality of violence, to make it stronger than the numbness about violence? Is it the magnitude of the threat that is numbing: nuclear war, the power of envy? What is particularly numbing is the difficulty of tolerating our own anxiety and rage over issues so basic as whether we are the same as others or different from others.

Numbing is the freezing of the self by fright, rage, and guilt. Emotional numbing is one of the major problems of our era. Primarily it is the threat of violence—remembered, real, or fantasized—that makes people numb.

Numbing conceals guilt, a paradoxical kind of guilt that can be dangerous to the self in two ways. Numbness follows the guilt of fantasizing violence, as well as the act of killing. Numb, too, are those who feel guilty for living while a loved one is dead. When guilt is unconscious, it immobilizes and disintegrates the self, blocking responsiveness to the self and to the world. When guilt is unconscious and denied, it can also release unchecked destructiveness. In Vietnam, when buddies died, soldiers tried to numb their feelings by taking drugs and muttering, "It doesn't mean anything," but the blocked grief at the loss of their loved ones and at the loss of meaning, turned into murderous rage. All that the soldiers who became numb *could* feel was murderous rage.

To reanimate a numb person is to help him suffer the feelings behind the guilt, grief, loss, and see the need for sacrifice and repair. There is a world of difference between frozen, denied guilt—a numbness that signifies despair about the value of human life—and the painful attempt to face one's own guilt. Dread of suffering guilt is the main barrier to perceiving the role violence plays in our lives, our communities, and our total historical world.

In everything we have observed earlier about the necessity for reconciliation with our fathers, our brothers, our mates, we have learned that avoiding the pain of suffering means missing the road to manhood. Manliness is not cool indifference to murder or addiction to vengeful violence. Manliness is taking full responsibility for our pain and insensitive acts, and if we can, taking responsibility for the pain of others, the violence of others. Denying the existence of violence does not eliminate violence; it simply blinds us to the violence in ourselves and in a world where numbness is a condition of survival. Men can function, but we cannot be human or manly if we cannot allow ourselves to feel guilt and responsibility about violence. To become men, we men must sacrifice our innocence about violence.

To hold men responsible for violence is to invite men to assume their proper role as protectors and defenders. A hero is a protector of the trust of his group. If a man protects his group from his violence and from their violence as well as from the violence of outsiders, his life will not lack meaning. And the best way to protect a group is to respect the pain of the most vulnerable, to promote their self-respect, to reduce differences.

The numb man cannot protect because he cannot identify with his own feelings, much less with the needs of others. His chief pursuit is to deny his vulnerability to others, to deny his responsibility for others. He will deny any victim's need and may blame or further victimize the victim, thus isolating himself not only from emotion and from membership in his group but also from his essence as a man, a protector.

Heroic men often fight to unify groups in the face of external enemies, as well as internal enemies, against the fission opened by envy and rebellion. So Moses, Mohammed, George Washington, and Charles de Gaulle held groups together. But if the leadership becomes unjust, a frozen hierarchy that inhibits growth and development, then the task of a man is to rebel. Martin Luther judged the hierarchy of the Roman Catholic Church to be inhibiting to the practice of Christianity, and he made a division that formed a new church. The entire history of Christianity illustrates the dialectic of holding together and splitting apart. Sometimes it has been necessary to suppress schism, and sometimes only schism could renew the life of the church.

Differences, stratification, make the structure of a complex society. Differentiation that releases social energy is positive; that which maximizes injustice is negative. To assert we are all the same is positive against tyranny, but envious when it is asserted against *earned* status differences. Men should inhibit rebellious juvenile envy; men should overthrow tyrannical envy.

When I say that facing violence is a criterion for manhood, I do not necessarily mean bearing arms but bearing responsibility for violence as it confronts us in ourselves, our families, our social and political lives. We men are responsible for violence that interferes with the human need to belong or for violence that threatens the equally basic need to be free, individual, different, equal.

The right of a person to be the same as other persons is just as basic as the right to be different. Both are essential to social trust. Both rights need defending, sometimes even to the point of using violence. Making painful and discriminating choices about the legitimate use of violence is the province of manhood.

When we are irrational, we deny others the right to be the same as we are, *and* we deny the right to be different.

The issue of homosexuality can serve to crystallize our understanding of how differentness evokes violence, and of men's responsibility to tolerate differentness. Two male friends recently told me they find homosexuality repulsive. Both men are secure in status, fathers of children, "masculine" by any index. But they grew up in a culture that contrasted its conception of manliness with the effeminacy called "queer." Now, twenty-five years after this conditioning, they still believe *manliness means not being homosexual.* Both men hastened to assure me that they did kiss and hug men—fathers, sons, workmates—and felt comfortable doing so. What made them queasy was the "other" kind of kissing.

Some men are enraged by the very sight of gay men: they are verbally abusive; they punish; they want to promote and even legalize discrimination; they attack. The gay community in New York estimates that three unprovoked assaults *each day* are committed against gays in the city. Why? If we can understand this kind of violence, we can understand a great deal about violence. We can also learn more about how much differentness is "allowable."

Allowable differentness is the fluctuating margin of security that protects a vulnerable minority group from acts of violence by the dominant majority that defines what is "normal." The folk knowledge version of allowable differentness states that you can think differently from others, speak differently, act differently, or dress differently, but you had better not try to do all of those things simultaneously, or you will surely be attacked. Dread of attack for being different has kept gays in the closet for a long time in the United States.

Dread of attack has also caused many gays to deny that

they are gay, both to themselves and to others. This same fear of violence has caused Jews and blacks to deny *their* group membership or to hide their differentness near a group of adult males who are sensed to be in a rage. Violence seeks discharge, and violent groups discharge their violence against others who are "too different" to belong. When people are terrified, they may often abandon their identities, individually or collectively, and to avoid being stigmatized seek to identify with the group that owns the violence.

Gays live under stigma in our society. They suffer from prejudice, from a process of progressive depersonalization that strips them of the protections accorded persons. Prejudice justifies hostility through overgeneralization that denies humanity to the "enemy." Thus, gays are considered "unnatural" in their sexual practices, rebels against God, perverted, dangerous to youth, dangerous to health. We have laws that discriminate against gays who seek custody of children, that deny them work and housing, and that criminalize their personal, private behavior.[17]

Similar actions are taken whenever the dominant group is threatened by the differentness of the others. The charges made against gays are also leveled against Jews, blacks, and women. Major religions still consider women inferior, unclean, and, therefore, subhuman.

The classical Greek world would not have understood the way we stigmatize homosexuals. For the Greeks, persons had complex, different natures. The Bible condemns homosexual *behavior,* but until the eighteenth century, personality was seen as distinct from specific sexual actions. Sexual actions such as pederasty or sodomy were punished as crimes, but the stigmatization of the person and the group as essentially diseased had to await the nineteenth-century medical theory of homosexuality. Then the soul of the homosexual was officially declared diseased, even criminally diseased, until homosexuality as a medical diagnostic term was recently dropped by the American psychiatric establishment.

The steps to violence are always the same. Insecurity about social control leads a dominant group to underscore the differences of a deviant group. Those differences are then exaggerated and become essential differences, separating the different ones, the "others," from the real human beings. Once the perverted ones are identified, they can be loaded with all the dread and venom of the dominant group. Scapegoating a stigmatized group is the next step; verbal abuse precedes restrictions and formalized penalties. The final step is violence, which may be either random or organized, like slavery or Hitler's Final Solution.

Acts of violence against gays are licensed by a culture that legitimizes denigration. Once a group is the target of vicious humor, negative projection, and stereotyping—as, for example, hairdressers, spies, perverters of children—it becomes vulnerable to attack. "Queers" was the term for gay men when I was a boy. They were different, *too* different for tolerance. We knew we could assault a gay male and be winked at by the police. The police still wink. And when gays are murdered, the crime often goes unpunished and unpublicized, as if gays were nonpeople.

Gay men are aware that they suffer because they deviate from and threaten images of manhood. Those most likely to feel threatened by the alleged effeminacy of gay men are men who dread that they are not manly. Such men cannot afford to notice that the spectrum of gay male behavior ranges from machismo to flaming queens to submissive "chickens," for every variation along the range is still different from the idea of manliness in a way that feels threatening.

When men violently deny that they are effeminate, they are only asserting their difference from the feminine, from women, and using the surrogate object of the homosexual as a safe target for unsafe rage at women who come too close to them for comfort.

Homosexuals are involuntary sacrificial victims, substitutes for the unclear objects of male dread, the women who evoke "weak" feelings in men. Men dread vulnerability to being "penetrated" by men as much as they dread being controlled by women.

Homosexuals are sacrificial surrogates for male rage, but they also *embody* male rage. The most explosive dimension of male homosexual behavior is rarely dealt with, by either neutral observers, apologists, or persecutors. It is the element of parody, the parody of relationships of maternal creativity, of male domination, and of subordination. Gay social parody strikes at the root of the social order itself.

In leather bars, uniformed men act out the roles of master and slave. In jails, this acting-out loses its play dimension and becomes serious in a way that is sometimes deadly. The submissive man is humiliated, often penetrated by force, degraded, enslaved.

Homosexuality assaults the *sacred* dimension of social order. It parodies hierarchy, submission, and deference, crucial violence-mediating behaviors, by sexualizing them and calling them into question. It confuses the boundaries of male affection. Some homosexual men rage at all women and seek to negate, incorporate, and exclude them, thus betraying envy of the mother's powers of creativity, which is one root of homosexual fantasy. As the progenitor of ongoing human life, motherhood *is* sacred as well as holy.

From a traditional political point of view, homosexuality is an envious parody by outsiders of a power structure that is based on hierarchy, sexual division, and dominance. Because hierarchy is sacred to social order, homosexuality is viewed as subversive. The outrage at violations of sacred social order will escalate if social order is seriously threatened.

The best that one can say about homosexuality from a social point of view is that parody of social dominance is not only healthy but possibly holy. Many cultures regard deviants of all kinds as holy *because* they are outside the sacred order. "Differentness" is a value that varies from holiness to lethal virus, depending upon the tolerance of the culture. The notion of the holy is important because it insists that no matter how different a person may be, he is our human brother or sister. All souls are one.

The problem of subordination is particularly explosive at this time because the traditional hierarchical dominance of men is being questioned and altered by women as well as parodied by gays. Parody, when confined to a holy day or relegated safely to the realm of entertainment, has long been considered a safeguard of the traditional structure of social relationships: carnivals reverse relationships of dominance and subordination—for a day—and create a safety valve for envy and rage against privilege and power.

When power becomes sacred, as it tends to do in every social order, we see paranoid behavior, such as that of Richard Nixon. Then, any action that protects the existing social order ostensibly becomes justifiable by an appeal to its sacred character. But the value of the holy, the value of the individual life, is that it stands against hierarchical social order and exposes it to the criticism of a moral order higher than the preservation of the given cast of characters acting in their status roles. The pretension of any government to sacred permanence is exploded by the wildness of the outsider, the deviant, the other, the different, the alternative, the spontaneous. The god Dionysius embodied this holy rage in Greece, as Shiva does in India. The holy is not the devil, but the destructive-creative challenge of change itself.

Men are willing to lie and kill to protect the "permanence" of what they perceive as the sacred social order. Men are

willing to kill and die to challenge that order in the name of
a difference, of a change. Yet in the long perspective, only
change is eternal; any pretension to permanence is illusory.
When men are caught between the contradictory commands
of the sacred—national security, family life, property, lib-
erty—and the commands of the holy—world peace, gay rights,
equality—conflict is inevitable. But tension and ambivalence
are necessary aspects of the social tolerance of differences. We
must face the need to accept the ongoing contradiction that
will always prevail between the sacred and the holy.

Hierarchy may be allowed to organize social life but not
to undermine the holy bonds of trust or to exclude parody,
deviance, or change. But those who seek to parody, deviate
from, or change social structure outside customary legal, bureaucratic, and artistic channels also must understand the rule
of allowable differentness. Social control systems are held
together and defended by violence. What is sacred is what
will be defended by legitimized social violence.

Jesus, Gandhi, and Martin Luther King, Jr., tried to teach
men how to make social change through sacrificial willingness
to absorb the violence of the system one seeks to change.
When reconciliation is impossible, the holy dominates the
sacred only through the willingness to die. When reconciliation is impossible, the sacred preserves itself only through
the willingness to kill. Men who can mediate such clashing
claims are desperately needed—men who can gaze at violence
with calm eyes. Gay men who have arrived at manhood will
accept responsibility for gay violence.

As victims, gay men were passive. They are now seeking
to define themselves, refusing definition by the violence of
others. When gay men "come out," they say to themselves
and to their families, "I am gay, and if you want to be my
family, you must accept me with my lover." Families resist,
but often, step by step, they cease trying to split a gay son or

brother from his mate and accept *the other,* first as a companion and then as a person with a name, a real individual.

Gay men in America today are at what is often a necessary stage in struggles for equality. When they identify themselves today as gay, they are not simply saying, "I am a person like you, only my sexual habits are different." Instead, they claim that gayness is something essential to identity, and they are claiming membership in a gay community that they define as different from the straight community. Gays offend and provoke heterosexuals when they claim that their sexual preferences and their culture are somehow "better." If they challenge and parody the norms of the dominant culture, they can expect to be attacked. But it is also our task to restrain the violence provoked by such violations of conservative social decorum.

The straight community will tolerate the differentness of gays if they live in a ghetto, restrict themselves to "gay occupations," gay bars, baths, and restrooms. But if two gay students wish to attend a prom together, they violate the allowable boundary of differentness by trying to become the same as boy and girl. The ambiguity of gay identity as an assertion of differentness in language, style, media, behavior, and communal participation exposes gays to violence at the pole of being "too different," but it also exposes gays to violence at the pole of nondifference from other men and women. They can be attacked for being too strange as well as for trying to join the familiar rituals of the straight community.

The gay community does not have the power to make itself secure from denigration, discrimination, and violence. It remains vulnerable to violence whenever it violates the vague, fluctuating limits of allowable difference established by a culture of insecure and easily threatened males.

A gay sociologist tells the story of moving into a house in a suburb. At first, his neighbor assumed that he was straight, but when she discovered he was gay, she came over and asked, "What color should I paint my walls?" When he responded that he was a sociologist and not particularly good at interior design, she was shocked. "But you're gay!" This woman would be surprised to know she was violent, but the kind of thinking that categorizes people in this rigid, impersonal way is precisely what prepares the ground for violence.

Gays are not themselves innocent of violence; none of us is. Some gay men are legitimately concerned about the treatment of gays as objects by other gays, about the failure within the homosexual community to evolve models for personal relationships, about the substitution of sometimes sadistic sexual behavior for loving behavior. The degradation of other persons for sex or by sex or because of sex is a legitimate ethical concern.

The Mattachine Society was founded in 1950 to create a positive ethical homosexual culture. Twenty years later, the gay liberation movement of the 1970s viewed homosexuals as an oppressed minority, and it sought to create a culture based on pride, community, shared identity, and on a well-organized base of homophile politics. In 1983, the AIDS hysteria created a potent scapegoating counterforce that rekindles and mobilizes the dread of homosexuals as contaminators of the social body.

The sacredness of male/female gender as an organizing principle of American society is reasserting itself once again, narrowing the zone of allowable difference. Efforts to drive doctors who treat AIDS patients from their offices and the refusal to rent apartments occupied by suspect gays, go far beyond the dread of a virus; they reveal again the power of purity as a symbolic force in social life. In the American caste system, no matter how prosperous or locally accepted they may have become, homosexuals are still always vulnerable to rapid social demotion to untouchability. Although a recent

Vatican statement on homosexuals views them more toler-
antly—as morally misguided and in need of help rather than
as pariahs or scapegoats—gays would be well advised to be
as vigilant as the Holocaust-scarred Jewish community about
the threat of violence.

We have learned now that the essence of violence is the
estrangement of the other. The kind of deprivation and estrangement the homosexual community suffers makes gays
targets for murder by strangers. And they are not the only
victims of the estranging languages of murder.

Killers must be trained to dehumanize their victims and
deprive them of individuality. Two mass murders, one in
Vietnam at My Lai conducted by Lieutenant William Calley
and one committed by the "Manson family," show how depersonalization precedes violence. Both Calley and Manson
were convicted by massacring innocent, helpless people, without provocation and without mercy. Both crimes were impersonal acts of murder. When Calley was asked at his trial
why he ordered his men to kill women and children, he was
puzzled by the question. "I didn't discriminate between individuals in the village, sir. They were all the enemy, they
were all to be destroyed, sir."[18] Manson and his companions
looked for victims among people they identified as "pigs"—
anyone who benefited from "the system." Any pig could be
killed by the righteous members of "the family" with a feeling
of impunity. They were not killing persons but ridding the
earth of parasites, of devils.

Killers legitimize killing by depersonalizing the enemy and
also by acting victimized themselves. For killers, it is always
"the others" that are the killers. They are merely sanitizing
the earth. Manson imagined that his random killing scenario,
Helter Skelter, would persuade whites that blacks were the
murderers and that whites would then unite against the blacks;
then the blacks would win the civil war. This crazy scenario

has the same legitimizing logic as any other murder scenario that appeals to future "purification"—of race, community, culture—as its rationale.

The language of love is individual, specific, concrete, and personal. The language of violence is a language of depersonalization. Violence begins in language that depersonalizes people, setting them up for physical, sometimes legalized, assault. Men of honor will not join in such assaults but will struggle instead against the persecution of innocent people. There is no manliness in scapegoating, only in interceding to protect and defend those who are vulnerable to irrational violence. If we can acknowledge our own vulnerability, what will be revealed is that, ultimately, we are all vulnerable to violence.

The prime task for manhood in our time is confrontation with violence, reduction of every step of violence: social injustice, depersonalization, verbal denigration, "legal" discrimination, acts of physical violence—in the home, the community, and in or by the nation state.

A boxing fan told me that America is going to have to get a lot more saintly before it can eliminate boxing. But boxing, hunting, and football are forms of socialized violence. They are rule-following, and they do not escalate into mass murder. They are *allies* in the effort to bring violence under control. Let men box, hunt, and tackle, but let us also focus on the problem of allowable differentness, on the denigration of differentness, discrimination against differentness, the depersonalization of those who are different. We must learn to rejoice in difference, contradiction, and opposition, to welcome it as men, and to struggle with our own rage for sameness, our childish need to be *different from and better than.*

We have said that vulnerability to our own suffering that turns men away from violence and toward sympathetic identification with other human beings who suffer. If we men

can experience the pain of our own fears—the dread of separation, of abandonment, of fusion, of change, of loss, of
violence—if we can desire to suffer the pain and the shame
that belongs to us, then we will not split emotionally or dread
differentness in compulsive or violent ways. If we are honest,
we will accept responsibility for our own suffering; if we are
not, we will inflict violence on others, scapegoating them,
making "others" responsible for our own unsuffered pain.

Should it be surprising that the same acts of denial of
suffering that cause men to become numb as persons and that
promote divisions and estrangement in the family endanger
the larger social world? For divided men *need* enemies as
objects upon which they can project and thus discharge their
rage and dread. The Russians, the *others,* do not cause our
violence, they merely provide an excuse for acting it out—
or for threatening to—and a rationale for the male military
domination of social life. Divided men deny others access to
dialogue as equals, deny credibility to the suffering of others.

To deny suffering is to kill one's own aliveness. Once they
become numb, men envy aliveness in others and wish to kill
it in them. A man who acknowledges his vulnerability and
goes on to suffer his pain and that of others will speak out
for compassion for all.

Denial of our *vulnerability* to Soviet attack has produced
hysteria about bigger military budgets and more competitive
arsenals, fostering a spiraling arms race that continues to hold
all of us hostage to the secret and partially paranoid dread
of the men who defend us and who prevent us from acknowledging our vulnerability. The "defense" quest for total
invulnerability, based on the belief that we must somehow
wield a total threat against the enemy, is largely an irrational
form of social control of our own citizenry. And so we are
taxed to build the new, computerized "defense" pyramids.

An aide to Senator Lyndon Johnson wrote in 1957 that

"the Russians have left the earth and the race for control of the universe has started."[19] Now, sophisticated military satellites circle the earth, crushing us with their cost—economically, politically, and psychologically. This symbolic crusade to achieve invulnerability is not pure fantasy, of course. There *is* a threat from the Russians, based on *their* male dread of vulnerability, which is partially based on the reality of the invasion they suffered in World War II. But one cannot achieve invulnerability—not to sudden attack and certainly not to loss. One *can* confront the threat of violence with deference and dialogue, a process that is far more difficult than making bombs.

Following the showing of the landmark television film about nuclear war, *The Day After,* on November 20, 1983, two former cabinet members, Robert McNamara and Henry Kissinger, discussed U.S. foreign policy. It seems clear that U.S. defense policy has been and continues to be based on an understanding that the United States and the Soviet Union may actually use tactical nuclear weapons, especially against upstart nations. What worries both camps is simply the failure of "crisis-control" systems that might lead to a war neither wants. What the United States and the Soviet Union want is continued dominance, as symbolized by the huge nuclear stockpiles of each. The reality is that not only the people of these two nations but the people of the world are held hostage to this outrageous balancing act performed by two governments that are unresponsive to the true political process of disarmament that would reduce their global dominance.

The men who rule both the United States and the Soviet Union are different, but they are alike in their wish to deny their own vulnerability and the vulnerability of state policy to the wishes of the public and the reality of other nations. No men should have the right to control such power in such secrecy. Secret government is a form of violence against those governed.

What is dangerous in U.S. foreign policy is what is dangerous in narcissistic men generally: the quest to be invulnerable through a process of violent withdrawal from real negotiations combined with faith in the power of magic technology. Only vulnerability is honest. Americans must admit vulnerability to our mirror-image Russian counterparts and also to the violence inherent in a system of nation-states that respects neither justice nor territorial integrity. The only true security possible lies in trust in a world of brothers.

Samuel Pisar's painful memoir of Auschwitz, *Of Blood and Hope,* reminds us powerfully of our radical vulnerability to political violence. Yet Pisar is able to regard his survival of Auschwitz as an ordeal of coping with violence that symbolized his full awakening to life. "It forced me to develop to the fullest such physical and mental faculties as I had."[20]

Pisar survived, but he became numb. To find his own voice, to live again, he had to acknowledge his living connection to the dead six million Jews, to speak for them, to remember them. He believes that the real enemy is the denial of violence, struggle, and evil, the inability to recognize that life is not an uninterrupted feast but a permanent, painful struggle.

For Pisar, the precondition of survival in the face of peril is clarity of mind. To summon and maintain clarity of mind is difficult in the face of violence and loss, but it is impossible if we forget the reality of violence and loss, because we are then in a state of illusion. Pisar was himself nearly seduced into believing that he had become invulnerable by having achieved status and wealth as a corporate attorney. Fortunately for him, he was able to remember who he was: a Jew, a man both vulnerable to violence and responsible for it. From the depth of his own suffering, Pisar has warned the West not to turn away from Russia. If Americans want peace, even as we reject Russian depreciation of freedom, we must trade—value Russian goods, currency, fears. Power cannot substitute for deference any more than deference can substitute for power.

The awareness of violence—of our own against others, of what we have suffered from others, of all against all—is the beginning of manhood. Without such awareness, we are defenseless against the violence of others, unprepared to set limits for it, and also vulnerable to being intoxicated by violence—the violence of liberation promised by the theologians of terror. A man must not dream that this is the best of all possible worlds nor must he dream that violence will create utopia. For only when we stop dreaming can we see what is there: a world potentially more human, in ourselves, our families, our communities, but one that is now distorted by terror, rage, greed, envy, and intolerance of human differences.

If we men can learn to tolerate and then to love what we first fear—alien faces, different-colored flesh, strange gods, vulnerable children, the dying elderly, power or neediness in women, our own imperfections and limits—we can take some steps to limit violence, especially the violence that first takes root in ourselves and then burgeons like a grapevine into our relationships with close others and beyond them, into the world of strangers.

Spiritual democracy develops in stages of consciousness about the need for sacrifice. First there were ritual sacrifices performed by priests as representatives of the community, then universal male temple attendance and rule observance, and then the notion of individual suffering of responsibility. All three phases of religious sacrifice involve the subordination of self-will to the sacred order of the social cosmos—its orderly process of work, its division of time, and its coordination of group behavior. The notion of voluntary sacrifice—by persons, of persons, for persons—is religion's most profound idea.

Hindu sages said that "to sacrifice is to be born ... [still] unborn is the man who does not sacrifice."[21] The narcissistic man still lives in a fetal trance, unaware of the social reality that sustains his life and of his debt to the fathers.

For our fathers' fathers, the sun rose with the morning sacrifice and because of it—not in a magical way, but as the wheel turns on its axle. Sacrifice is the essence of the ethical cosmos, the ritual and moral control of the narcissistic violence that lies at the core of social life. That is why Buddha's sacrificial compassion for suffering founds a world religion, why Jesus's crucifixion is the axis of another, why Judaism bears witness to its own history as a record of sacrifice, and why Islam worships its martyrs in the ongoing drama of its own sacrificial history.

The less than just distribution of goods fuels the violence of envy that rages now between persons, communities, and nations. The wheel of sacrifice revolves around the reality of injustice. The powerless among us are sacrificed to the power of the existing social system, its sacred millwheels grinding faces, bodies, and minds. Those who are enraged at their own share of social goods may rob and kill, inflicting violence randomly, making sacrificial victims of people who are merely acting their social roles. And there are those who are conscious of the inequality, who may sacrifice their own advantages and share their goods. Some have no choice about their sacrifice; some violently choose others as substitutes for their own sacrifice; and some choose to sacrifice.

Our obligation is clear: manhood requires us to reduce injustice so that we may repair the bonds of trust. We must do this by reducing the powerlessness of the poor, by aiding them to become more productive instead of encouraging them to worship demagogues as heroes. We can increase the levels of our voluntary, exemplary, and inspirational sacrifices of time, energy, and goods to bind others more securely to the life of our communities. We can reduce the rage of the outsiders or limit and control their violence by respecting the outsiders' need to belong. Alienation breeds violence; access to social goods, including deferential attention, human warmth, and recognition from successful men, reduces violence.

Most of human history reflects the puerile phase of personality development. To a large extent, history is the history of envy, of the differentiation of one's group at the expense of others. To a large extent, the concept of personality is the history of a claimed superior differentiation from others.

All religions agree that the spoken word of God inside the heart of a person stabilizes the person's life, uniting thought, belief, emotion, and action. But they all agree, too, that such a state is unhappily evanescent, easily lost. How quickly we return to our divided states of being!

The fullest realization of this elusive state of devotion occurs in certain rare spirits who are able to suffer the resonance of vulnerability. These saints remain near God and can transmit the word with all its inspiring and radiant power to others. The test of the witnessing of God's word is, in fact, the congruence of speech, intention, emotion, and action. That is why the spirit of the truth is found to fulfill the law, not to contradict it, to reveal the law's meaning, not to undermine it. And what do saints do? They sacrifice their self-will to become living links of trust between divided people, absorbing the violence of others into themselves, turning strangers into kin.

The essence of religion is the realization that God's will is not subject to human choice. For the saint, especially, suffering is not denied but welcomed and freely chosen because it is a sign of election. Sanctity is the suffering by the innocent of

God's will, for others, as ransom for their sins. All major religious traditions recognize that the true misfortune is not suffering but hardness of the heart.

The suffering servant in the Jewish tradition, the martyr al-Hallaj in Islam, Jesus, and the compassionate Buddha all teach the redemptive power of suffering compassionately for others. What distinguishes these heroes is their *spiritual* difference, a quality they establish by their radical *refusal to be different from others*. Saints like Gandhi and King deliver themselves as hostages to the ignorance and violence of those they serve, making a link between those who are deluded by differences in status and the one God who recognizes no differences between souls. When Gandhi or King follow this holy path, they know it leads to martyrdom, but they accept it as part of their role as suffering servants.

Religion at its best is the record of the heroism of the human spirit. It is there that we will find the paradoxical notion that heroism is humility that rises to the heights of glory. Louis Massignon devoted his life to telling the story of the Islamic mystic al-Hallaj. He claims that those saints who have "substituted" their own evolved souls for those of their community, sacrificing themselves to intercede for the injustice and violence of their people, deserve a place above those benefactors of humanity who invent machines, create wealth, or preserve states, because their heroic acts of humility are the axis of human spiritual progress, the cornerstones of the city of God on earth.[22]

Struggling against social injustice is one way to diminish envy, but the redistribution of wealth by itself, without spiritual renovation and social enlightenment, is a highly temporary method of creating wealth, either for society or persons. The wealth of a person in the Kingdom of God is measured not by goods, prestige, or power but by the objects of the person's desire, by what the person loves. To love is to overcome envy, to replace denigration with deference, to surrender the narcissism of competition, to feel others as one feels oneself. What a man loves is the measure of his soul.

Saint Augustine identifies envy as the primary sin, that of Satan, of Cain, of Adam. The primary quality of the sin of envy is its narcissistic and self-isolating assault on the reality of the creation—on its plenitude, on its variety, on its otherness. The attack on the angels, the brother, the limits of life in the garden, is a denial of the limits of selfhood and an assertion of wholeness and completeness that is only delusion. It is the demonic self that seeks to be a totality, poaching on the preserve of God, the only proper inclusive totality.

Envy is doomed to torment because it cannot appreciate anything outside its own selfhood. The envious man is ungrateful about the gift of the world, because he cannot experience it. Saint Augustine is at pains to argue that the love of this world is not so much evil as it is ignorant and doomed to envy; those who are attached to the goods of this world cannot comprehend higher goods—the goods of aesthetic, social, and divine love—because they cannot empathize or identify with anything they themselves do not own, dominate, or control.[23] "When a man is born, whoever he may be, there is born simultaneously a debt to the gods, to the sages, to the ancestors, and to men."[24]

Like the wise men and women who taught me that I am not alone, I bow to the memory of my mother, to my father, to my brother, to my friends. I am grateful to be able to feel guilt and shame and to have the opportunity to repair the bonds of trust, to repay my debts.

Our debts are gifts; our guilt is our treasure. If men can learn to accept the need to *give back* to the world, their violence and resentment will diminish. Resentment is puerile because every man born inherits the wealth of the universe, of wisdom, of the ancestral gene pool, and of the goods of social life.

Envy arises from spiritual impoverishment, from fixating on deprivation in the midst of plenitude. The more a man can forgive the insults and deprivation of his childhood and welcome the hardships of a life of work and responsibility, the more he has the capacity to appreciate the gifts he has received from life, and to comprehend the reality of his debt to others and his need to sacrifice to restore the balance. Just as envy and violence are expressions of poverty, so is sacrifice an expression of wealth. Paradoxically, the sacrifice of egocentricity and narcissism opens the way to enjoying others and to embracing the world, not resenting it. By clinging to deprivation, revenge, violence, envy, the idea of one's own sole importance, one casts a blinding shadow. It is by acknowledging the certainty of our own deaths that we free ourselves from the violence of denying loss and vulnerability, to opening our eyes to beauty, our hearts to empathy.

Violence destroys human life and negates its value. Men can overcome their envy of women's power to make and nurture life only by acknowledging the value of that human life and defending it against violence. And we men can value the gifts of life not by fantasizing new and more perfect worlds and people but only by suffering our vulnerability to needing those gifts, suffering the guilt of denying or damaging them and of needing to repay them.

True presence and honest speech break the lock of deception, withdrawal, and refusal to give that characterizes puerile men. The admission of one's own violence—in fantasy, in feeling, and in action—is the first step toward overcoming violence. Let us move one step beyond violence, one step closer to trust.

NOTES

1 FROM NARCISSISM TO HEROISM

1. Alasdair MacIntyre, *Against the Self-Images of the Age,* London: Duckworth, 1971, p. 22.
2. John M. del Vecchio, *The 13th Valley,* New York: Bantam Books, 1982.
3. Michael Herr, *Dispatches,* New York: Avon Books, 1978.
4. Phyllis Chesler, *About Men,* New York: Simon and Schuster, 1978, p. xiii.
5. Christopher Lasch, *The Culture of Narcissism,* New York: Warner Books, 1979.
6. Erik H. Erikson, *Young Man Luther: A Study in Psychoanalysis and History,* New York: Norton, 1978; *Gandhi's Truth,* New York: Norton, 1969.
7. The entire Jungian tradition is guilty of this one-sided view of heroism.

2 THE REVOLT AGAINST MANHOOD

1. Barbara Ehrenreich, *The Hearts of Men,* New York: Anchor Press, Doubleday, 1983.
2. Luise Eichenbaum and Susie Orbach, *What Do Women Want,* New York: Coward-McCann, 1983, p. 14.
3. William E. Geist, "Second String to Football: Ignored Wives Study the Enemy," *New York Times,* October 5, 1983.
4. Natalie Gittelson, *Dominus: A Woman Looks at Men's Lives,* New York: Harvest Books, Harcourt, 1978, p. 29.
5. "A National Anti-Sexist Men's Organization," National Organization for Men, Box 93, Charleston, IL. This well-intentioned group does excellent work in bringing men together in consciousness-raising groups. But their analysis of men's plight gets stuck in victimization by "sex roles" and in the vulgarity of being against "the whole rotten mess."

As a movement, the men's movement is inert, whining, and a hodge-podge of men against alimony, patriarchy, oppression of gays, pornography, rape, and for better fathering, ERA, etc.

6. Cited in Winthrop D. Jordan, "Searching for Adulthood in America," in *Adulthood*, ed. Erik H. Erikson, New York: Norton, 1978, p. 193.
7. "A Contempt of Court," *Time*, July 4, 1983, p. 66.
8. "The Timeless Boyhood of an American Hero," *New York Times Magazine*, September 11, 1983, p. 53f.
9. Johan Huizinga, *In the Shadow of Tomorrow*, New York: Norton, 1964, p. 170. For examples of puerile writing about male issues, see Norman Mailer, *The Prisoner of Sex*, New York: Signet Books, 1971; Warren Farrell, *The Liberated Man*, New York: Random House, 1974; Marc Fasteau, *The Male Machine*, New York: McGraw-Hill, 1974; Herb Goldberg, *The Hazards of Being Male*, Plainview, NY: Nash, 1975.
10. Glenn Collins, "Why Fathers Don't Pay Child Support," *New York Times*, October 17, 1983.
11. Some good new books about heroism are: William Manchester, *Goodbye Darkness: A Memoir of the Pacific War*, Boston: Little Brown, 1980; John Bierman, *Righteous Gentile*, New York: Bantam Books, 1983; Thomas Keneally, *Schindler's Ark*, London: Coronet Books, 1983.
12. On demonic heroism, see the discussion in chapters 7 and 8. See also Ernest Becker, *Escape from Evil*, New York: Free Press, 1976; Ernst Nolte, *Three Faces of Fascism*, New York: Signet Books, 1969; and Robert Jay Lifton, *Revolutionary Immortality: Mao Tse-tung and the Chinese Culture Revolution*, New York: Random House, 1968.
13. See especially Hemingway's journalism: Ernest Hemingway, *By-Line*, ed. William White, New York: Scribner's, 1967.
14. Eric Skjei and Richard Rabkin, *The Male Ordeal: Role Crisis in a Changing World*, New York: Putnam, 1981, p. 239.
15. Sigmund Freud, *The Future of an Illusion*, in *Standard Edition*, XXI, London: Hogarth Press, 1962, p. 49.
16. Maurice Friedman, *Martin Buber's Life and Work: The Middle Years*, New York: Dutton, 1983, p. 73. Martin Buber is one of the great teachers of the twentieth century. He was one of the few modern philosophers to realize that freedom from traditional bonds means that a person must replace habitual, shared behavior with *more* personal responsibility and responsiveness.
17. John Kenneth Galbraith, "About Men," *New York Times Magazine*, January 22, 1984, p. 39.

18. Gustave Thibon, Introduction in Simone Weil's *Gravity and Grace,* London: Routledge, 1963, p. xxii.

3 FATHERS AND SONS: TOWARD RECONCILIATION

1. See William S. Appleton, *Fathers and Daughters,* New York: Doubleday, 1981; Christoper P. Anderson, *Father: The Figure and the Force,* New York: Warner Books, 1983; Suzanne Fields, *Like Father, Like Daughter,* New York: Little Brown, 1983.
2. There are no precise statistics. See Flora Colao and Tamar Hosansky. *Your Children Should Know,* New York: Bobbs-Merrill, 1983. For good discussions of parental violence against children, see Leon Sheleff, *Generations Apart: Adult Hostility to Youth,* New York: McGraw-Hill, 1981; Lloyd de Mause, *Foundations of Psychohistory,* New York: Creative Roots, 1982.
3. John Munder Ross, "Oedipus and the Laius Complex," *Psychoanalytic Study of the Child,* vol. 37, New Haven: Yale University Press, 1982.
4. David Bakan, *And They Took Themselves Wives: The Emergence of Patriarchy in Western Civilization,* New York: Harper & Row, 1980, p. 12.
5. William Wharton, *Dad,* New York: Knopf, 1981. Another fine book about an absent father is Paul Auster's *The Invention of Solitude,* New York: Sun, 1982.
6. Homer, *The Odyssey,* Fitzgerald trans., New York: Doubleday, 1961, pp. 31, 307.
7. Franz Kafka, *Dearest Father,* New York: Schocken Books, 1954, p. 138.
8. Ibid., p. 191.
9. Sigmund Freud, *Interpretation of Dreams,* in *Standard Edition,* vol. v, London: Hogarth Press, 1953. On the role of silence in psychoanalysis, see Jacques Lacan, *The Four Fundamental Concepts of Psychoanalysis,* trans. Alan Sheridan, New York: Norton, 1978; *Ecrits: A Selection,* trans. Alan Sheridan, New York: Norton, 1977.
10. See Philip E. Slater, *The Glory of Hera,* Boston: Beacon Press, 1968.

4 THE BOND OF BROTHERHOOD

1. See Stephen P. Bank and Michael D. Kahn, *The Sibling Bond,* New York: Basic Books, 1982. As a contrast to the feebleness of the formal study of brothers, see *Brother Songs: A Male Anthology of Poetry,* ed. Jim Perlman, Minneapolis: Holy Cow Press, 1979. The most powerful

classical statement of brotherhood is that of the great Islamic philosopher al-Ghazali, *On the Duties of Brotherhood,* trans. Muhtar Holland, Woodstock, NY: Overlook Press, 1979. Al-Ghazali writes: "Know that the contract of brotherhood is a bond between two persons, like the contract of marriage between two spouses . . . the contract of brotherhood confer[s] upon your brother a certain right touching your property, your person, your tongue and your heart. . . ." p. 21.

2. Wilson Carey McWilliams, *The Idea of Fraternity in America,* Los Angeles: University of California Press, 1973, chapter 1. For a fascinating discussion of the fraternal ritual of blood-brotherhood, see Harry Tegnaeus, *Blood Brothers: An Ethno-sociological Study of the Instructions of Blood-brotherhood with Special Reference to Africa,* New York: Philosophical Library, 1952.

3. Thomas Merton, *The Seven Storey Mountain,* New York: Signet Books, n.d., p. 28.

4. R. D. Laing, *The Divided Self,* New York: Penguin Books, 1965.

5 MEN AND WOMEN: THE CRISIS OF MISTRUST

1. Joseph Epstein, *Divorced in America,* New York: Penguin Books, 1974, p. 22.

2. Henry Adams, *Education of Henry Adams,* Boston: Houghton-Mifflin, 1974, p. 383.

3. Mary-Lou Weisman, "Hers," *New York Times,* October 13, 1983.

4. Chuck Wachtel, *Joe the Engineer,* New York: Morrow, 1983.

5. William Leach, *True Love and Perfect Union: The Feminist Reform of Sex and Society,* New York: 1980, p. 9. See also Ann Douglas, *The Feminization of American Culture,* New York: Basic Books, 1980. On a new tendency toward conservatism in relationships, see Jane E. Brody and Richard D. Lyons, "Sex in America: Conservative Attitudes Prevail," *New York Times,* October 4, 1983, p. C1. On gender, see Ivan Ilich, *Gender,* New York: Pantheon, 1982.

6 TURNING FORTY: THE PASSION FOR SELF-RESPECT

1. Elliott Jaques, "Death and the Mid-Life Crisis," in *Work, Creativity, and Social Justice,* New York: International Universities Press, 1970.

2. Roger L. Gould, *Transformation: Growth and Change in Adult Life,* New York: Simon and Schuster, 1978, p. 236f. I had the privilege of seeing my friend Jerome Chazen face his need to change his work at the end of his forties. A very successful executive, he became restless.

His children were successfully leaving the family nest. He needed to make something of his own, to be more like Jerome Chazen. It was not enough to make money. Consulting with his wife about the risk of failure if he made a change, he got her full support and encouragement, not without much mutual agonizing. Then he met with Liz Claiborne and other old friends he trusted, and they began their own firm, Liz Claiborne, on slender capital but great courage, skill, experience, and determination. Eight years after founding, this firm employs 1,100 people.

Liz Claiborne serves the need of a rising class of women for stylish professional clothing that could be quickly mixed and matched, saving them time. Jerome took risks, increasing the scale of the company rapidly while maintaining quality.

For Chazen, success also means responsibility for the welfare of others. Business means social trust. His firm started the Liz Claiborne Foundation, which supports many charitable groups. He gives his own time and energy to social causes he believes in, some of them the same causes his father supported.

3. The poll of values by the Yankelovitch Organization is cited in Barbara Goldsmith, "The Meaning of Celebrity," *New York Times Magazine,* December 4, 1983, p. 75.
4. W. R. Bion, *Attention and Interpretation,* in *Seven Servants; Four Works by Bion,* New York: Aronson, 1977, p. 19.
5. Rebecca West, *Black Lamb and Grey Falcon,* New York: Viking, 1943, p. 3.
6. Plutarch, *Moralia,* Cambridge: Harvard University Press, 1960, vol. 1, p. 449.
7. Henry Mitchell, *The Essential Earthman,* New York: Farrar, Straus and Giroux, 1981, p. 3.
8. William C. Chittick, *The Sufi Path of Love: The Spiritual Teachings of Rumi,* Albany: State University of New York, 1983, p. 8.

7 HEROISM: TIME BLAZING WITH MEANING

1. Benjamin Constant, *Prophecy from the Past,* ed. Helen Byrne Lippman, New York: Reynal and Hitchcock, 1941, p. 25.
2. David K. Shipler, "Russia: A People without Heroes," *New York Times Magazine,* October 16, 1983.
3. Joseph Campbell, *The Hero with a Thousand Faces,* Meridian Books; New York: 1956, pp. 30, 359, 390. For other discussions of the hero

in myth, see Lord Raglan, *The Hero,* New York: Vintage Books, 1956; Otto Rank, *The Myth of the Birth of the Hero,* New York: Vintage Books, 1959; Dorothy Norman, *The Hero: Myth, Image, Symbol,* New York: New American Library, 1969.

4. James M. Markham, "Russians and Americans Bury G.I. by the Elbe," *New York Times,* November 27, 1983, p. 1.

5. William L. Shirer, *Gandhi: A Memoir,* New York: Simon and Schuster, 1979, p. 91.

6. Philippe Ariès, *The Hour of Our Death,* New York: Vintage Books, 1982, p. 346.

7. Jean Lacouture, *The Demigods: Charismatic Leadership in the Third World,* New York: Knopf, 1970.

8. Richard Slotkin, *Regeneration Through Violence,* Middletown, CT: Wesleyan University Press, 1973. The expectation of political violence exerts tremendous influence on the formation of hierarchy within a state and also draws the state into an international system of polarized alliances—against the real interests of social life. Xenophobia thrives on the dread of violence from strangers. See Harold D. Lasswell, *World Politics and Personal Insecurity,* New York: The Free Press, 1965.

9. Peter H. Merkl, *Political Violence under the Swastika,* Princeton, NJ: Princeton University Press, 1975.

10. Peter Brown, *The Cult of the Saints,* Chicago: University of Chicago Press, 1982.

11. Freeman Dyson, *Disturbing the Universe,* New York: Harper Colophon, 1981, p. 224. In a recent essay, Mr. Dyson expresses skepticism about the ability of a nonviolent resistance movement to build a stable world order. The forces of envy, hatred, and vengeance are too strong for such groups to overcome. See *The New Yorker,* February 27, 1984, p. 86.

8   VIOLENCE OR SACRIFICE

1. October 5, 1983. On violence in the family, see Susan Schechter, *Women and Male Violence,* Boston: South End Press, 1982; Phyllis Frank and Beverly Houghton, *Confronting the Batterer: A Guide to Creating the Spouse Abuse Educational Workshop,* Rockland County, NY: Volunteer Counseling Service Publication, 1983.

Treatment of family violence as a criminal justice issue has been an important development in exposing violence as violence in child abuse, incest, child sexual abuse, and spouse abuse. It has been difficult to create a unified conceptual or service approach to family violence. Evan Stark and Ann Flitcraft have written about the ideological problems of partial perception of family violence as a health issue. The fragmentation of our perception of this problem reflects the resistance in our culture to seeing male violence and injustice mirrored in families. See "Social Knowledge, Social Therapy and the Abuse of Women: The Case Against Patriarchal Benevolence," in *Family Violence: The Problem and the Response,* ed G. Hotaling, New York: Russell Sage, 1982. The evidence that the psychiatric profession is still misdiagnosing and mistreating women who suffer violence is found in Elaine Carmen, M.D., et al., "Victims of Violence and Psychiatric Illness," *American Journal of Psychiatry,* 141:3, March 1984. Even those of us working for years with the issue of family violence have been slow to realize that family violence is the primary cause of injury to women, both as direct physical injury and as a cause of alcoholism, suicide, depression and disturbances in capacity to work.

2. de Mause, *op. cit.*

3. R. W. Apple, Jr., "New Stirrings of Patriotism," *New York Times Magazine,* December 11, 1983, p. 96.

4. Ted Robert Gurr, "A Comparative Study of Civil Strife," in *The History of Violence in America,* ed. Hugh Davis Graham and Ted Robert Gurr, New York: Bantam Books, 1969, p. 572.

5. Edwin I. Megargee, "Psychological Determinants and Correlates of Criminal Violence," in *Criminal Violence,* ed. Marvin E. Wolfgang, Beverly Hills: Sage Publications, 1982, p. 122. See the same editor's, "International Terrorism, in *The Journal of the American Academy of Political and Social Science,* Beverly Hills: Sage Publications, 1982.

6. Ted Honderich, *Violence for Equality,* London: Penguin Books, 1980, pp. 19, 188. See also, Carl Leiden and Karl Schmitt, *The Politics of Violence: Revolution in the Modern World,* Englewood Cliffs, NJ: Spectrum Books, 1968.

7. Alain Joxe, "Introduction," *Violence and Its Causes,* Paris: UNESCO, 1981.

8. Bryce Nelson, "Acts of Violence Against Therapists Pose Lurking Threat," *New York Times,* June 14, 1983.

9. Melanie Klein, "The Oedipus Complex in the Light of Early Anxieties," in *Love, Guilt, and Reparation,* New York: Delacorte Press, 1975.

10. Margaret S. Mahler, et al., *The Psychological Birth of the Human Infant: Symbiosis and Individuation*, New York: Basic Books, 1975.

11. Carl and Shelley Mydans, *The Violent Peace*, New York: Atheneum, 1968, p. 4.

12. W. R. Bion, *Experiences in Groups*, New York: Basic Books, 1961. See also Philip E. Slater's *Microcosm: Structural, Psychological, and Religious Evolution in Groups*, New York: Wiley, 1966.

13. René Girard, *Violence and the Sacred*, Baltimore: Johns Hopkins Press, 1977, p. 221. Girard has written a very great book, a complex meditation on the psychological and cultural transformations of violence. Other recent books about violence, hierarchy, and the sacred are: V. S. Naipaul, *Among the Believers: An Islamic Journey*, New York: Vintage Books, 1982; Elaine Pagels, *The Gnostic Gospels*, New York: Random House, 1979; Jack Beeching, *An Open Path: Christian Missionaries: 1515–1914*, Santa Barbara: Ross-Erikson, 1982; Carlos Franqui, *Family Portrait with Fidel: A Memoir*, New York: Random House, 1984.

14. The Safer Foundation is located at 10 S. Wabash Ave., Chicago, IL 60603.

15. See for example, Ronald Fernandez, *Excess Profits: The Rise of United Technologies*, Reading, MA: Addison-Wesley, 1983.

16. Robert Jay Lifton, *The Broken Connection*, New York: Simon and Schuster, 1979, p. 173f.

17. John D'Emilio, *Sexual Politics, Sexual Communities: The Making of a Homosexual Minority in the United States*, Chicago: University of Chicago Press, 1983.

18. Peter L. Berger, "Languages of Murder," in *Facing Up to Modernity*, New York: Basic Books, 1977, p. 86.

19. Fred Kaplan, *The Wizards of Armageddon*, New York: Simon and Schuster, 1983, p. 135.

20. Samuel Pisar, *Of Blood and Hope*, New York: Macmillan, 1980, p. 310.

21. Amanda K. Coomaraswamy, in *The Hero*, New York: New American Library, 1969, p. 234.

22. Louis Massignon, *The Passion of al-Hallaj: Mystic and Martyr of Islam*, trans. Herbert Mason, Princeton: 1982, vol. 1, p. lxv. Massignon considers heroism to be "humility that rises to the heights," p. 5.

23. Saint Augustine, *City of God*, trans. by David Knowles, New York: Penguin Books, 1972, pp. 477, 601.

24. Cited in Raimundo Panikkar, *The Vedic Experience; Mantrammanjari*, Berkeley: University of California Press, 1977, p. 393.

READING LIST

ADAMS, HENRY, *The Education of Henry Adams*, Boston: Houghton-Mifflin, 1974.

AUSTER, PAUL, *The Invention of Solitude*, New York: Sun, 1982.

BECKER, ERNEST, *The Denial of Death*, New York: Free Press, 1975.

BION, W. R., *Experiences in Groups*, New York: Basic Books, 1961.

BLACK-MICHAUD, JACOB, *Cohesive Force: Feud in the Mediterranean and the Middle East*, New York: St. Martin's, 1975.

BOWKER, JOHN, *Problems of Suffering in Religions of the World*, Cambridge: Cambridge University Press, 1975.

BROWNING, FRANK, and GERASSI, JOHN, *The American Way of Crime*, New York: Putnam, 1980.

BUBER, MARTIN, *Between Man and Man*, New York: Macmillan, 1965.

———, *I and Thou*, New York: Scribners, 1970.

CHAFE, WILLIAM H., *Women and Equality*, Oxford: Oxford University Press, 1977.

DEGLER, CARL N., *At Odds: Women and the Family in America*, New York: Oxford University Press, 1980.

DE MAUSE, LLOYD, *Foundations of Psychohistory*, New York: Creative Roots, Inc., 1982.

D'EMILIO, JOHN, *Sexual Politics, Sexual Communities: The Making of a Homosexual Minority in the United States*, Chicago: University of Chicago Press, 1983.

DOUGLAS, MARY, *The World of Goods*, New York: Basic Books, 1979.

DRESNER, SAMUEL, *The Zaddik*, New York: Schocken, 1974.

DUBBERT, JOE L., *A Man's Place: Masculinity in Transition*, Englewood Cliffs, NJ: Prentice-Hall, 1979.

DWORKIN, ANDREA, *Pornography*, New York: Putnam, 1981.

DYSON, FREEMAN, *Disturbing the Universe*, New York: Harper Colophon, 1981.

ELLUL, JACQUES, *The Technological Society*, New York: Knopf, 1964.

Reading List   259

ERIKSON, ERIK H., ed., *Adulthood*, New York: W. W. Norton, 1978.

FERNANDEZ, RONALD, *Excess Profits: The Rise of United Technologies*, Reading, MA: Addison-Wesley, 1983.

FRANQUI, CARLOS, *Family Portrait with Fidel: A Memoir*, New York: Random House, 1984.

GANDHI, M., *An Autobiography*, Boston: Beacon Press, 1957.

GELLES, RICHARD, *Family Violence*, Beverly Hills: Sage Publications, 1979.

GIRARD, RENÉ, *Violence and the Sacred*, Baltimore: Johns Hopkins Press, 1977.

GOODE, WILLIAM J., *The Celebration of Heroes*, Berkeley, California: University of California Press, 1978.

HOFSTADTER, RICHARD, ed., *American Violence*, New York: Knopf, 1970.

HUIZINGA, JOHAN, *In the Shadow of Tomorrow*, New York: W. W. Norton, 1964.

ISAACS, HAROLD, *Idols of the Tribe*, New York: Harper Colophon, 1975.

JOHNSON, PAUL, *Modern Times*, New York: Harper and Row, 1983.

KAKAR, SUDHIR, *Shamans, Mystics, and Doctors: A Psychological Inquiry into India and its Healing Traditions*, Boston: Beacon Press, 1982.

KAPLAN, FRED, *The Wizards of Armageddon*, New York: Simon and Schuster, 1983.

KEEGAN, JOHN, *The Face of Battle*, New York: Penguin, 1978.

KLEIN, MELANIE, *Envy and Gratitude and Other Works*, New York: Delacorte Press, 1975.

LAING, R. D., *The Divided Self*, New York: Penguin Books, 1968.

LASCH, CHRISTOPHER, *The Culture of Narcissism*, New York: Warner Books, 1979.

LASSWELL, HAROLD D., *World Politics and Personal Insecurity*, New York: Free Press, 1965.

LIFTON, ROBERT JAY, *The Broken Connection*, New York: Simon and Schuster, 1979.

MACINTYRE, ALASDAIR, *After Virtue*, Notre Dame, IN: University of Notre Dame Press, 1981.

MANCHESTER, WILLIAM, *Goodbye Darkness: A Memoir of the Pacific War*, Boston: Little Brown, 1980.

MANERI, SHARAFUDDIN, *The Hundred Letters*, New York: Paulist Press, 1980.

MYDANS, CARL and SHELLY, *The Violent Peace*, New York: Atheneum, 1968.

NAIPAUL, V. S., *Among the Believers: An Islamic Journey*, New York: Vintage Books, 1982.

OATES, STEPHEN, *Let the Trumpet Sound—The Life of Martin Luther King, Jr.,* New York: Harper Torch Book, 1983.

PANIKKAR, RAIMUNDO, *The Vedic Experience,* Berkeley: University of California Press, 1977.

PISAR, SAMUEL, *Of Blood and Hope,* New York: Macmillan, 1980.

ROSENZWEIG, FRANZ, *The Star of Redemption,* Boston: Beacon Press, 1972.

SAMPSON, ANTHONY, *The Arms Bazaar,* New York: Viking, 1977.

SARSBY, JACQUELINE, *Romantic Love and Society,* London: Penguin, 1983.

SCHACTER, ZALMAN M., *Sparks of Light: Counseling in the Hasidic Tradition,* Boulder, CO: Shambala, 1983.

SCHECTER, SUSAN, *Women and Male Violence,* Boston: South End Press, 1982.

SCHILLEBEECKX, EDWARD, *Jesus,* New York: Seabury, 1981.

SCHIMMEL, ANNE MARIE, *Mystical Dimensions of Islam,* Chapel Hill, NC: University of North Carolina Press, 1975.

SCHOECK, HELMUT M., *Envy,* New York: Harcourt, Brace and World, 1969.

SHAPIRO, STEPHEN A., and RYGLEWICZ, HILARY, *Feeling Safe,* Englewood Cliffs, NJ: Prentice-Hall, 1976.

———, *Trusting Yourself,* Englewood Cliffs, NJ: Prentice-Hall, 1976.

SHIRER, WILLIAM L., *Gandhi: A Memoir,* New York: Simon and Schuster, 1979.

VAN GENNEP, ARNOLD, *The Rites of Passage,* Chicago: University of Chicago Press, 1960.

WALZER, MICHAEL, *Spheres of Justice,* New York: Basic Books, 1983.

WEIL, SIMONE, *Gravity and Grace,* London: Routledge, 1963.

WHYTE, WILLIAM H., *The Organization Man,* Garden City, NY: Anchor Books, 1957.

INDEX